W A G O N S   F O R   T H E   S A N T A   F E   T R A D E

DATE DUE

MARK L. GARDNER

Wagons for the Santa Fe Trade

WHEELED VEHICLES AND THEIR MAKERS, 1822–1880

University of New Mexico Press   Albuquerque

Library of Congress Cataloging-in-Publication Data

Gardner, Mark L.
Wagons for the Santa Fe Trade : wheeled vehicles and their makers, 1822–1880 /
Mark L. Gardner.— 1st ed.
p. cm.
Includes bibliographical references and index.
ISBN 0-8263-1846-0 (cloth : alk. paper)—ISBN 0-8263-2196-8 (paper : alk. paper)
1. Wagons—West (U.S.)—History. 2. Santa Fe Trail. I. Title.

TS2010.G37 2000
688.6—dc21   99-006948

William A. Gardner (left) and Loyd Gardner in front of log wagon and mammoth walnut log, Pettis County, Missouri, circa 1919.

For my great grandfather William A. "Willie" Gardner

(1880–1970), a skilled worker of draft horses

during a time when draft horses and wagons were

a part of everyday life.

And for my grandpa Ernest G. Carter (1909–1981),

friend and companion on many an adventure afield

in the Missouri hills of my youth.

Contents

Figures

We are told that on this great thoroughfare, from early spring until late autumn, not a day passes but large trains of these wagons may be seen.

COUNCIL GROVE PRESS, JUNE 15, 1863

Preface

In frustrating moments during the long time I have been working on this book, I would get the feeling that I somehow got "stuck" with the topic of Santa Fe Trail freight wagons. For in the beginning, I did not specifically choose this subject to pursue as an area of expertise. My interest in wagons was a general one, connected, quite naturally, with my affinity for the history of the Santa Fe Trail. This pleasant state of affairs immediately started to change, however, when I began to realize that while strong convictions concerning Trail wagons were quite abundant, they usually came without documentation in the known primary sources. Here was a challenge. I began to gather any information I could find on Santa Fe Trail wagons, particularly historic references, and in 1989 I published some of my research in an article on Conestoga wagons. In 1994, the National Park Service, aware of my work on wagons, asked me to write a study on Trail wagons to be used as a resource for the Santa Fe National Historic Trail. It was not that I was necessarily the best choice for this project; it was simply that they knew of no other scholar who was pursuing this subject, even considering how limited my efforts had been up to that time.

Thus began a frenzied period of more research, more digging. After the NPS study was finally completed, it became evident that here were the makings of a book. Also, a book would allow me to incorporate more subjects—such as the changing technology of wagon making in the nineteenth century—that were beyond the scope of the original NPS contract. So again I delved into a plethora of primary sources, which, because of my passion for research, was quite easy to do. Much new material was discovered during the course of this work, and it has resulted in both important revisions and the addition of key evidence to some of my earlier conclusions.

But this was not all that happened. As I conducted the research for my chapter entitled "From Shop to Factory," as I read about power-driven saws, planers, and other woodworking machines, a flood of memories began to come over me. I thought back to my childhood in the 1960s, when my dad owned and operated a small sawmill near a curving blacktop road in the country north of the little Missouri town in which we lived. I remembered the big diesel engine which, with long belts, powered the large circular saw blade (sixty inches in diameter). And I remembered how the saw shrieked as it sliced through the logs: cottonwood, oak, maple, etc. I remembered the mountain of sawdust behind the mill that, of course, had to be scaled, and I remembered how extremely itchy a shoe containing sawdust can be. One especially pleasant memory was of the times when the saw needed to be sharpened. Everything in the mill was shut down, cold bottles of pop were opened, and stories and jokes were told as my dad methodically worked a file over each individual tooth of that steel blade.

My family has been involved in the logging and sawmill business for at least the last four generations. My dad logs in Missouri even now. Thinking back to my dad's mill and the countless days I spent in the woods with him as a helper—perhaps a generous use of that term—made the wagon makers and factory workers of the past much more real to me. I felt a connection to these people and their time, an era that historian Brooke Hindle has coined "America's Wooden Age." For my family, though, that age has not ended. Needless to say, I no longer feel like my work on wagons and wagon making has been an unwanted burden. Quite the contrary, I consider myself most fortunate to have had the opportunity to tell this important story.

This book is a "first" in many respects. No previous volume has focused on the wagons of a single overland route. Most histories of the various western trails devote very little text to identifying wagon types, and even those books on freighting contain surprisingly little information on the vehicles which were a key component of that business. And no other volume has closely examined the wagon makers and their factories, the power sources employed, and the common woodworking machines found in those factories. Of course, having worked on this subject for several years, I know firsthand how daunting, confusing, and elusive a study of wagons can be, and fully understand why most scholars have stepped lightly around this subject—and I cannot blame them.

Many extremely important primary sources were used for this book that have been sadly neglected by historians and others. For example, the famous legend of the "monster" wagon made by Joseph Murphy is explored using, in part, Murphy's own account books, which reside at the Missouri Historical Society in St. Louis. For the first time, the U.S. industrial census has been used both to identify Missouri wagon makers and to reveal many hitherto unknown facets of their operations. Additionally, rare historic images and photographs have been given the same weight as documents in regard to the information they can provide as to wagon types and construction.

A significant first is found in the chapter devoted to the legendary windwagon of Westport. Although the primary record notes that William Thomas received a U.S. patent for his windwagon invention, no scholar has previously pursued this important lead. From the National Archives I obtained both Thomas's original patent application and the scale drawings that accompanied that application. These wonderful drawings are reproduced in this volume.

Even with the great variety and number of primary sources consulted for this book, the reader will find within the following pages much educated guesswork (at least I like to think it is educated). And there are some questions that, when all is said and done, remain very good questions. My goal, however, has not been to provide a definitive work on wagons, but to examine this subject using the available evidence and letting that evidence speak for itself. It is my hope, then, that this volume will serve as a sourcebook more than "the last word," for there remains much to be discovered. With that in mind, I have attempted to provide detailed notes as to sources and an extensive bibliography. I now pass the torch on to my fellow researchers, historians, craftsmen, and trail buffs. Be forewarned, though: this subject can suck you in like a Missouri River whirlpool and hold on like a snapping turtle.

One final note: It should be remembered that the emphasis of this study is on civilian freight wagons. Yet because carriages and other personal vehicles were usually a part of the freight wagon caravans, a brief discussion of these vehicles has been included. The chapter on the windwagon was added because that vehicle was intended for freight, as well as passengers, and it was tested on the Santa Fe Trail (and it's a fun story, too). The wagon types adopted by the U.S. Army, while they may be mentioned in the following pages, have purposely been left out of this volume. Most of the freight shipped west over the Santa Fe Trail for the army was transported by civilian contractors using civilian wagons. U.S. Army wagons and carriages, however, are deserving of their own book. So, too, are Santa Fe Trail stagecoaches, which also are beyond the scope of this work. Stagecoaches were for passengers and mail, not heavy freight.

Many thanks are due to all those who have assisted me in this project, particularly the able staffs of numerous historical agencies and libraries throughout the country. These include the State Historical Society of Missouri; the Kansas State Historical Society; Leavenworth County, Kansas, Public Library; the inter-library loan department of the Pikes Peak Library District; the Special Collections and Government Documents departments of Tutt Library at Colorado College; and several others. I am grateful for the many comments provided by the readers who perused a draft of my NPS wagon study: Doug Thamert, Stanley B. Kimball, Marc Simmons, Leo E. Oliva, William Y. Chalfant, Harry Myers, Jane Elder, Charles Bennett, William "Pat" O'Brien, and the staff of the Long Distance Trails Group Office. Also, historians and friends Marc Simmons, Harry Myers, Pat O'Brien, the late Pauline Fowler, and the late W. Earl Givens graciously shared their research with me, and this study has benefited as a result.

Other individuals who went out of their way to help are Lonn Taylor and Peter Liebhold at the National Museum of American History, Daniel Brown at Bent's Old Fort NHS, Martha Clevenger at the Missouri Historical Society, Mike Dickey and Richard Forry at Arrow Rock State Historic Site, Luther Hanson at the U.S. Army Quartermaster Museum, Sylvia Knight at the University of Vermont Libraries, Peter Blodgett at the Huntington Library, Jane Elder, Daniel T. Kelly, Jr., Gabrielle Palmer, Anna Belle Cartwright, and the late Kathryn Hinchey Cochran. To those I have left out, I beg your forgiveness, my only excuse being that this book has left me somewhat addled.

Deserving of special thanks is wagon maker, transportation historian, and friend Doug Thamert. Doug generously provided me with reams of obscure published materials on wagons and carriages (many of these are in this study's bibliography) as well as his own valuable insights on his craft. During our many conversations (and some friendly arguments) I never failed to learn something about this fascinating subject. If this book meets with Doug's approbation, then I will consider the effort to have been worthwhile.

Finally, I would like to thank my wife and friend, Katie, and my daughter, Christiana, who, for the last several years, have been forced to accommodate my research on, of all things, freight wagons.

MARK LEE GARDNER
Ute Pass Wagon Road, Colorado
February 17, 1999

WAGONS FOR THE SANTA FE TRADE

ONE

Early Wagons on the Santa Fe Trail

When William Becknell and five companions from the Boonslick country of Missouri arrived in Santa Fe in November of 1821—the first overland traders to open commerce with the newly independent Mexican nation—they had in tow a few pack animals loaded with a meager assortment of trade goods. The goods-starved New Mexicans, however, welcomed Becknell and his merchandise with "apparent pleasure and joy," as Becknell would tell it later.[1] The Missourians reaped outrageously high profits on their goods, and the New Mexican governor "expressed a desire that the Americans would keep up an intercourse with" his country.[2] Now here was a market indeed.

Becknell returned to Missouri, his packs bulging with silver, and within a few short months he was back on the trail to Santa Fe, this time accompanied by a much larger party of enthusiastic adventurers—and something else. According to his now-famous "journal," first published in the pages of the *Missouri Intelligencer* in 1823, Becknell's 1822 company consisted of "21 men, with *three* waggons."[3] No one had ever attempted to take wagons from Missouri to Santa Fe, but, put simply, the more goods one brought, the more profits there were to be made. And Becknell, having traversed the prairies twice, was apparently confident that loaded wagons could successfully make the journey. He was right.

Becknell's second Santa Fe expedition was another great success. Of the three wagons that arrived safely in Santa Fe with their loads, only one, it appears, belonged to the expedition's leader.[4] This wagon, it was later reported, had cost 150 dollars in Missouri and was sold by Becknell in New Mexico for 700 dollars.[5] The other wagons were probably disposed of in a like manner; they do not seem to have returned to Missouri. What these wagons looked like, their hauling capacity, where they were made and by whom—all this is unknown. Their importance, however, is unquestioned. They—and Becknell—proved that merchandise-laden wagons could navigate the eight hundred–plus miles between Franklin, Missouri, and Santa Fe, a remarkable feat that did not go unnoticed.

No wagons were reported on the Santa Fe Trail in 1823, but the 1824 caravan contained an amazing assemblage of vehicles. Meredith Miles Marmaduke, a member of this company, recorded in his diary on May 24 that they traveled with "2 road waggons, 20 dearborns, 2 carts and one small piece of cannon."[6] Augustus Storrs, another member of the expedition, wrote some months later that there had been "twenty-three four-wheeled vehicles, one of which was a common road wagon."[7] While Marmaduke and Storrs do not agree on the number of vehicles in the caravan, it is important to note their use of the term *road wagon*. According to transportation historian Don Berkebile, in his *Carriage Terminology: An Historical Dictionary*, the term has two definitions. One describes a vehicle also known as a buggy. The term was "also loosely applied," Berkebile tells us, "to larger WAGONS that were employed in the movement of materials or merchandise over the roads."[8] The second definition is probably the one intended by Marmaduke and Storrs; Santa Fe trader and historian Josiah Gregg uses "road-wagon" in his *Commerce of the Prairies* (1844) to denote freight wagons.[9] While the term leaves us to speculate on the appearance of these vehicles, it is possible that the road wagons in the 1824 caravan were the first actual freight wagons to travel the Santa Fe Trail.

Where the road wagons of the 1824 caravan were manufactured is unknown. They could have been made in Missouri, however. James D. Earl and Andrew Light, blacksmiths and wagon makers of St. Louis, advertised, in the 1821 directory for that city, that they had "made such arrangements as will enable them to manufacture Road Wagons, Dearborn Carriages, Carts & Drays, Hand & Wheel Barrows."[10] At the same time, it is possible that the traders' wagons were brought from the East, a practice that became commonplace in the Santa Fe trade in the 1830s and 1840s.

The caravan for 1825 reportedly contained thirty-four wagons. The *Intelligencer* declared simply that the "wagons and carriages, of almost every description are numerous."[11] Also on the Trail that season were seven wagons purchased for the use of the U.S. government survey party, which was charged with surveying and marking a road from Missouri to Santa Fe. George C. Sibley, one of three commissioners for the survey appointed by President John Quincy Adams, ordered six wagons for the expedition from two unidentified St. Louis makers (the seventh wagon acquired for the survey may have been purchased used). The vehicles were described as "seven strong light wagons (painted light blue) — 2 of them drawn by 4 horses each and 5 by 2 horses." These wagons appear to have had a capacity of at least two thousand pounds.[12]

The year 1826 saw a substantial increase in wagons traveling the Santa Fe Trail. Josiah Gregg estimated that a total of sixty rolled to New Mexico that year. Also according to Gregg, 1826 was the first year that pack animals were not part of the yearly caravan, and he notes that from that date forward only wagons were used to transport goods to Santa Fe.[13] Some of those wagons belonged to Mexican Manuel Escudero. The *Intelligencer* of June 9, 1826, reported that "Six or seven new and substantial built waggons arrived in this place on Tuesday last, heavily laden with merchandise on their way to New Mexico, owned exclusively, we believe by Mr. Escudero. . . . This gentleman has expended a very large sum in the purchase of goods, waggons and equipments." Where Escudero purchased his "new and substantial built waggons" is unclear, although he did travel to St. Louis and Washington, D.C., during the previous year and undoubtedly passed through St. Louis again on his return.[14]

"SANTA FE WAGGONS FOR SALE" was the bold title for an advertisement that appeared in the *Intelligencer* on April 1, 1828. "There will be sold for cash," the ad stated, "at public sale, on Monday the 10th inst. in the town of Fayette, several light running Waggons, but strongly constructed, and well suited for the Santa Fe trade — for families removing — for market or plantations." Unfortunately, like most of the references to wagons during this period, the ad simply poses more questions. A light running wagon was one of light draught, but what did those in the ad look like, and how were they constructed? Were they perhaps comparable to the light wagons constructed for Sibley's government survey party?

Sixty wagons and approximately 120 men are supposed to have made up the Santa Fe caravan of 1830. "The goods of the adventurers are now almost exclusively transported in waggons, dearborns, &c.," reported the *Missouri Intelligencer*. "Some of the waggons are of the largest class, with four horses or mules."[15] The wagons of "the largest class" were almost certainly a type of freight wagon.

The first known graphic depiction of Santa Fe Trail wagons is a small engraving (Fig. 1.1) found in *Scenes of American Wealth and Industry in Produce, Manufactures, Trade, The Fisheries, &c. &c. For the Instruction and Amusement of Children and Youth* (Boston: Allen and Ticknor, 1833). The engraving, titled "Santa Fe Traders," pictures a train of mule-drawn wagons; the wheels of the wagons are quite wide and the wagons have a very boxlike shape. The artist is unknown, as is the artist's inspiration for the image. Was "Santa Fe Traders"

SCENES

OF

AMERICAN WEALTH AND INDUSTRY

IN

PRODUCE, MANUFACTURES, TRADE,

THE FISHERIES, &c. &c.

Santa Fe Traders.

FOR THE INSTRUCTION AND AMUSEMENT

OF

CHILDREN AND YOUTH.

BOSTON:
ALLEN AND TICKNOR.
1833.

1.1.   "Santa Fe Traders." From *Scenes of American Wealth and Industry . . . For the Instruction of Children and Youth*, Boston, 1833. (Courtesy of the Winterthur Library: Printed Book and Periodical Collection.)

created from personal observation or a written description? Whatever the source of the image, the presence of palm trees (not native to the region of the Santa Fe Trail) in the scene renders the engraving highly suspect.

In the absence of additional artist renderings or more detailed references to vehicles, the hundreds of wagons used to transport merchandise on the Santa Fe Trail during the 1820s and even into the 1830s must remain somewhat of a mystery. What is clear, though, is that the early years of the trade

saw an odd assortment of vehicle types traveling to Santa Fe, a characteristic of Trail travel that would never entirely disappear.

A Note about Draft Stock

Horses were used almost exclusively during the first years of the trade.
Alphonso Wetmore wrote in 1824 that Santa Fe goods were "transported
by means of horses raised here [Missouri], which are fed on the herbage
found in abundance on the route."[16] However, the horse was rapidly re-
placed in the harness by the mule "as soon as the means for procuring these
animals increased," wrote Josiah Gregg.[17] In 1829 oxen were introduced to
the Trail by the U.S. Army. They drew the baggage wagons and carts for
the first military escort to accompany the traders' annual caravan, com-
manded by Major Bennet Riley. Trader Charles Bent experimented with
one yoke of these oxen after leaving the military escort behind at the Arkansas River, taking the animals all the way to Santa Fe.[18] From that date
forward, according to Gregg, "upon an average about half of the wagons in
these expeditions have been drawn by oxen."[19]

A Santa Fe Trail caravan composed of both ox-drawn and mule-drawn
wagons was a common sight during Gregg's day, primarily because these
caravans were composed of several merchant owners, each of whom made
his own arrangements regarding the draft stock to pull his goods-laden
wagons. Once large-scale contract freighters began operating on the Trail
after the Mexican-American War, however, it became the norm to see either bull trains or mule trains, not a combination of the two, for these trains
had a single owner or operator who made the decision about stock, and an
important decision it was. According to Gregg, oxen could pull "heavier
loads than the same number of mules, particularly through muddy or sandy
places; but they generally fall off in strength as the prairie grass becomes
drier and shorter, and often arrive at their destination in a most shocking
plight." Mules were more expensive than oxen but made better time and
generally maintained their strength.[20]

Captain Randolph Marcy echoed Gregg's comments in his own observations published in his *The Prairie Traveler* in 1859:

There has been much discussion regarding the relative merits of
mules and oxen for prairie traveling, and the question is yet far from
being settled. Upon good firm roads, in a populated country, where
grain can be procured, I should unquestionably give the preference to

1.1a. This rare occupational tintype of a wagoner dates to 1865. The "blacksnake" whip he is holding indicates that he drove a team of mules or horses. Bullwhackers (ox drivers) did not use this type of whip; their whip consisted of a long wooden stock (often a hickory sapling) to which was attached a rawhide lash ten or more feet in length. (© Mark L. Gardner Collection.)

mules, as they travel faster, and endure the heat of summer much better than oxen; and if the journey be not over 1000 miles, and the grass abundant, even without grain, I think mules would be preferable. But when the march is to extend 1500 to 2000 miles, or over a rough sandy or muddy road, I believe young oxen will endure better than mules; they will, if properly managed, keep in better condition, and perform the journey in an equally brief space of time. Besides, they are much more economical, a team of six mules costing six hundred dollars, while an eight-ox team only costs upon the frontier about two hundred dollars. Oxen are much less liable to be stampeded and driven off by Indians, and can be pursued and overtaken by horsemen; and, finally, they can, if necessary, be used for beef.[21]

Santa Fe Trail stage driver James Brice recalled the considerations behind the choice of draft stock many years after the last wagon train unhitched in Santa Fe. "When a load of freight was to go through in quick time," Brice commented in 1905,

mules were the motive power.. . . They made better time than the oxen.. . . Mules were also used in the fall and winter when the Indians had burned the grass off the prairies to interfere with the freighters. At that time of the year enough corn would have to be carried to feed the mules on the trip, and the price of hauling freight under such circumstances was, of course, more. In the spring and summer when the grass was green the oxen sustained themselves by grazing.[22]

Some freighters purposely matched their teams by color or other distinguishing characteristics. Colonel James F. Meline described the ox trains he saw in Leavenworth, Kansas, in 1866 as "remarkable, each wagon team consisting of ten yokes of fine oxen, selected and arranged not only for drawing but for pictorial effect, in sets of twenty, either all black, all white, all spotted, or otherwise marked uniformly."[23] How frequently teamsters followed this practice is unknown to the author. However, it is clear from surviving bullwhacker accounts that once a team was selected for a wagon, whether by the wagonmaster or the teamster, that team remained with the assigned wagon for the entire journey.[24] What Meline deemed a "pictorial effect" was likely the bullwhackers' system for quickly identifying their oxen in a train's large herd at yoking time each morning.

In the following chapters, many references will be made to ox wagons and mule wagons—the wagons themselves were different. It was not the style of the wagons, however, that distinguished one from the other, for they looked quite alike; the difference was in how the draft animals were hitched to the vehicles. A mule wagon came with a doubletree mounted by a pin on top of the front hounds and tongue. Hooked to the doubletree were two singletrees, and to these singletrees the traces of the leather harness were attached (to limit the movement of the doubletree, which swiveled in place, stay chains ran back from near each end of the doubletree and were secured to the front axle). For a four-mule (or horse) team, a spreader bar with two singletrees was added by short spreader chains to the end of the tongue. An additional span of mules (making a six-mule team) again required its own spreader bar with singletrees, which was connected to a ring in the end of the tongue by a length of chain, called a fifth chain (Fig. 1.2).[25] The team was driven by a muleskinner, who rode not in the wagon, but on the "near wheeler" (the mule closest to the front wheel on the left side of the wagon).

On an ox wagon, there was no doubletree, nor were spreader bars and singletrees used. Instead, an ox wagon was equipped with a hook attachment on the end of the tongue to which the ring of a double ox yoke was secured. The next yoke was fastened via a fifth chain to the end of the tongue (to relieve this strain on the tongue, there was often a chain that ran from the end of the tongue back to the front axle). Each additional yoke required its own length of chain, which was fastened to the ring of the yoke behind it. The bullwhacker, or ox driver, walked alongside his team; he did not ride like the muleskinner.[26]

1.2.   A six-mule hitch. The harness is not
completely pictured in this drawing.
(Illustration from George Shumway and Howard C. Frey,
Conestoga Wagon, 1750–1850. Courtesy George Shumway.)

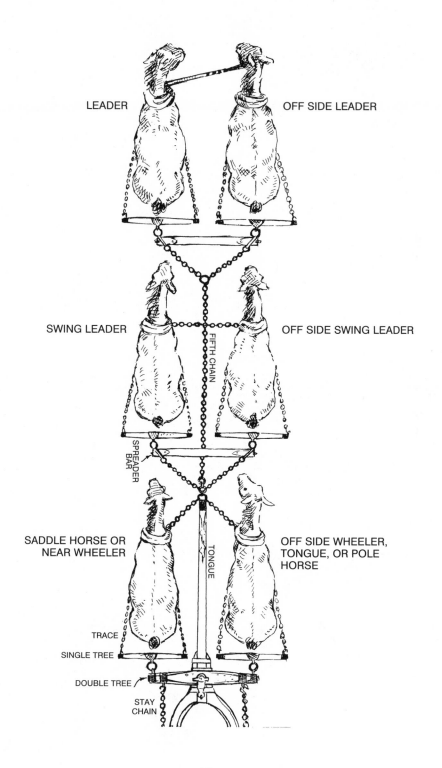

LEADER

OFF SIDE LEADER

SWING LEADER

OFF SIDE SWING LEADER

FIFTH CHAIN

SPREADER BAR

SADDLE HORSE OR
NEAR WHEELER

OFF SIDE WHEELER,
TONGUE, OR POLE
HORSE

TONGUE

TRACE

SINGLE TREE

DOUBLE TREE

STAY
CHAIN

TWO

Wagons from Pennsylvania

It is not known when the first Pennsylvania-made wagons rolled down the Santa Fe Trail. By the late 1830s, however, they had become a prominent fixture of the trade. Thomas J. Farnham, who was in Independence, Missouri, in 1839, wrote: "In the month of May of each year, . . . [Santa Fe] traders congregate here, and buy large Pennsylvania wagons, and teams of mules to convey their calicoes, cottons, cloths, boots, shoes, &c., &c., over the plains.. . ."[1] It is well documented that most of these Pennsylvania wagons were manufactured in Pittsburgh. *Niles' National Register* of July 10, 1841, related the following information obtained from a Pittsburgh newspaper: "Six horse wagons are constructed in Pittsburg, loaded with assorted goods from New York and Philadelphia, transported to Independence in Missouri, and there driven across the country to Mexico, where they were sold and paid for in specie or the best funds." The following year, the *Pittsburgh Morning Chronicle* boasted of the purchases made in Pittsburgh by three Hispanic traders, which included twenty-six large wagons and forty packages of harness sets for 172 mules. In 1843, a party of Santa Fe traders spent twenty thousand dollars in Pittsburgh, some of that total going to the purchase of fifty new wagons, as well as harness for 700 mules.[2] Finally, Josiah Gregg, in his *Commerce of the Prairies*, states plainly that "the wagons now [1844] most in use upon the Prairies are manufactured in Pittsburg; and are usually drawn by eight mules or the same number of oxen."[3]

Why Pittsburgh? By the 1840s there were several wagon shops and factories located in and around Pittsburgh. Here, they had access to supplies of coal, iron, and lumber as well as the immense overland freighting business of the roads from Philadelphia and Baltimore. Pittsburgh was also an

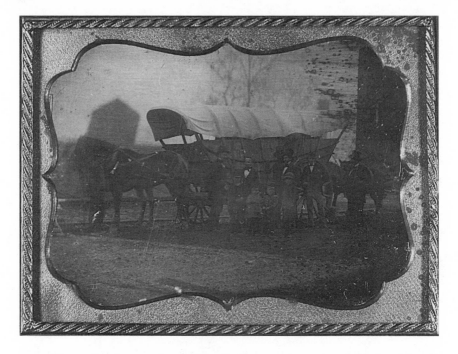

2.1.   The earliest known photograph of a Conestoga wagon, a half-plate daguer-reotype, ca. 1849. (Courtesy of William Welling.)

important shipping point on the Ohio River through which goods purchased or imported at New York, Philadelphia, and Baltimore were funneled to the West.[4] Santa Fe traders on their way to these cities to make their selections passed through Pittsburgh and made purchases of convenience while there; Pittsburgh wagons were easily shipped on board steamboats along with the boxes and bales of new merchandise destined for the Southwest.[5] And the price was right. One Santa Fe trader informed the *Pittsburgh Morning Chronicle* in 1842 that wagons and harness could be "contracted for at a cheaper rate in Pittsburgh than in any other place in the United States."[6]

The type of freight wagon purchased by Santa Fe traders at Pittsburgh, and perhaps elsewhere in Pennsylvania, was the Conestoga (Figs. 2.1, 2.2, and 2.3), or variations thereof. This distinctive freighter is believed to have first come into general use in southeastern Pennsylvania around the middle of the eighteenth century. Its name is thought to have been taken from the Conestoga River Valley of Lancaster County. The wagon's beginnings do not rest entirely in Pennsylvania, however, for the Conestoga was undoubtedly a product of the

2.2. A large Pennsylvania Conestoga wagon in the collections of the Hagley Museum at Wilmington, Delaware. (Courtesy of Hagley Museum and Library.)

2.3. A Pennsylvania Conestoga wagon, without its cloth cover, currently housed at Fort Larned National Historic Site, Kansas. Note the decorative tool box on the side of the wagon, a feature associated with the classic Conestoga. The wheels on this vehicle are not original to the wagon. (© Mark L. Gardner Collection.)

backgrounds of the settlers who came to America from the British Isles and
Europe.[7] According to one authority, the "Conestoga wagon of North
America was based on the large vehicles of Western Germany and the road
wagons of eighteenth-century Britain."[8]

The Conestoga has been described as "a huge affair, very heavily built,
with a bed higher at each end than in the middle, and topped by a dull-white
cloth cover which had a similar curve of still more pronounced degree."[9]
Another distinguishing characteristic was the paneled look of the wagon's
body. The wagon's two side panels were constructed of three longitudinal
rails, several vertical uprights or standards mortised through these rails, and
thin board planking. The front and rear end gates also were made up of rails,
uprights, and planking. The paneled look came from the fact that the rails
and uprights were visible on the outside of the wagon body (the technical
term for this is *raved body*). Traditional colors for the Conestoga were blue
for the wagon bed and red for the running gear.[10]

By the 1830s, Conestogas had for years been the primary freight carri-
ers on the roads between Philadelphia and Pittsburgh and Baltimore and
Pittsburgh. Indeed, the business of wagon freighting in Pennsylvania had
reached amazing heights. In the early months of 1837, the average daily ar-
rivals of wagons in Pittsburgh were estimated at "50 six-horse teams, loaded
with groceries and all kinds of foreign and domestic merchandise." In this
period of just three months time, the total came to "4,500 wagons loaded
with goods amounting to 27,000,000 pounds."[11] It is not surprising, then,
that the Conestoga freighter, which had already demonstrated its merits on
the uneven routes over the Appalachian Mountains, would be acquired in
large numbers by Santa Fe traders. In fact, with this wagon type being so
prevalent around the Pittsburgh environs, one wonders if the traders had
much of a choice.

Still, even though Santa Fe traders were purchasing Pennsylvania-built
Conestogas, it is important to note that many of these freighters differed
in some significant aspects from the "classic Conestoga" traditionally associated with southeastern Pennsylvania and of which several examples survive in museums. While virtually all of the Conestoga literature focuses on
the "classic" wagon, Conestoga-type wagons were also manufactured in
other regions and states. A recent and revealing study of several existing
early Virginia freight wagons has concluded that, while these wagons contained several features that distinguished them from the Pennsylvania
freighters, they "can properly be classified as Conestogas" (in fact, surviving Pennsylvania Conestogas vary from one to the other, in size and other
small details, although they are still readily recognizable as Conestogas).[12]

Similarly, it is clear that many Conestogas used on the Santa Fe Trail had their own distinguishing characteristics (discussed in chapter 4 of this book), perhaps a result of several factors: cost, the specific demands of the traders themselves, stylistic preferences of the Pittsburgh makers, recent innovations in wagon construction, and so on. It is obvious from contemporary descriptions and artist renderings, however, that, like the Virginia Conestogas, these Santa Fe Trail freighters properly belong in the Conestoga class. Indeed, they were identified as such at the time.[13]

Several firsthand accounts confirm the presence of Conestoga-type wagons on the Santa Fe Trail. Thomas Farnham described the freight wagons he saw in 1839 as "long sunken Pennsylvania wagons," an obvious reference to the Conestoga's curved, downbowed, body.[14] A similar observation comes from the pen of Lewis Garrard, who was on the Trail in 1846. He writes of "the heavily laden, *high before and behind*, Pennsylvania wains careening from side to side in the ruts...." (emphasis added).[15] Some individuals mention Conestogas by name. At a camp on the Santa Fe Trail near the Missouri state line in 1841, Rufus Sage observed "four large Connestoga waggons, with ample canvass tops."[16] Lt. James Abert, a member of the Topographical Engineers, was in New Mexico with the Army of the West in 1846 and, according to his official report, on November 10 camped on the Chihuahua Trail within sight of a train of "forty large Conestoga wagons."[17] Another reference is found in an 1857 issue of *Harper's New Monthly Magazine*, where author Charles Hallock describes (apparently from personal observation) an 1852 Santa Fe Trail caravan that included "fourteen white-tilted Conostoga wagons."[18]

The Conestoga also appears in some noteworthy western fiction of the time. Englishman George A. F. Ruxton traveled through New Mexico and over the Santa Fe Trail to Missouri in 1846–47. Shortly thereafter he wrote a novel about the mountain men based on his observations made in the West. That novel, *Life in the Far West*, first published serially in 1848, is noted for its valuable insights into the everyday life and material culture of the 1840s frontier. Here is Ruxton's description of traders' wagons in a camp near Independence, Missouri:

Upward of forty huge wagons, of Conostoga and Pittsburg build, and covered with snow-white tilts, were ranged in a semicircle, or rather a horse-shoe form, on the flat, open prairie, their long "tongues" (poles) pointing outward; with the necessary harness for four pairs of mules, or eight yoke of oxen, lying on the ground beside them, spread in ready order for "hitching up."[19]

By far the most graphic description of Conestoga wagons used by South-west traders was written by a young Missouri volunteer in the Army of the West by the name of Frank S. Edwards. About December 22, 1846, Edwards viewed the traders' caravan that was following Colonel Alexander W. Doniphan's Chihuahua expedition. The caravan was then spread be-tween camps at San Diego and Robledo, at the southern end of the Jornada del Muerto on the Chihuahua Trail. Edwards described what he saw thus:

> Encamped here . . . were about three hundred wagons belonging to the traders; and to one who has never seen these traveling merchants on their journey, the whole is interesting. Their wagons, called Con-estoga or Pennsylvanian, are of the largest kind, covered with three or four cotton covers or sheets drawn close at each end so as to exclude moisture, and these are supported by high hoops, and, as those at the ends of the wagon are much higher than those in the middle, it has a very singular appearance. The height to the top of these end-hoops is usually from eighteen to twenty feet. They are each drawn by ten mules or six yoke of oxen, and contain about forty hundred weight of goods each.[20]

In support of the written accounts are several contemporary engravings, woodcuts, and drawings picturing Conestoga-type wagons on the Santa Fe and Chihuahua trails. Josiah Gregg's *Commerce of the Prairies*, first published in 1844 by Henry G. Langley of New York City, contains four illustrations showing freight wagons with Conestoga features, the most notable being the engraving entitled "March of the Caravan" (Fig. 2.4). This engraving distinctly portrays wagons on the Trail with curved bodies and outward-canted end gates. While it is almost certain that the artists who created the illustrations for *Commerce of the Prairies* never traveled the Santa Fe Trail, it is known that Gregg was in New York City for the first half of 1844, paying close attention to his book's production, and thus may have super-vised to some degree the artists' efforts.[21] In fact, many of the illustrations in *Commerce of the Prairies* contain authentic details that would have been impossible to render accurately simply from studying Gregg's text. And although it was a common practice for illustrators to "borrow" from ear-lier published works, the author has been unable to locate any previous depictions of the Santa Fe Trail that contain similarities to the illustrations in Gregg's book.[22]

A now-famous engraving of Independence, Missouri, (Fig. 2.5) an im-portant outfitting point for Santa Fe Trail traffic, pictures a Conestoga-type

2.4. "March of the Caravan," an engraving from the 1855 edition of Josiah Gregg's *Commerce of the Prairies*. This engraving is identical with the image that appeared in the 1844 first edition of Gregg's work. (Courtesy of the State Historical Society of Missouri.)

2.5. Independence, Missouri, an engraving from *The United State Illustrated: The West*, New York, 1853. (Courtesy of the Kansas State Historical Society.)

wagon on the town square. This engraving, part of a series of views of western towns published by Herrmann Meyer of New York City in 1853, is
believed to represent Independence as it appeared about 1847–1850 and
may have been based upon a daguerreotype.[23] However, it has been shown
that other views in the above series are not entirely faithful to the earlier
images they were drawn from; in at least two cases, various vehicles appear
in the engravings that are not in the original source images.[24] It is possible,
then, that the unknown artist for the Independence engraving could have
added the Conestoga to the scene — and the other vehicles as well. Yet without the original source for the engraving, this will never be known. Artis-
tic license or not, the fact that the engraving includes a representation of a
Conestoga, a wagon type mentioned in the contemporary Trail literature,
bears consideration. Additionally, two firsthand Trail accounts of the late
1840s also contain illustrations containing Conestoga-type wagons, although the provenance of these images is impossible to document.[25]

Fortunately, there exist three early images featuring overland freight
wagons where the artist is both identified and known to have rendered his
work from on-the-spot observation. In 1840, a young British army lieuten-
ant by the name of William Fairholme and several companions struck out
along the Santa Fe Trail for a grand hunting excursion on the Great Plains.
Fairholme kept a detailed journal of the trip and also made several wonderful sketches.[26] One of the latter, a view of their "Ground Ash Camp" of
October 28–29, pictures all four vehicles that were a part of the expedition
(Fig. 2.6). Three wagons had been purchased in St. Louis to transport the
personal belongings of the adventurers. Two of these were drawn by a pair
of mules each and sported striped canvas covers; the third, a smaller wagon,
was drawn by a single mule. A fourth wagon was "hired" at Independence
to haul the Indian corn that was purchased for the many horses taken on the
expedition.[27]

The Independence wagon, apparently a freighter, was drawn by oxen;
Fairholme described it in his journal as a "large box-waggon." In Fairholme's sketch of the Ground Ash Camp, a nice profile of the ox wagon is
provided, and it is instantly recognizable as a Conestoga-type vehicle. Its
curved body with a definite rise to the rear, the outward-canted end gates,
and cloth cover echoing the curve of the wagon's top rail, stand out sharply
from the simple box forms of the personal vehicles in the scene.

The second early depiction (Fig. 2.7) is an engraving made from a drawing
by M. Rondé, a Frenchman who visited the state of Chihuahua, Mexico, in
1849.[28] Titled "Chariots de Chihuahua," the engraving depicts Conestoga-type
wagons and a Mexican *carreta* at the hacienda or village of Corralitos, the home

2.6. "Ground Ash Camp" by William Fairholme, from his 1840 journal. (Courtesy of the Henry E. Huntington Library and Art Gallery.)

2.7. "Chariots de Chihuahua," an engraving based on a sketch by M. Rondé. From *Le Tour Du Monde*, vol. 4 (1861), p. 147.

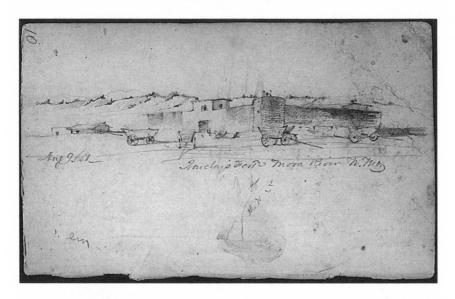

2.8.   Barclay's Fort, New Mexico, August 9, 1851. A sketch by Edward Kern. (Courtesy of the Henry E. Huntington Library and Art Gallery.)

of merchant José María Zuloaga, an operator of local silver smelters. Mexican merchants, including many from Chihuahua, are known to have purchased and used American freight wagons, and from Rondé's account of his experiences in Chihuahua, it is probable that the Conestogas pictured in his rare illustration were the property of Zuloaga.[29]

The third important image is found on the inside cover of a diary kept by artist Edward Kern. It is a sketch of Barclay's Fort, on the Santa Fe Trail near Watrous, New Mexico, dated August 9, 1851 (Fig. 2.8).[30] In this view, several wagons can be seen parked haphazardly around the walls of the adobe stronghold. Although the sketch is rough and the wagons are missing their hoops and cloth covers, distinct Conestoga characteristics are visible, primarily the overhanging end gates and the slightly curved lines of the wagon bodies.

Pennsylvania Wagon Makers

In 1826, Pittsburgh had "7 establishments where wagons and ploughs of a dozen different kinds are made—employ 35 hands, and manufacture per year to the amount of 12,000 dollars."[31] A survey of existing Pittsburgh city directories for the 1830s, 1840s, and 1850s reveals the identities of several wagon makers situated in and near the city (some of the wagon manufactories of this period were actually located in the village of Manchester, a short distance downstream from Pittsburgh, although warehouses for these establishments were often in Pittsburgh proper). In the 1837 directory are advertisements for Samuel Kissick, who kept "on hand, ready to ship at short notice, a good stock of the best Wagon Work," and Marlatts & Hall, "Plough and Wagon Manufacturers."[32] The wagon-making firm of Townsend & Radle, Manchester, advertising in the directory for 1839, stated that they had

> on hand and are daily manufacturing a good supply of all kinds of WAGGONS, CARTS, WHEEL BARROWS, &C. either for town or country, for the river trade or for western and southern planters. They manufactured last year, about $40,000 worth, and are preparing to extend their business by a steam engine.[33]

An interesting list of nine coach and wagon makers appears in the 1844 directory for the cities of Pittsburgh and Allegheny: Thomas Donahu, John Donahu, Jacob Fedder, Jacob Wise, Neal McIlwayn, Wm. McCegua (M'Cague, later M'Kee) (Fig. 2.9), Robert D. Nicholson, David Sloan, and Cyrus Townsend. Manufacturers who advertised themselves as wagon makers in the 1850 directory were William M'Kee, and Daniel T. Johnston & Brothers. In the 1854 volume there were advertisements for Phelps, Carr & Co., F. Aeschlemann, and J. & M. Fischer.[34]

Not all wagon makers placed advertisements in the directories, however. Some shops changed hands over time or went out of business, and there were undoubtedly those small establishments who catered only to local trade. According to an 1854 article on the commerce and manufactures of Pittsburgh, there were then seven carriage manufacturers in the city and

> 2 very extensive wagon factories, where are manufactured every year an incredible number of light and heavy wagons of every description.... Most of their products go far West.... The larger of these establishments supplied our army while in Mexico [1846–1848] with most of the camp and baggage wagons, gun-carriages, &c.[35]

By this time, Pittsburgh had clearly established a national reputation as a wagon manufacturing center. German traveler Julius Froebel wrote of twenty freight wagons purchased in 1853 for the Chihuahua trade that "had been ordered at one of the celebrated manufactories in Pittsburg."[36]

WM. M'CAGUE,

Manufacturer of

WAGONS, CARTS, DRAYS, TRUCKS,

TIMBER WHEELS, &C.

Head of Seventh Street,

PITTSBURGH.

Work of all kinds kept on hand, or made to order.

2.9. Wm. M'Cague's advertisement in *Harris's General Business Directory of the Cities of Pittsburgh & Allegheny* (1847).

It is difficult to determine which Pittsburgh shops did the most business with Santa Fe and Chihuahua traders. However, two are known to have catered to this particular clientele—William M'Kee and Cyrus Townsend. M'Kee's 1850 directory advertisement announced: "Those engaged in the Santa Fe trade, and Furnace men, are requested to give him a call before purchasing elsewhere." M'Kee had been in business in Pittsburgh at least as early as 1839. Townsend, a native of New York, is found in the 1839 directory as a blacksmith and a member of the firm of Townsend & Radle, noted above. By 1841 he was the sole owner of what he advertised as the Manchester Wagon Factory (Fig. 2.10).

Surviving records indicate that Cyrus Townsend was patronized by more Southwest traders than any other Pittsburgh wagon maker of his time. According to the *Pittsburgh Morning Chronicle* of March 5, 1842, three Hispanic traders by the names of Otero, Armijo, and Perea purchased from

FOR SALE

BY ISAAC HARRIS,

No. 120, Liberty Street,

Pittsburgh.

And generally by agents in all the principal cities and towns throughout the West.

MANCHESTER WAGON FACTORY.

CYRUS TOWNSEND,

(*Successor to Townsend & Radle,*)

WHOLESALE AND RETAIL

Carriage, Sleigh, Wagon, Cart, & Timber Wheel

MANUFACTURER:

Warehouse, St. Clair Street,

Adjoining the Bridge,

PITTSBURGH, PA.

2.10.   Cyrus Townsend's advertisement in *Harris' General Business Directory, of the Cities of Pittsburgh and Allegheny* (1841).

Townsend "twenty-six large wagons, suitable for the trade in which they are engaged." They paid for the vehicles in gold. The following year, a party of Santa Fe traders acquired "50 good new wagons made by Mr. Townsend."[37] A surviving invoice book for the Southwest trading firm of Owens & Aull records a purchase of fifteen wagons and five "Sleeping Wagons" from Cyrus Townsend in April of 1846.[38] It was these very wagons, apparently, that became the subject of controversy in the press later that year.

On September 9, 1846, the St. Louis *Missouri Republican* reported that a letter received from Bent's Fort spoke "in disparaging terms of the wagons purchased by the traders at Pittsburgh. A great portion of the time was occupied in repairing them, and on their arrival at the Fort much the largest

portion of the timber in them was not that with which they started." The
paper went on to encourage wagon purchases in St. Louis. It did not take
long for this little news item to make its way east. The *Republican* noted on
September 30 that the *Wheeling Times* (Virginia) had responded to the statements in the letter by proclaiming that "Wheeling furnishes the right kind
of wagons." The Pittsburgh *Chronicle* quickly rejoined this attack on its
manufactures: "The wagons of which the complaints were made, were *not*
Pittsburgh wagons. They were manufactured elsewhere. The statement
made in St. Louis papers was most emphatically denied by Mr. Townsend,
the principal carriage maker in our city. Mr. Townsend showed that no
wagons from this city had reached St. Louis at the time when the complaints
were made.. . ." But the *Republican* stood by its story and also took the opportunity to slip in another taunt. The Pittsburgh "wagons not only reached
St. Louis, but had, as stated, made the trip to Fort Bent, so much, at least,
as was left of them. . . ."

Cyrus Townsend's denial may have resulted from confusion over the
delay involved in receiving letters from the plains. Or, in the interest of
business, he may have conveniently forgotten his transaction with Owens
& Aull, who indeed traveled the Santa Fe and Chihuahua trails that year.
Townsend seems to have quit the wagon business or retired by 1854, when
the firm of Phelps, Carr & Co. listed themselves as the successors to Townsend, Carr & Co.

Despite the popularity of Pittsburgh wagons, it is probable that Southwest traders also purchased wagons from manufacturers in Philadelphia,
another center for wagon making in Pennsylvania at that time and an important stop for western merchants. *O'Brien's Philadelphia Wholesale Business Directory . . . for the Year 1844 . . .* lists twelve firms and individuals under
the heading of wagon, dray, cart, and wheelbarrow manufacturers: Nicholas Coleman; Everham & Colsher; B. Flum; Isaac Potts; George Richards;
Robert B. Scott; Henry Simons; Adam F. Sylvestor; T. W. Simpers; Samuel
Ware; D. G. Wilson, J. Childs & Co.; and William Wood. Three of the
above makers, William Wood, Henry Simons, and Wilson, Childs & Co.,
had advertisements in the directory that stated they gave "prompt attention"
to orders from, in addition to the United States, South America, the West
Indies, Texas, and Mexico.[39]

Wilson, Childs & Co. (Figs. 2.11 and 2.12) had been in business in Philadelphia since 1829, when Wilson, a wheelwright, and Childs, a blacksmith,
formed a partnership. The firm built the prototype of the six-mule army
wagon, designed by Major George H. Crosman of the Quartermaster's Department shortly after the Mexican War. Once Crosman's design (notable

2.11. Portrait of David G. Wilson, Philadelphia wagon maker. (© Mark L. Gardner Collection.)

primarily for its "uniformity of construction in all the parts" and its ability to be drawn by either mules or oxen) was adopted by the army, Wilson, Childs & Co. manufactured many of the wagons subsequently used by the military in the West.[40] Percival G. Lowe, a civilian wagonmaster with the Quartermaster's Department in the 1850s, wrote: "Until the Mormon War [1857], nearly all the Government wagons used at Fort Leavenworth were made in Philadelphia—The Wilson Wagon,' so called—and they were absolutely perfect."[41]

Beginning in the 1860s, heavy freight wagons manufactured by Wilson, Childs & Co. were sold by August Staacke of San Antonio, Texas, for use

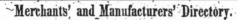

BEGGS & ROWLAND,

WHEELWRIGHTS,

Nos. 220 and 222 North Front Street.
PHILADELPHIA.

Where they continue to manufacture extensively, and in the most substantial manner for home use and exportation, every description of Light and Heavy Wagons, Drays and Carts, Timber Wheels and Wheelbarrows. Orders from any part of the United States, South America, West Indies, Texas and Mexico, will meet prompt attention and will be executed on the most reasonable terms. Planters and others may depend upon the most satisfactory attention, care and despatch, being paid to all their orders for wheelwright work by addressing their commands to them at their establishment above mentioned.

D. G. WILSON, J. CHILDS & CO.,
WHEELWRIGHTS,

No. 305 North Third Street,
BETWEEN NOBLE AND TAMANY STREETS,
PHILADELPHIA.

Where they continue to manufacture extensively and in the most substantial manner, for home use and exportation, every description of light and heavy Wagons, Carts, Drays, Timber Wheels, Ox Carts, Wheels and Wheelbarrows, all of the very best materials and workmanship.

Orders from any part of the United States, South America, West Indies, and Mexico, will meet prompt attention, and will be executed on the most liberal terms.

Planters and others may depend upon the most satisfactory attention, care, and despatch being paid to all their orders for Wheelwright work, by addressing their commands to them, at their establishment above mentioned, or to their Agents, D. G. Wilson, No. 24 Perdido st, New Orleans ; Messrs. Barnwall & Filler, Mobile.

2.12. Advertisements of Philadelphia wagon makers in *O'Brien's Philadelphia Wholesale Business Merchants and Manufacturers' Directory . . . for the Year 1853.*

in the overland trade between that place and Chihuahua, Mexico.[42] An 1867 advertisement of Wilson, Childs & Co. lists "Chihuahua Wagons" among the many vehicle types available from its factory.[43] These wagons, however, were larger than those employed on the Santa Fe Trail, and they were apparently only available with iron axles.[44] According to Texas freighter August Santleben, the wagons "were constructed to withstand the wear and tear of the rocky and mountainous roads in western Texas and Mexico, and they could not be used to advantage elsewhere on account of their weight, which was estimated to be about four thousand pounds."[45]

Although firms like Wilson, Childs & Co. continued to sell wagons to western customers through the 1860s and undoubtedly later, the dominance of Pennsylvania-made freight wagons (civilian wagons are being referred to here) appears to have waned beginning in the 1850s, if not earlier. This was due primarily to competition from wagon makers in other states, especially Missouri and Illinois, some of whom were conveniently located at trail outfitting points.[46] The increasingly large numbers of freight wagons employed each year in the West drove the wagon-making business and encouraged the establishment of additional shops and factories. One man wrote of the Santa Fe trade in 1848: "Very little of the stock or wagons ever return [from New Mexico], which keeps up the demand for wagons and stock."[47] And those wagons that did make more than one eight-hundred-mile trip could not be expected to last for long. Isaac Jones Wistar, who was in Independence in 1849, remembered seeing in "some low-lying ground and meadows adjacent, at least fifty or more acres of old and worn-out Santa Fé wagons . . . falling to decay."[48] Less than ten years later, a total of 9,784 wagons are reported to have traveled to New Mexico from Kansas City in one year alone.[49] While some of these were certainly made in Pittsburgh, Pennsylvania's near monopoly of the business of the early 1840s was never to return.

THREE

A Missouri Wagon Industry

By necessity, Santa Fe traders, fur trappers, emigrants, military expeditions, and various travelers either passed through or began their western journeys from various Missouri towns, among them St. Louis, Franklin, Lexington, Independence, and Westport. Merchants and mechanics located in these communities were obviously in an extremely advantageous position to capitalize on this steady traffic. They did so in what was known as the "outfitting trade": the selling of various needed supplies for an overland trip, including clothing, firearms and ammunition, fresh foodstuffs, saddles, horses, mules, and oxen, and, eventually, wagons and carriages. William H. Eisele's memories of Westport are typical of an outfitting town during its heyday: "There were many harness shops, blacksmith shops and wagon shops to equip the freight trains and supply the Mexican trade. Also many farmers made yokes and bows in the winter time and there was good demand for them."[1]

Although Independence, Missouri, became the primary outfitting point for Santa Fe expeditions soon after it was laid out in 1827, several years passed before wagon making became a significant industry. At first, local blacksmiths made minor repairs or modifications to wagons that were purchased elsewhere and shipped to that place (a common job was the resetting of tires). Beginning in the 1840s, however, Independence supplied a considerable number of locally made wagons for the "commerce of the prairies." Statistics for the Santa Fe trade published by an Independence newspaper in 1844 show that out of a total of ninety-two wagons estimated to have traveled down the Santa Fe Trail that season, fifty were made in Independence. And, according to the paper, the town's wagon makers had orders for seventy-five wagons for the following spring.[2]

3.1. Lewis Jones (1799–1876), Independence blacksmith and entrepreneur. (Courtesy of the Local History Center, Public Library, Canon City, Colo.)

The demand for iron for wagons was such that in March 1846, Independence merchants W. & J. McCoy wrote to the proprietors of the Meremac Iron Works, near present-day St. James, Missouri, inquiring about the price and availability of various types of iron. The letter was written on behalf of a local blacksmith who had "worked up during the past year 32 Tons of Iron for the Santa Fe trade. His prospects the coming one is better than usual and he has contracts out at present for from 20 to 30 large waggons to be completed by June." The merchants added that a "Mexican Trader has just come in and has engaged from our Blksmiths [sic] 34 waggons & pays cash on their delivery."[3] Four years later, Independence boasted "several large Wagon and Carriage Manufactories in which are between 40 and 50 forges."[4] German traveler Julius Froebel found the town in 1852 "surrounded by wheelwrights' shops, large premises filled with new waggons, painted red, green, or blue."[5]

NOTICE

To Santa Fe Traders and Oregon
EMIGRANTS.

THE subscriber is now prepared to ex-ecute all orders in his line of business, and will keep on hand all the different sizes of *Mule and Ox*

Wagons, suited either for the Mexican trade, or the Emierants to Oregon or California.— He is also prepared to supply the Farmers with all the various kinds of farming utensils, and at prices that cannot fail to please.— Having on hand between 15 and 20 tons of assorted Iron, and wagon boxes of all sizes, he respectfully invites all wishing to purchase and to have good work done, to give him a call. Remember the old established stand on Main street, opposite the Locust Grove Hotel.

JOHN W. MODIE.

October 25, 1845.   3m7

3.2.   Advertisement for Independence wagon maker John W. Modie in *The Western Expositor*, Jan. 31, 1846.

Among the very early wagon makers in Independence was Lewis Jones (Fig. 3.1). Jones established a blacksmith shop on the town square in 1827 and for several years in the 1830s worked as the government blacksmith for the nearby Shawnee Indian tribe. The number of wagons he produced for the Santa Fe trade was probably minimal, for he appears to have eventually quit the life of a smith to partake of other business opportunities, including trading expeditions to New Mexico and Chihuahua (beginning in 1829); he built the Nebraska House Hotel in Independence in 1849.[6]

Independence wagon makers active in the 1840s included John W. Modie, Robert Stone, Andrew J. Hoyal, Frank Simpson, and Robert Weston.[7] In 1845 and 1846, Modie published an ad in *The Western Expositor* (Fig. 3.2) in which he stated that he would keep "on hand all the different sizes of *Mule and Ox Wagons*, suited either for the Mexican trade, or the Emierants [*sic*] to Oregon or California."[8] Andrew J. Hoyal, formerly of the wagon-making firm of Hoyal & Bean, gave notice in the same paper in 1846 that he was "prepared to fill orders for Santa Fe, Oregon and California wagons, made in the most substantial manner of the very best materials."[9] Trader James Josiah Webb purchased approximately five wagons from Robert Stone in the spring of 1846, taking them all the way to San Juan de los Lagos, Mexico. Webb arrived back in Independence with four of the wagons the next year and dropped them off with Stone for sadly-needed repairs—they had traveled eight thousand miles.[10]

Eleven individuals and/or firms are listed as wagon makers in the 1850 industrial census for Jackson County, Missouri: G. I. (or G. J.) Biggs, Frederick Klaber, Leven P. Wills, James C. Mason, George Rider, Dennis Dale, Shaw & McClellen (listed as wagon and carriage makers), David Vance, Benjamin Dresser, Enoch Moore, and Henry Long.[11] Seven of the shops were relatively small operations, employing only one to three people apiece. The remaining four manufacturers employed more workers and, significantly, they each have an additional entry in the census as blacksmiths. For example, James C. Mason is listed as a blacksmith with sixteen workers and then as a wagon maker with six, thus making a total of twenty-two individuals employed in his overall operation. The advantage of running both blacksmith *and* wagon shops was that one firm could produce an entire wagon. Traditionally, a wagon maker fashioned only the wooden parts of a vehicle and then sent his work off to a blacksmith to be "ironed" (skeins for axletrees, hub bands and tires for wheels, various hooks, chains, and so on). In some cases, an arrangement or partnership existed between the two craftsmen whereby the sale price of the finished wagon would be divided. Probably more often, however, the wagon maker simply figured the blacksmith's fees into his prices.[12] This system still prevailed with some of the smaller shops in Independence at this time. For example, blacksmith Thomas C. Peers's annual product is listed simply as "Iron 50 Wagons." The value of this work is given as 1,750 dollars, which indicates that Peers received roughly 35 dollars for each wagon ironed.[13] This practice soon disappeared as large wagon "manufactories" became the norm.

In a very short time during the 1850s, a former Tennessee slave rose to become the leading wagon manufacturer in Independence. Hiram Young came to Missouri as the property of a George Young, but in 1847 he purchased his freedom, afterward settling in Liberty, Missouri, with his family before finally locating in Independence about 1850. Young is listed in the 1850 population schedules for Jackson County as a carpenter. By the next year, however, he had established himself as a manufacturer of ox yokes

and freight wagons for government contractors and others. Sometime before July of 1854, Young took on a partner, another free black by the name
of Dan Smith. Yet this partnership, operating under the firm name of
Young & Smith, lasted only until August of 1855. After the firm's dissolu-
tion, Young continued in the wagon-making business "on his own hook."[14]
By the late 1850s, Young had captured a respectable share of the business
with overland freighters, his wagons competing successfully with those
produced in much larger cities. James Thomas, a fellow free black, recalled:
"People who had to deal with Hiram Young, a tall, dark skin colored man,
found him to be a good business man. He had a large plant and gave employment to all white and black. Wagons of his make could be seen on the
plains from Kansas City to San Francisco."[15] Percival G. Lowe remembered:
"Contractors and nearly all big freighters crossing the plains used wooden
axle wagons made by Murphy or Espenscheidt [Espenschied] of St. Louis,
or Young and others of Independence, Missouri, and were able to carry
their 6,000-pound loads anywhere."[16] William B. Napton, who traveled the
Santa Fe Trail with a freight caravan in 1857, stated that the wagons in their
"train were made by Hiram Young, a free negro at Independence, and they
were considered as good as any except those with iron axles."[17] In 1860,
Young employed twenty-five men in his wagon and yoke factory, producing approximately three hundred wagons and six thousand yokes a year.[18]

Although Independence and its rival neighbor, Westport, boasted several
wagon makers in the 1850s, St. Louis was a much larger wagon-making center, with more than double, if not triple, the number of builders. St. Louis–
made wagons had seen service on the Santa Fe Trail at least as early as 1825, a
full two years before Independence's founding.[19] Of all the St. Louis wagon
makers, Joseph Murphy (Fig. 3.3) is by far the best known today. Indeed, his
wagons have become an integral part of Santa Fe Trail lore, often being referred
to as the "standard" plains freighter (this is especially interesting considering
that no Murphy freight wagon is currently known to exist, nor are there any
surviving images identified as depicting Murphy freight wagons). As it turns
out, much of the legend that has grown up around Murphy, particularly his
supposed development of a "monster" wagon used by Santa Fe traders in the
1840s, is not substantiated by primary sources.

Murphy, a native of Ireland, apprenticed in the shop of St. Louis wagon
maker Daniel Caster from 1819 to 1825. After completing his apprenticeship, he worked for short periods under James Earl, John B. Gerard, Samuel
Mount, and Edward Harrington before establishing his own business on
June 22, 1826.[20] According to Murphy's surviving account books, much of
his livelihood for the first several years consisted not in constructing wag-

3.3.   Joseph Murphy (1805–1901), St. Louis wagon maker. (© Mark L. Gardner Collection.)

ons, but in repairing a variety of vehicles, including wheelbarrows. He took on such piecemeal work as replacing handles in hammers and augers, constructing cart wheels on order, and, for local farmers, fashioning and repairing plows.[21] Actually, this type of work was an important side business for many wagon makers.

The first reference to a Santa Fe wagon in the Murphy business records appears in the account of a Jacob Jarrett under the date of March 19, 1827: "by Making santafee waggon.... 27.00."[22] A number of historians and writers have mistakenly interpreted this entry to mean that Jarrett purchased the wagon. However, it is clear from a close study of Murphy's accounts that Jarrett was an employee of Murphy who *made* the wagon, thus receiving a credit of twenty-seven dollars for his work.[23] Murphy employed several wagon makers over the years, and instead of the employees working jointly to fill various wagon orders, it appears that they were individually assigned wagons to make. They then received a credit in the account books for the completed vehicles. One of many examples of this system is the 1849 account of Murphy employee Henry Beters, who received a credit of seventy-five dollars "by Making 4 heavy Santa fee wagons."[24]

After the Jarrett entry of 1827, the next specific reference to a Santa Fe wagon does not appear in Murphy's records until twenty years later. However, Murphy did not consistently identify wagons intended for use on the Santa Fe Trail in his accounts.[25] Also, there is an unfortunate gap in the Murphy records from December 1840 until May 1847, the very same period that supposedly saw Murphy's "monster" wagons gain premier status among merchants and freighters on the Santa Fe Trail.

The Murphy legend has its origins in an article published in the *Missouri Historical Review* in 1952: "Joseph Murphy's Contribution to the Development of the West," by Emily Ann O'Neil Bott.[26] According to this article, when New Mexico governor Manuel Armijo imposed a new customs duty of five hundred dollars per wagon in 1839, Santa Fe traders would have been "ruined" but for Murphy, who began building them a much larger wagon. Bott then quotes a description of this new wagon written by Murphy's son, Anselm, in 1938. Following is the quotation as it appears in Bott's essay:

> the wheels were seven feet high, the height of the bed was such that a man standing inside would barely disclose the top of his head. The wagon was moved by four pair of oxen. The rim of the wheels were eight inches wide, the spokes, young oak saplings, and the tongue was fifty feet long. The wheels were not bound with iron, which could not be obtained.[27]

Contemporary accounts do indeed confirm the impact of Armijo's new policy on wagon size. Josiah Gregg writes in his *Commerce of the Prairies* (1844) that "the traders soon took to conveying their merchandise only in the largest wagons, drawn by ten or twelve mules."[28] David H. Coyner, in his *The Lost Trappers* (1847), states that to "take the advantage of this regulation, the traders have wagons made that will contain seventy or eighty hundred weight, with very wide tire."[29] A more conservative estimate of the hauling capacity comes from Lt. James W. Abert, who encountered a train of forty-two wagons on the Cimarron Route of the Santa Fe Trail in 1845, "most of them capable of carrying 5000 lbs. The wagons are made large on account of the duty being charged per wagon."[30] It is significant, however, that no contemporary source gives Murphy (or any wagon maker, for that matter) credit for the innovation of larger wagons on the Trail. In fact, Murphy wagons are not mentioned in any extant 1840s Santa Fe Trail accounts. And if Murphy is to be credited for single-handedly providing the means for the merchants to take advantage of Armijo's duty, then how does one explain the numerous wagons that Southwest traders continued to purchase yearly in Pittsburgh, Independence, and elsewhere?

There are also major problems with Anselm Murphy's description of the "monster" wagon. First, a wagon tongue fifty feet long is simply ludicrous (unless it served double duty as a flagpole). Also, such a large wagon, fully loaded, would undoubtedly require more than four yoke of oxen to pull it. Additionally, the eight-inch width of the wheels is very questionable, particularly the subsequent assertion by historians that this width became standard for Santa Fe Trail freight wagons.[31] While it was possible for a wagon maker to construct such wheels (and contrary to Anselm Murphy's statement, iron was available at the time for the tire, although it probably would have required the piecing together of several sections, an operation called straking), contemporary references from the 1840s and later consistently note tire widths that are far narrower than the eight inches claimed.

In 1845, James M. Maxey wrote from Independence to James Frazier Reed, advising him that if he intended "to go by Santefee—you had better in the first place get you a large waggon made about 3 inches on the tread and will beare about 6 thousand pounds."[32] Even Joseph Murphy's own account books contradict the wide-wheel story. Of all the wagons described in the Murphy accounts (1847–1853) that can be safely identified as intended for the Santa Fe trade, the largest specified tire width found was three and one-half inches. The remainder are three inches or less. If the eight-inch width was truly ideal, one would expect to see its continued use on freight wagons, especially by the man who is credited with developing the prototype. And although there is the David H. Coyner reference to large wagons with "very wide tire," we are left to guess at what Coyner judged to be wide. Thomas Searight tells us that the "broad wheeled, or 'broad tread wagon,'" used on the National Road in the first half of the nineteenth century had tires "about four inches" wide.[33]

Like many a colorful story, the tale of the "invention" of a huge Murphy wagon in response to Armijo's per-wagon duty is more folklore than fact. Certainly a wagon with all the dimensions and features provided by Anselm Murphy never existed, nor did any kind of "monster wagon" become the standard plains freighter (Anselm was not yet born when this episode is supposed to have taken place, so his information obviously did not come from personal observation).[34] However, it is indeed probable that Murphy constructed some of the large wagons known to have been used by the traders in the 1840s. Like any wagon maker, he built vehicles to his customers' specifications. But, contrary to the legend, he was not alone in this endeavor. Wagon makers from Pittsburgh and Independence surely filled orders for large wagons too.[35]

Another feature of the Murphy legend is his reputation as a "painstaking master craftsman."[36] It seems that no Murphy product was less than perfect. According to one writer, his "wagons were made of only the best selected, well seasoned lumber."[37] In this regard, there is contemporary evidence that Murphy did manufacture a superior product. The St. Louis *Missouri Republican* reported in 1850 that "of all the wagons taken to Santa Fe this year, those only that were manufactured in this city, by Mr. J. Murphy, have withstood all the injurious effects of the heat."[38] Yet an 1856 letter from a Santa Fe merchant reveals that Murphy, human after all, could experience the occasional problem with quality control. "I am told," wrote John Kingsbury to his partner, "that many of Murphy's Waggons turned out mean last year. [Henry] Connelly had 6 out of 7 new ones entirely used up."[39]

While an attempt has been made here to strip Murphy of much of the myth that surrounds him, there is no denying that he was one of the important manufacturers of wagons used on the Santa Fe Trail. Indeed, by the late 1850s his wagons were among the few actually favored by freighters. His surviving business records, which only go to 1853, contain several accounts with Southwest traders, both Mexican and American, including Richard Owens, Alexander Barclay, Branham & McCausland, Seth E. Ward, Beck & Brent, and F. X. Aubry. Murphy also received numerous government contracts for wagons. According to the 1850 industrial census, Murphy's business employed twenty-five men and had an annual product of four hundred wagons and drays valued at thirty-two thousand dollars.[40] An 1894 account (published seven years before the wagon maker's death) claims that "over 200,000 wagons were built by Mr. Murphy [or] under his immediate supervision."[41] Although this figure is probably far too high, it does reflect Murphy's preeminence as a wagon maker.

Despite the name recognition that Murphy's wagons would come to enjoy, he was not without strong competition from other St. Louis makers. The 1850 St. Louis city directory lists eleven individuals under the heading of Wagon Makers: Christian Augustin, Benj. M. Backensto, Saml B. Bellis, Peter Conrad, Fredk Hackman, Joseph Jahla, H. W. Knollhoff, John F. Knollhoff, Joseph Murphy, Henry Steidman [or Steidemann], and James Virden.[42] Yet this list obviously represents only those wagon makers who paid to be so noted in the directory. United States census statistics for St. Louis for 1850 specify thirty-two wagon makers with a total of 121 workers and an annual production valued at 146,585 dollars.[43] After Murphy, the two largest St. Louis wagon manufacturers were Jacob Scheer and John Kern, and neither appear in the directory listing. Scheer had an annual product in 1850 of 200 wagons with an estimated value of 12,000 dollars, while Kern is listed as a blacksmith and wagon maker with an annual product of 150 wagons valued at 14,500 dollars.[44] In the absence of account books for these builders, however, it is virtually impossible to determine how much of their business was with Santa Fe traders and contract freighters.

Among those wagon makers not found in the 1850 industrial census for St. Louis but believed to have begun manufacturing wagons during this period are Louis Espenschied and John Cook. Espenschied, a native of Germany, established a blacksmithing business in St. Louis in 1843. At what time he expanded to wagon making is unknown. By the late 1850s, however, his freight wagons were among the most popular makes on western trails.[45] W. L. Kuykendall, in discussing the government freighting contracts of Russell, Majors, & Waddell, wrote that to "properly handle the contract there was required the employment of hundreds of big Murphy and Espenschied wagons made in St. Louis, each with a capacity of ten thousand pounds." [46] During the Civil War, Espenschied provided large numbers of wagons and wagon wheels for the Union army.[47]

John Cook supposedly established a wagon manufactory in St. Louis in 1848, and ten years later it was said to be "one of the largest houses in the western country." Cook manufactured wagons, carts, drays, and wheelbarrows "of every description and quality." It was also claimed that "every thing is superintended by the proprietor in person, materials of the most reliable character only allowed to be used, and workmen of superior skill and experience employed in every department of their work." Cook also manufactured army wagons during the Civil War.[48]

Missouri Wagon Makers in New Mexico

In a discussion of New Mexico's mechanical arts, Josiah Gregg commented in 1844: "Wagons of Mexican manufacture are not to be found; although a small number of American-built vehicles, of those introduced by the trading caravans, have grown into use among the people."[49] W. W. H. Davis seconded Gregg's claim thirteen years later, writing that "I do not recollect to have ever seen a wagon of Mexican manufacture."[50] Instead of wagons, Hispanos and Pueblo Indians in the Southwest crafted the well-known *carreta*, or two-wheeled cart. But what about Anglo wagon makers who may have immigrated to New Mexico?

Some Missouri craftsmen did indeed travel to the end of the Santa Fe Trail and set up shop, although documentation is slim. Antonio Barreiro noted the presence of a "few Anglo-American craftsmen" in New Mexico in 1832. "Among the foreign craftsmen," he wrote, "there are tailors, carpenters, blacksmiths, hatters, tinsmiths, shoemakers, excellent gunsmiths, etc., etc."[51] Perhaps the earliest wagon maker to leave the States behind was B. D. Long, who apparently joined a Santa Fe trading venture in 1830. His story is known only because he left two outstanding notes with merchant James Aull of Lexington, Missouri. In 1833, after it was clear that Long had remained in Mexico to practice his profession, Aull instructed his agent in Santa Fe to attempt to collect on the debt. Long, Aull believed, was "working somewhere in the 'lower country.'"[52] The outcome of this bill-collecting effort is not recorded. Nor, unfortunately, is any additional information available on Long and his activities.

Much more information is available on blacksmith James Pool. A native of Virginia, Pool was employed variously as a gunsmith and blacksmith at the Delaware Agency in Kansas from 1830 to 1833, and in 1841 he served as the blacksmith at the Neosho Subagency.[53] Pool eventually located in Independence, Missouri, near the town's southwest corner. Recorded in the Jackson County deed books is a deed of trust executed on May 20, 1846, in which Pool mortgaged all the tools in his shop, including two "full and complete sets" of blacksmith's tools, and a cherry bureau and eight-day metal clock in his home against a promissory note for 180 dollars.[54] Pool's exact movements after this date are unclear.[55] By 1849, however, he was operating in Santa Fe. In September of that year Pool's shop repaired nine freight wagons for the firm of St. Vrain & McCarty to the amount of $207.86. When $98.36 of this debt went unpaid, Pool took the merchants to court. Included in the surviving district court case file is a valuable itemized statement showing some of the various repairs made, as well as charges for sundry wagon parts and accessories.[56]

James Pool is found in the 1850 U. S. population schedules for New Mexico as a blacksmith residing in Santa Fe with real estate valued at forty thousand dollars—an incredible amount considering the small promissory note he executed just four years earlier in Independence.[57] There is no evidence that Pool ever made wagons, either in Independence or Santa Fe, although his shop was probably capable of such work. If Pool did construct any wagons in Santa Fe, they would have been quite costly compared to those manufactured in the East, where many sources of timber and iron were readily available to wagon makers. Pool undoubtedly had plenty of business in just repairing a portion of the many vehicles that annually came down the Santa Fe Trail.

3.4.   1912 postcard of "Santa Fe Trail Wagon, made complete at [Francis] Hahn's Wagon shop, south of Westport." (Courtesy of the Jackson County Historical Society.)

The Look of the Missouri Wagon

It should now be clear that there is considerable information on who was making freight wagons in Missouri. What is not so readily available is conclusive evidence that associates a particular style or design with Missouri wagons. Were Missouri wagons during the period preceding the Civil War similar in design to their Pennsylvania counterparts, what we might call a Missouri Conestoga? Or were Missouri craftsmen turning out something quite different?

An interesting postcard (Fig. 3.4) dated 1912 features a sketch of a "'Prairie Schooner' Santa Fe Trail Wagon, made complete at [Francis] Hahn's wagon shop, south of Westport." Since it is evident that the wagon pictured is a Conestoga, this would seem to be confirmation that Missouri wagon makers were producing Conestoga-type wagons. However, the caption goes on to say that the "Side boards with mail box [tool box?], showing hand made wrought iron nails may be seen at 432 Westport Ave.," which leads one to suspect that all that was really left of Hahn's wagon were the sides of the body or bed. But what about the complete wagon in the sketch? Curiously, it exactly matches a photograph published in *The Missouri Magazine* of January 1935 (Fig. 3.5). The caption for this photo reads: "Wagon in Which Kentucky Immigrants Came Overland to Jacksonville, Randolph County, Mo."[58] There is no doubt that the sketch of the wagon on the postcard was made from this photo, but the photo was not published until 1935, so how did the artist gain access to the image in

3.5. "Wagon, in which Ky. Immigrants Came to Jacksonville, Randolph County, Missouri." Originally published in *The Missouri Magazine*. (Courtesy of the State Historical Society of Missouri.)

1912? And which caption are we to believe? Was the vehicle built by Hahn and used on the Santa Fe Trail, or did it come from Kentucky? The Hahn wagon pieces would definitely shed some light on this matter, but, unfortunately, the fate of these relics is unknown.[59]

An 1859 directory advertisement for Joseph Murphy featuring an intriguing cut of a Conestoga-type wagon (Fig. 3.6) is well known. Not so well known is the appearance of this very same cut on an 1853 billhead of J. T. Johnson & Co., of Boonville, Missouri. The billhead was printed by Keemle & Hager of St. Louis.[60] It is unclear if the cut was made in St. Louis or was purchased from an engraver or founder in an eastern city. The cut may indeed be representative of the wagons being produced in 1853, but there is not enough evidence to proclaim it as an example of a Missouri-made wagon. Its repeated usage does suggest that the Conestoga style had come to exemplify the typical American freight wagon.

Although conclusive proof is lacking, it is not unreasonable to suggest that Missouri wagon makers were turning out vehicles very similar in look or style to wagons of the eastern United States, at least during the first three decades or so of the Trail's history. The Conestoga was the standard freighter in the East from the early 1800s through the 1840s. That its distinctive design received acceptance outside of Pennsylvania is evidenced by the fact that these wagons, or variants thereof, are known to have been manufactured in Virginia, and it is believed that they were being built in

J. MURPHY,

WAGON MANUFACTURER,

No. 362 Broadway

{ NORTH OF O'FALLON

SAINT LOUIS.

3.6.   Advertisement for Joseph Murphy in the St. Louis directory for 1859. (Courtesy of the State Historical Society of Missouri.)

New Jersey, Maryland, and Ohio as well.[61] Also, the fact that Santa Fe traders purchased large numbers of Pennsylvania wagons must have had an influence on wagon makers competing for this business in Missouri. And what of those Missouri wagon makers trained in the eastern tradition or "school"? Certainly this training came to bear on their craft.

The birthplaces of Missouri wagon makers, as found in the U.S. population schedules for 1850, are intriguing. Of course, there is no way of determining from the census records whether or not a wagon maker served his apprenticeship in the state or country of his birth (Joseph Murphy, for example, was born in Ireland but apprenticed to a wagon maker in St. Louis). Still, the very high number of Missouri wagon makers with birthplaces east of the Mississippi River suggests that there was a very strong eastern, and even European, influence in their work. Thirty-eight individuals were found in the 1850 U.S. population schedules for Jackson County.[62] Following is a list of their birthplaces as given in the schedules with the number of craftsmen who claimed each.[63]

Virginia	9	North Carolina	2
Kentucky	8	Ohio	2
Tennessee	5	Ft. Laramie	1
Pennsylvania	3	Indiana	1
Germany	3	Massachusetts	1
Missouri	2	South Carolina	1

The author was unable to review the entire population schedules for St. Louis County; however, six of the eleven wagon makers listed in the St. Louis city directory for 1850 were located. Of these, two were born in Germany, and one each in Missouri, New York, Virginia, and Ireland. Living in the household of wagon maker Henry Steidemann, a native of Germany, were five other wagon makers, obviously employees, two of whom were sons. All five were born in Germany. Joseph Murphy's household included five wagon makers also, natives of Ireland, Germany and New York.[64] Louis Epenschied, it will be recalled, was a native of Germany.

Again, except for a very few individuals, it is impossible to ascertain how many of these wagon makers received their training in their native states or countries. Of those craftsmen whose careers are documented, however, perhaps the most interesting case is that of Independence wagon maker Jacob Leader. Leader was born in Lancaster County, Pennsylvania, in 1814, and, at about age seventeen, learned the wagon-making trade there. Lancaster County is located in a region firmly linked with the classic Conestoga; as noted in the previous chapter, its Conestoga River Valley is believed to be the source of the wagon's famous name. It is highly probable that Leader learned his craft building Conestogas. Leader moved to Pittsburgh in 1834, then to St. Louis the next year. After remaining in St. Louis for only a few months, he moved to Illinois. Sometime between 1835 and 1839, he located in Independence, Missouri, but only for about a year. Leader returned once more to Illinois, where he was married in 1839, before finally settling again in Independence in 1840. In the latter place, Jacob Leader became "the head of [Robert] Weston's wagon-making division," where he could easily have produced Conestoga-type wagons for the Santa Fe trade.[65]

FOUR

Characteristics of Freight Wagons on the Santa Fe Trail to circa 1855

In this chapter are gathered together the various features and specifications for Trail wagons of this period as identified in a wide range of primary sources, supplemented at times with secondary works. Unfortunately, no single primary source provides every detail of a Trail wagon's construction (far from it, actually). Yet by piecing together the scattered references in journals, account books, court records, and the occasional artist's rendering, several distinctive characteristics clearly emerge.

Wagon Body or Bed

As detailed in chapter 2, the curved, raved bodies of Conestoga wagons (see Fig. 4.1) are well documented in contemporary accounts and artwork. The bodies of the wagons pictured in the M. Rondé engraving, "Chariots de Chihuahua" (Fig. 2.7) clearly have sides with three horizontal rails and a number of vertical uprights, a distinctive characteristic of the Conestoga wagon. A departure from the classic Pennsylvania Conestoga design, however, is visible on the front end gate of one of the Rondé wagons. The top and middle rails of this gate are straight or without curvature; classic Conestogas have front end gates with the top and middle rails downbowed, or curved downward, and rear end gates with the top rails bowed upward (see Figs. 2.2 and 4.2). It is worth noting that straight top rails on end gates are a feature common to Virginia-made Conestogas.[1]

Removable sideboards, which "could be added above the top rail to increase the carrying capacity," were standard with Conestogas and were

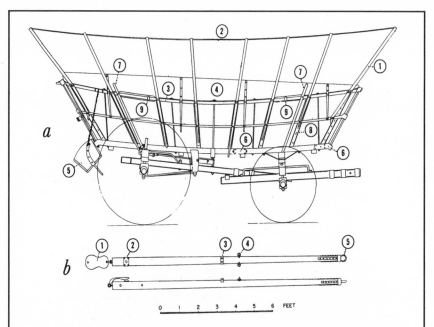

4.1.   Drawing of Conestoga wagon; *a:* Bed and Running Gear, Right Side,
(1) bows for supporting cover, (2) ridgepole or stringer, (3) top rail, (4) sideboards, (5) feedbox, (6) rubbing plates, (7) side-board standards, (9) securing
rings; *b:* Tongue or Pole, Top and Side Views, (1) double-tree hasp, (2) wear
plate, (3) feedbox staple, (4) hitching rings, (5) end ring. (Illustration by
Donald W. Holst from *Contributions from the Museum of History and Technology,* Smithsonian Institution, 1959.)

undoubtedly common with Santa Fe Trail wagons as well.[2] The 1851 Kern
drawing (Fig. 2.8) pictures one wagon that appears to have sideboards in
place.

An additional feature of the Conestoga is a tool box, usually attached to
the left side of the wagon body. A tool box is visible in two contemporary
illustrations that are Trail related, one of which is pictured in chapter 2 (see
Fig. 2.5).[3] The Hahn wagon, discussed in chapter 3, was supposed to have
had "side boards with mail box," which in reality was probably a tool box.
At some point, it appears that the tool box was also made as a separate unit
which was suspended from either the front or rear end gate of the wagon
by chains, thus allowing it to be easily removed (see chapter 7). A feedbox
was also attached to a wagon's rear end gate in the same fashion.

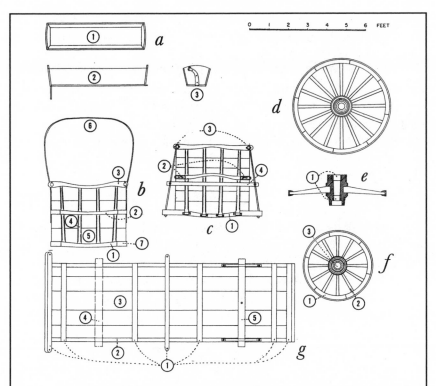

4.2. Details of Conestoga wagon; *a:* Feedbox, (1) top, (2) side, (3) end; *b:* Front End Panel, (1) bottom end rail, (2) middle end rail, (3) top end rail, (4) standard or upright, (5) end boards, (6) bow, (7) corner plates; *c:* Rear End Gate, (1) staples, (2) end-gate hasps and hooks, (3) pins, (4) crossbar; *d:* Rear Wheel; *e:* Cross Section of Wheel, (1) boxings; *f:* Front Wheel, (1) felly or felloe, (2) spoke, (3) hub or nave; *g:* Floor of Wagon from Underside, (1) cross-beams, (2) bottom side rails, (3) floorboards, (4) rear bolster, (5) front bolster. (Illustration by Holst from *Contributions from the Museum of History and Technology*, Smithsonian Institution, 1959.)

Classic Pennsylvania Conestogas display many decorative details, in both the iron and woodwork (for example, ornate hinges and hasp on the tool box and chip carving on the edges of front and rear gates). Whether or not Conestoga-type wagons used on the Santa Fe Trail contained such decorative work is unknown. It seems questionable, however, particularly considering the speed with which the wagons were being produced, as well as the fact that many of the wagons did not remain in the original owners' hands for more than a trip or two. Decorative work was time consuming and undoubtedly added to the price of the wagon. Would a Santa Fe trader pay for such details on a vehicle he did not plan to keep?

Dimensions for the bodies of Santa Fe Trail wagons of this period are virtually unrecorded in the primary sources consulted.[4] Frank Edwards's otherwise valuable description of "Conestoga or Pennsylvanian" wagons on the Chihuahua Trail in 1846 provides a measurement of height that is an obvious exaggeration. Edwards stated that the wagons he saw measured, vertically, eighteen to twenty feet to the top of the "end-hoops."[5] This, of course, would make the wagons taller than they were long.

Dimensions are known for several surviving Pennsylvania Conestogas of various sizes. Don Berkebile states, in his *Carriage Terminology*, that the Conestoga "body is frequently twelve to thirteen feet long on the bottom, and sixteen to seventeen feet at its top (exclusive of bows)."[6] The width inside the wagon body is typically forty-two inches.[7]

Primary sources reveal little about the types of wood used to construct Santa Fe Trail wagons of this period. Woods used in the bodies of the Pennsylvania Conestoga were white oak, poplar, and ash.[8]

Bows and Covers

Wagon bows support the cloth covering; their number depends upon the size of the wagon. Conestogas, according to Berkebile, can have from eight to twelve.[9] The wood favored for bows seems to have been hickory.[10] Spread over the wagon bows, as one observer noted in 1839, were "two or three thicknesses of woolen blankets; and over these, and extended to the lower edge of the body, is drawn a strong canvass covering, well guarded with cords and leather straps."[11] An account from 1852 states that the

> waggons are provided with a double covering of sailcloth, drawn over wooden hoops, and long enough to be pulled down to the point of the axletree: this forms a roof, under which, placed upon the axletree, the leathern harness can be kept dry; and this is the place where the driver usually sleeps.[12]

Josiah Gregg goes into great detail regarding the wagon covering:

> [I]n order to make a secure shelter for the cargo, against the inclemencies of the weather, there should be spread upon each wagon a pair

of stout Osnaburg sheets, with one of sufficient width to reach the bottom of the body on each side, so as to protect the goods from driving rains. By omitting this important precaution many packages of merchandise have been seriously injured. Some have preferred lining the interior of the wagon-body by tacking a simple strip of sheeting all around it. On the outward trips especially, a pair of Mackinaw blankets can be advantageously spread betwixt the two sheets, which effectually secures the roof against the worst of storms. This contrivance has also the merit of turning the blankets into a profitable item of trade, by enabling the owners to evade the customhouse officers, who would otherwise seize them as contraband articles.[13]

Osnaburg, according to a modern reference work on fabrics, "is the name of a fabric originally woven in the city of Osnabruck in north west Germany. At one time it was made of linen but now it is a rough, strong, plain-woven, cotton cloth."[14]

Axles or Axletrees

Wooden axles were the norm for this period; oak and hickory were the preferred raw materials.[15] Some axle dimensions are found in Joseph Murphy's account books. Seth E. Ward's ox wagon, purchased in 1847, was equipped with five-inch axles. Two ox wagons built for an unnamed Mexican in 1849 had five and one quarter-inch axles, and three six-mule wagons constructed the following year had four and one quarter-inch axles.[16] According to modern-day wagon maker Doug Thamert, these are measurements of width taken midway between the axle-arms.[17]

One feature of the axle should be explained. Attached to each axle-arm were two metal skeins (also called clouts). The skein was an iron strip mounted lengthwise on the top and bottom of the axle-arm to receive the wear of the wheel's hub (see Figs. 4.3 and 4.4). Owens & Aulls' 1846 invoice with wagon maker Cyrus Townsend of Pittsburgh included "12 Bottom skeins" (costing one dollar each), probably because the bottom skein received most of the wear.[18] The wheel was held in place on the axle-arm by a linchpin, which slipped through a slot at the end of the arm. The same Owens & Aull invoice also contains the purchase of forty linchpins. At Santa Fe in 1849, St. Vrain & McCarty purchased thirty linchpins from blacksmith James Pool.[19]

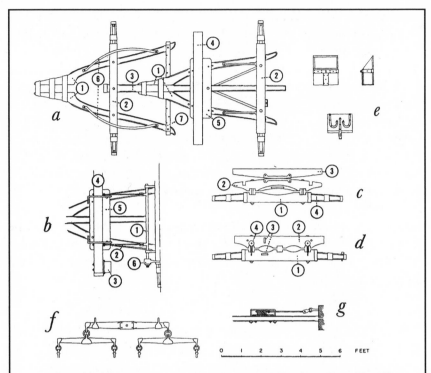

4.3.   Details of Conestoga wagon running gear; *a:* Running Gear, Top View, (1) front and rear hounds, (2) bolsters, (3) coupling pole, (4) brake beam, (5) brake-beam shelf, (6) segments forming fifth wheel, (7) rear brace; *b:* Brake Mechanism, Detail, (1) brake rocker bar, (2) rods connecting rocker bar to brake beam, (3) rubber or brakeshoe, (4) brake beam, (5) brake-beam shelf, (6) brake lever; *c:* Front Axletree and Bolsters, Front View, (1) axle-tree, (2) bolster, (3) upper bolster, (4) axle; *d:* Rear Axletree and Bolster, Rear View, (1) axletree, (2) bolster, (3) hook and staple, (4) hound pins; *e:* Toolbox, Showing Front, End, and Top; *f:* Doubletree with Singletrees Attached; *g:* Brake Mechanism, Side View. (Illustration by Holst from *Contributions from the Museum of History and Technology*, Smithsonian Institution, 1959.)

No evidence was found of the use of the thimble skein during this period. The thimble skein was a single piece of thin iron (later steel) that completely enveloped the wooden axle-arm; it was made for use with either a linchpin or nut (Fig. 4.5). Thimble skein freight wagons were being offered by 1860.[20]

According to trader James Josiah Webb, iron axles were introduced on the Trail in 1845:

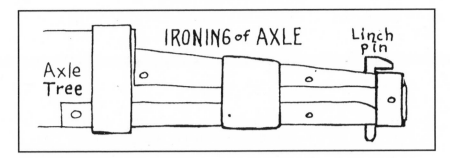

4.4. Illustration of axle-arm showing top and bottom skein and linchpin, drawing by H.K. Landis from originals at the Landis Valley Museum, in John Omwake, *Conestoga Six-Horse Bell Teams* (1930).

Solomon Houck had bought a lot of wagons in Pittsburgh, and among them were two heavy wagons with iron axles—a new experiment for freight wagons and one looked upon as quite hazardous. What if an axle should break or get badly sprung on the plains? No chance of fitting a wooden axle to the box for an iron one, or straightening the iron one if badly bent. Wagons were scarce, and Houck proposed

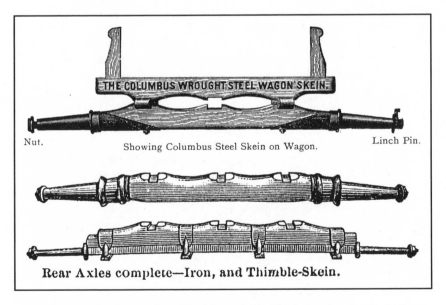

4.5. An example of a wooden axle with steel thimble skeins showing both the nut and linchpin types; and a comparison of a wooden axle with thimble skeins and an iron axle (bottom). (© Mark L. Gardner Collection.)

selling one of these; and after due consideration I made up my mind
to take the risk. This, I believe, was the first freight wagon with iron
axles that ever went over the plains, and Mr. Houck followed some
weeks after with the second—the mate to it. Gradually they came into
use for the Santa Fe trade, but not for the low country.[21]

The first reference to iron-axle Trail wagons in Joseph Murphy's account
books is in two 1851 entries recording wagons built that year for F. X. Aubry.[22]

Primary references are contradictory regarding the iron axle's utility.
Percival G. Lowe wrote that one army contractor's Utah-bound train in
1858 "had much trouble with wagons; some wheels broken down—iron axle
wagons."[23] Wagon maker Doug Thamert surmises that the iron-axle wagons did not have the elasticity or springiness of wooden-axle wagons, thus
the shocks of the road were primarily absorbed by the wheels.[24] Lowe went
on to say: "Contractors and nearly all big freighters crossing the plains used
wooden axle wagons made by Murphy or Espenscheidt of St. Louis, or
Young and others of Independence." Trail traveler William B. Napton
stated that Hiram Young's wagons were "considered as good as any except
those with iron axles." Unfortunately, Napton's claim can be interpreted
two ways: Young's wooden-axle wagons were inferior only to wagons with
iron axles, or Young's iron-axle wagons were inferior to all other wagons.[25]

It is important to note that if iron axles were used on wagons with Con-
estoga-styled bodies, and this may have been the case with Houck's Pittsburgh wagons, then this would be a significant modification of the classic
Conestoga wagon, which is only known with wooden axles.

Wheels and Tires

Wheels were made up of a hub, spokes, and felloes. The felloes, or rim, were
bound with an iron tire. On a Conestoga wagon, "front wheels average forty-
five inches in diameter, while those in the rear are often sixty inches or more."[26]
These wheels were "dished"; that is, the spokes, instead of being perpendicu-
lar, flared out at an angle from the hub (Fig. 4.6). This was intended "to give
stiffness, to resist lateral shocks, as when the wheel slips sideways, into a rut or
hole."[27] The dished wheels were so mounted on the axle that the tops of the
wheels inclined slightly away from the wagon body, and the bottoms, which
contained the load-bearing spokes, rested in a more vertical position.[28]

Hubs were usually made of elm and white oak; oak was standard for
spokes and felloes.[29] Randolph Marcy, writing in 1859, recommended
wheels made of Osage Orange as "best for the plains, as they shrink but

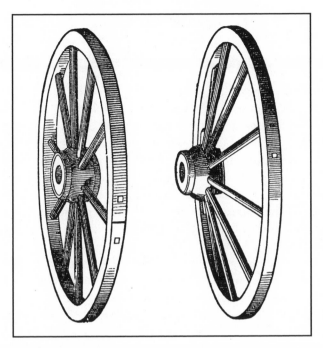

4.6.   Illustration of wheels with and without dishing. The dished wheel is on the right. (© Mark L. Gardner Collection.)

little, and seldom want repairing." But because this wood was difficult to obtain "in the Northern States, white oak answers a very good purpose if well seasoned."[30] No matter how well seasoned, however, wheels made in the humid East or Midwest were always susceptible to shrinkage after exposure to the dry atmosphere of the western plains. Josiah Gregg writes that on "some occasions, the wagon tires have become so loose upon the felloes as to tumble off while traveling."[31]

There were a few stopgap measures traders could resort to for the shrinkage problem. One was to give the wheels a good soaking in water "whenever an opportunity offers."[32] But this was only a temporary solution, for the wooden components would simply dry out and shrink again after each "watering." Gregg states that the

> most effective mode of tightening slackened tires (at least that most practiced on the plains, as there is rarely a portable forge in company), is by driving strips of hoop-iron around between the tire and felloe—simple wedges of wood are sometimes made to supply the place of iron.[33]

And there was always the ubiquitous rawhide. According to one old-timer, "Mexicans were experts in the way of mending almost any part of their wagons with rawhide with the hair on and wrapped spokes, felloes, singletrees or any other part very tight with it and when the strips dried, they shrunk and dented the wood."[34]

An essential component of the wheel sometimes noted in contemporary wagon makers' accounts from this period is the "box," or more correctly, the axle-box, a cast-iron bushing set into each end of the hub to receive the wear of the axle-arm. The box, like the axle, came in various sizes. Joseph Murphy sold a large ox wagon to Richard Owens, "Santafee trader," in 1847 that had five-inch boxes (a diameter measurement). The 1846 Owens & Aull invoice includes one and a half sets of "Wagon Boxes" for $2.52.[35] This *axle*-box should not be confused with the wagon body or bed, also sometimes called a "box."

Numerous contemporary references provide tire dimensions. As noted in an earlier chapter, James M. Maxey wrote from Independence in 1845, advising James Frazier Reed that if he intended "to go by Santefee—you had better in the first place get you a large waggon made about 3 inches on the tread and will beare about 6 thousand pounds."[36] A written deposition for Santa Fe blacksmith James Pool's 1850 court case against St. Vrain & McCarty, in which James Pool was attempting to obtain payment for repairs made to nine freight wagons, contains the following:

> the waggons that were returned were not the waggons that they re-paired[.] the waggons that they repaired had not pole tongs in them with the bark on them and one of the waggons the wheels are not alike[—] some of the wheels are two and a half inch tread others of three inch tread of the same waggon[.][37]

Joseph Murphy's accounts usually provide tire dimensions. Richards Owens's 1847 ox wagon had tires three inches wide by three quarters of an inch thick. Tires made the following year for two wagons "for [the] Santafee trade" were three inches wide by seven-eighths of an inch thick. Four "heavy Santa fee wagons" made in 1849 had tires three and one-half inches wide. F. X. Aubry's iron-axle wagons of 1851 rolled out of the shop with tires two and one-half inches wide.[38] In 1856, wagon maker Hiram Young mortgaged "twenty five large new Santafe Wagons [with] two and a half inch tread."[39]

Because Mexican traders used American-made freight wagons almost exclusively, a Mexican presidential decree of 1842, which prohibited the use of wagons with wheels less than eight inches wide or carrying freight of more than five thousand pounds, met considerable protest from Chihuahua merchants. According to historian Max L. Moorhead, the Mexican merchants complained to the central government, insisting

> that not only their commercial livelihood but also their very defense depended upon these newly-acquired vehicles; whereas pack mules were easily stampeded by attacking Indians, the wagons made excellent parapets; and the narrower tires did no harm whatsoever to the roads of northern Mexico, which were natural highways and never had to be resurfaced or improved artificially. On the strength of such arguments as these the national authorities agreed to submit the regulation to the congress for possible amendment in 1846 and meanwhile to allow a number of Chihuahua traders to use American wagons, but the outbreak of the war with the United States in that year prevented further modification. Actually this objectionable regulation was never enforced in the northern provinces.[40]

Brakes

No references were found to mechanical brakes on Santa Fe Trail freight wagons of this period, although brakes were being added to some classic Conestogas beginning about 1830.[41] Instead of mechanical brakes, lock-chains and shoes were employed to slow vehicles on steep grades. A lock-chain, wrapped around the felloe and tire of a rear wheel and then fastened to the wagon, kept the wheel from turning. But this method, over time, could produce uneven wear to the tire. This wear could be avoided by the use of a shoe (a wood or iron runner), which was placed under the wheel and secured to the wagon by a drag-chain.[42]

Tongues or Poles

In early horse- and mule-drawn wagons, the tongue, also called pole, was solidly attached to the front hounds (a hound is "one of the crooked timbers framed through the front axle to receive the pole, the back ends supporting the fifth wheel or sway bar," see Fig. 4.3).[43] Known as a "stiff tongue," it would stick straight out, suspended above the ground. However, the "drop tongue," which pivoted up and down, was decidedly more popular in the West because of the uneven nature of trails.[44] Randolph Marcy recommended a type of drop tongue when he wrote that the "pole of the wagon should have a joint where it enters the hounds, to prevent the weight [of the wagon] from coming upon it and breaking the hounds in passing short and abrupt holes in the road."[45] Joseph Murphy was referring to wagons with drop tongues when he recorded "loose tong ox wagons" in his account books.[46] Stiff and drop tongues can be found on both ox and mule wagons.

Three important early Trail wagon images, those by Fairholme, Ronde' and Kern (Figs. 2.6, 2.7, and 2.8), picture Conestoga-type wagons with drop tongues. Because the classic Pennsylvania Conestoga is believed to have been constructed only with a tongue "rigidly fixed to front hounds," this is another significant modification of the Conestoga design.[47]

Colors and Distinguishing Marks

On the classic Conestoga wagon, the "running gears . . . were painted red, though the shade varied to orange if red lead was used, while the bodies ranged from dark blue to gray-blue."[48] This traditional color scheme held true for western wagons as well. It will be recalled from chapter 1 that George Sibley's survey wagons were painted "light blue." An 1840 colored lithograph of the St. Louis waterfront features a Conestoga wagon with a blue body.[49] A large ox wagon valued at two hundred dollars was the object of an 1847 court case in Platte County, Missouri; it was described as having "a blue bed & red running gears."[50] In 1852, Julius Froebel described Independence's wheelwrights' shops as "large premises filled with new waggons, painted red, green, or blue."[51]

Early on, some wagon makers signed or otherwise identified their finished products; this appears to have become much more prevalent with the increased rivalry between various wagon manufactories. Hiram Young's wagons are known to have carried his name, probably applied through the use of a stencil.[52] A surviving wagon provision box in the local museum in Weston, Missouri, is stenciled with the St. Louis maker's name and address, as is an Independence-made ox yoke of the 1850s in the collections of the Colorado Springs Pioneers Museum.[53]

Hauling Capacity

The hauling capacity of the very early freight wagons on the Santa Fe Trail is a matter of speculation. J. Evarts Greene stated in a paper published in 1893 that Trail wagons made before Armijo's per-wagon duty of 1839 hauled "from one to two tons each," but he gives no authority for this information.[54] James Hall described the Conestoga wagons hauling goods from the Atlantic cities to Pittsburgh in the 1820s as "carrying from thirty-five to fifty hundred pounds each."[55] According to Trail journalist Matt Field, one wagon in the train he was accompanying in 1839 abruptly overturned in Raton Pass, "leaving twenty-five hundred weight of merchandise in the water, while the relieved mules dashed up the bank with the wheels."[56] Yet this may not have been the maximum hauling capacity of the wagon.

Writing in 1844, after the implementation of the per-wagon duty, Josiah Gregg stated that lately he had "seen much larger vehicles employed, with ten or twelve mules harnessed to each, and a cargo of goods of about five thousand pounds in weight."[57] Lt. James W. Abert provides the same estimate for Trail wagons in 1845.[58] Also that same year, James M. Maxey wrote his now-familiar letter from Independence recommending a large wagon that would "beare about 6 thousand pounds."[59] Three hundred thirty-five military contractors' wagons hauling supplies to Santa Fe in 1850–51 averaged 5,235 pounds per wagon.[60]

The wagons in the 1852 caravan that Julius Froebel accompanied "generally carry five to six thousand pounds weight, and are yoked [harnessed] with five pairs, if drawn, like ours, by mules."[61] John Russell Bartlett, writing in 1854, noted that the "large Missouri wagons" used in the Chihuahua trade transported "from five thousand to five thousand five hundred pounds" each.[62] Percival G. Lowe wrote that contractors using wooden-axle wagons made by Murphy, Espenschied, and Young in the late 1850s were "able to carry their 6,000-pound loads anywhere."[63]Although the six-thousand-pound load became the norm for Santa Fe Trail freight wagons, it was certainly not the maximum load. William B. Napton states that the Hiram Young wagons in his train in 1857 were "designed to hold a load of seven or eight thousand pounds of merchandise each."[64]

Price

William Becknell's 1822 wagon is supposed to have cost 150 dollars. Over twenty years later, in 1846, fifteen Pittsburgh wagons purchased by Owens & Aull were priced at $149.47 each![65] Joseph Murphy's account books are a good source for wagon prices. In 1848 Murphy sold to Pierre M. Chouteau of Kansas City "4 ox wagons for the Santafee trade/Bowed off with provision Boxes at the/rate of 130.00 Each." Two years later, Murphy made for Beck & Brent of Lexington, Missouri, twelve large ox wagons "to go to

Santafee at 165 Dollars Each" and "3 lighter wagons at 145 Dollars Each."[66] In 1854, John Russell Bartlett estimated that the "large Missouri wagons, which carry from five thousand to five thousand five hundred pounds, cost about two hundred dollars each."[67]

An 1852 deposition by trader John S. Jones provides a revealing assessment of the worth of wagons in New Mexico. According to Jones, in the spring of 1851, the firm of J. S. Lightner & Co. sold to William O. Ardinger & Co., at Santa Fe

> a lot of thirteen second-hand wagons, and their teams of six mules each, for between $750 and $800 each; and, as nearly as deponent recollects, at the price of seven hundred and ninety and odd dollars each. That he estimated the wagons at $160 each, the mules at $90 to $100 each, and the harness at $7 per set. Deponent says that the wagons referred to were not the largest sized wagons usually taken to New Mexico, being about 3,500 pounds freight; that a larger class of wagons, of from 4,500 to 6,000 pounds freight, cost more in the States and bring a better price in Santa Fe. That large sized wagons are the only ones used in [the] trade to New Mexico, and are generally in demand in August and September of each year, when they are required principally for the southern trade, and that they bring at these times one hundred and sixty dollars each. That wagons in good repair, in demand in New Mexico, bring their full value; but when not in demand they cannot be sold at any price, and a sale cannot be forced.[68]

FIVE

From Shop to Factory

Within the sixty-year lifetime of the Santa Fe Trail, the wagon and car-riage–making trade of the United States went through an amazing transfor-mation. A rapidly growing nation with commercial and emigrant routes penetrating the far reaches of the North American continent translated into a tremendous demand for more and more wagons. The response of many wagon makers was to increase the size of their shops, employ more work-men, and, as they became available, add machine tools and motive power. As mentioned in chapter 3, wagon makers also incorporated the blacksmith-ing work into their operation, so that all the processes needed to complete a wagon were now under one roof—along with all the profits. John Cook, who established a wagon manufactory in St. Louis in 1848, added "a large blacksmith shop" to his operation in 1853 because, he claimed, "complaints . . . had been made to him of the bad manner in which the iron work was executed. In having the blacksmithing done under his immediate supervi-sion, he was enabled to obviate for the future all such complaints."[1]

Another extremely significant change implemented by wagon and carriage builders sometime before the Civil War was the division of labor, a system of manufacturing that had already been successfully employed in other industries. Previously, under what one carriage manufacturer termed in 1860 the "old plan," each workman performed "all the different parts in turn until the car-riage was completed."[2] This traditional process is evident in the surviving ac-count books of St. Louis wagon maker Joseph Murphy (see chapter 3). The new, "novel," practice, however, involved "systematizing, dividing, and sub-dividing . . . work, in such a manner that each man had but a single part to perform, thereby enabling him to learn it to such perfection that he could ex-ecute it very rapidly and at a great reduction of cost."[3]

5.a.   The interior of a wheelwright shop of the early 1840s. The man with the mal-
let is driving spokes into a hub. Note the hub lathe at the right; its power source is
the apprentice turning the large pulley. From Edward Hazen, *Popular Technology;
or Professions and Trades* (1846).

    This system was in place at the huge Philadelphia wagon manufactory of
Wilson, Childs & Co. in 1857, where an observer noted that the wagon
"bodies are made by a number of men, each having his particular work assigned him; and, by such subdivision of labor, greater excellence and celerity
is attained."[4] And it was also a feature of M. T. Graham's wagon factory
established at Westport, Missouri, in 1860. In a glowing article about the
factory, the *Westport Border Star* compared Graham's wagon works to "factories for the construction of locomotives, [where] every thing is reduced
to a system.... [I]n the various departments, machine shops, painting room,
furnishing and trimming room, and lathe room, we find men engaged on
some particular part of a wagon."[5] True interchangeability of parts, however, something often associated with the division of labor, did not come
to the wagon industry until much later.

The power source employed in the larger mechanized wagon factories was often a stationary steam engine. Not only could the engine propel woodworking machinery, but it could also work power hammers and blowers for the many forges.[6] One of the earliest wagon makers to use steam power may have been the Pittsburgh firm of Townsend & Radle, who announced in 1839 that they were "preparing to extend their business by a steam engine."[7] Steam power seems to have been adopted much later in the West, however. In 1850, none of the prominent Missouri wagon makers supplying the Santa Fe trade utilized steam power in their shops. This was due, in part, to the fact that steam engines were expensive; in 1856, a steam engine with boiler capable of producing fifteen horsepower could cost nine hundred dollars, not counting shipping costs.[8] There were also considerations of fuel and water for the engine once installed, as well as subsequent maintenance. The only steam-powered wagon shop found in the 1850 industrial census for Missouri was one operated in the Missouri State Penitentiary at Jefferson City by lessees Price, McKee & Co., and that engine was apparently shared by cooper and rope and bagging shops at the penitentiary, also under Price, McKee & Co.[9] Interestingly, the annual product for the prison shop was 115 wagons, only slightly more than a quarter of Joseph Murphy's production, who was then without steam power. Ten years later, though, at least three Missouri wagon makers had acquired a steam engine. These were Murphy and James Virden, both of St. Louis, and M. T. Graham of Westport. Murphy used a fifty-horsepower engine, Virden a fifteen-horsepower engine, and Graham one of twenty-two horsepower.[10]

Other power sources available to wagon makers included water, wind, and animal power. Manufacturing statistics compiled for the 1870 U.S. census reveal that there were then more waterwheels in use at carriage and wagon shops across the country than there were steam engines (363 waterwheels to 279 steam engines). Pennsylvania counted twenty-one wagon or carriage establishments using a waterwheel, and Illinois and Indiana each had five.[11] One of the Indiana factories, then managed by Adolphus Eberhart and George Milburn at Mishawaka, sold its freighters through a branch "depot" in Westport, Missouri, for a short time in the late 1850s.[12] It appears that water power was not utilized by wagon makers within the state of Missouri, however, at least according to census records and the additional information on Missouri makers compiled for this study.

Wind seems rarely to have been considered as a power source by wagon makers. One known example is the wind-powered wagon factory operated by Wilder & Palm of Lawrence, Kansas. In 1864, this firm began the manufacture of wagons and agricultural implements with machinery propelled by

5.1.   A crosscut saw operated with a "four horse power." Horse powers, cheaper and much simpler than steam engines, were used by some wagon shops to provide motive power for saws and other woodworking machines. From *Scientific American*, September 10, 1864.

a windmill built specifically for that purpose. Their windmill, a local landmark, could produce eighty horsepower in a twenty-five-mile-per-hour wind.[13]

As for animal power, this was easy to take advantage of with the use of what was known as a "horse power." A horse power was a simple mechanical device of gears and shafting which, when put in motion by one or more horses or mules, could transmit power to various woodworking machines (Fig. 5.1). In Independence, Missouri, two establishments used horse powers. According to the 1860 industrial census, Hiram Young's wagon and yoke-making factory used a "4 Horse pow."; that is, a horse power designed for use with four horses. Ten years later, the industrial census reported that Robert Weston's blacksmith shop, then doing business as Weston & Strode, operated with a horse power.[14] Wagon maker Frederick Klaber of Westport is also known to have used animal power; a horse power is listed in his estate inventory of 1866, valued at 150 dollars.[15] "In places where a light power is required for but a portion of the time," commented the *Scientific American* in 1864, the horse power "has advantages over steam-power, as they are worked with less cost, and require less care, than an engine."[16]

The power-driven machine tools found in mechanized wagon factories are well documented in contemporary sources. Wilson, Childs & Co. boasted

two Upright and six Circular Saws; a machine for boring holes in the centre of the hub; another for boring holes for the spokes; four Drills (self-feeding) for drilling iron.. . . a Planing Machine, a Mortising

5.2. A Daniels planer, ca. 1870, in the collections of the Smithsonian Institution (Neg. No. 72–10951).

Machine, two machines for turning spokes, machines for driving in the Spokes and for shaping the Felloes, and finishing them complete, and a machine for boring Hubs so as to put the boxes in properly, and to ensure accuracy and a solid bearing.[17]

Graham's Westport wagon factory contained a comparable assortment of woodworking machines: a Daniels planer, Woodworth planer, hub mortiser, two lathes, one scroll saw, one felloe saw, three circular saws, one swing saw, one spoke lathe, one tenoning machine, one iron drill, one emory machine for spokes, one lath cutter, one rounding machine, and one boring machine.[18]

The Daniels planer (Fig. 5.2), a common piece of machinery in wagon factories, could accommodate lumber both large (up to sixteen inches thick by twenty-two inches wide and sixteen feet long) and rough. It was used to provide "the finishing touch to all the axles, bolsters, tongues, and other heavy timber about a wagon."[19] The Woodworth planer (Fig. 5.3) was notable for its ability to plane a board and, during the same operation, cut a tongue and groove along the board's edges.[20] This machine was presumably used to plane the boards that went into the wagon's body. Hub mortising machines varied widely in design, but their primary purpose remained the same: to cut the mortises in the hub into which the spokes were driven (Fig. 5.4). A tenoning machine—

5.3. A Woodworth planer as offered by the Fitchburg Foundry & Machine Co., Fitchburg, Mass., in 1857. (Courtesy of Special Collections, University of Vermont Libraries.)

and again, many varieties existed—cut the rectangular tenons on the ends of the spokes that were to be fitted into the hub mortises. On the opposite spoke ends, those to be inserted into the felloe, round tenons were cut by a tenoning machine equipped with a hollow auger (Fig. 5.5).

The first scroll saws were jigsaws, and they were used for cutting intricate shapes; jigsaws later lost favor to bandsaws in the factory.[21] The most interesting, and presumably most dangerous, saw in the workplace was the swing or pendulum saw (Fig. 5.6), an example of which was a feature in Graham's wagon factory. Designed for crosscutting, it was a circular saw

5.4. A hub mortising machine of 1854. The mortise was made by first drilling a hole with the auger (visible directly above the hub in the engraving), after which the two chisels were used, one at a time, to chip out the wood. From *Scientific American*, April 29, 1854.

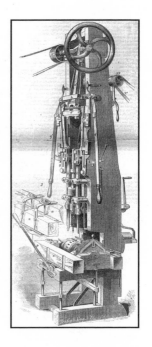

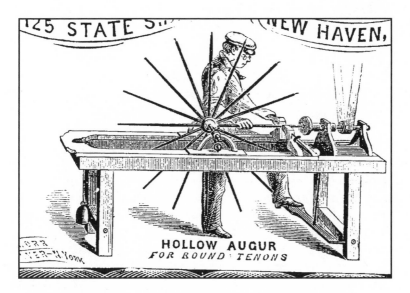

5.5. Tenoning machine manufactured by G. F. Kimball of New Haven, Connecticut. This machine is cutting tenons on the spokes of a carriage wheel. From *G. & D. Cook & Co.'s Illustrated Catalogue of Carriages and Special Business Advertiser* (1860).

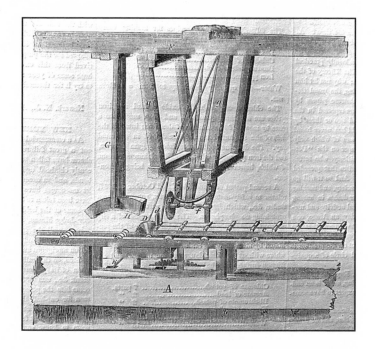

5.6.   A swing saw (K), here illustrated in combination with a trimming saw (D). A swing saw was used in Minor T. Graham's Steam Wagon Factory in Westport, Missouri. From the *Scientific American*, August 13, 1859.

suspended from the roof of the factory by a pendant frame. A simple handle allowed the operator to pull the saw across the lumber to make the cut. As is clearly seen in the accompanying illustration, early models had a completely exposed saw blade. The swing saw was popular, though, because of its "cheapness and overhead attachments."[22] The "emory machine for spokes," also mentioned as being in Graham's factory, was a sanding or polishing machine probably very similar to that depicted in an 1860 advertisement of wheel-making machinery (Fig. 5.7). Its purpose was to remove the cutter marks left after the spoke had been shaped on a lathe.[23]

Much was made at the time of the labor saved by these various machines. The hub mortiser in Graham's factory made all the mortises for a set of hubs in exactly eighteen minutes, "a job that would occupy a man all day and even then he could not do the work with near the niceity and exactness that the machine does."[24] A Daniels planer performed "a day's labor of one man in 20 minutes."[25] And a Woodworth planer, which cost 150 dollars (circa 1857) and required steam power of four horses, dressed ten thousand feet of

5.7.   Spoke polishing or emory machine manufactured by G. F. Kimball of New Haven, Connecticut. *G. & D. Cook & Co.'s Illustrated Catalogue of Carriages and Special Business Advertiser* (1860).

boards a day; "to do this work by hand would require 100 men."[26] But there was another benefit to woodworking machines in wagon factories beyond the obvious. As one authority noted in 1872, machines were "not made to supplement manual effort or hand labour alone, but also to supply the want of intelligence or 'brain power.'"[27] By 1860, the demand for wagons and the proliferation of wagon shops and factories had outstripped the supply of skilled craftsmen (who, not incidentally, were more expensive to employ). One can easily see, then, why the proprietor of a wagon factory would appreciate a Daniels planer that was "so simple [to operate] as to be easily managed by a boy."[28]

In 1860, the *Westport Border Star* reported that Graham's factory employed thirty-five men and could turn out 53 freight wagons per month, which made for an annual product of over 600 wagons (that year's industrial census says twenty men with an annual product of 450 wagons and plows). Joseph Murphy operated his factory with fifty employees and claimed an annual product of 250 freight wagons and 450 lumber wagons. Those numbers are minuscule, however, when compared to the feat accomplished by two Philadelphia wagon manufactories in 1857. That year,

Measuring Wheel

Measuring Tire

5.7a.   In the top drawing, a wagon factory worker measures the circumference
of a wagon wheel with a tool called a
traveler, or tire measuring wheel. In the
bottom drawing, the traveler is used to
measure the iron tire.
(© Mark L. Gardner Collection.)

Wilson, Childs & Co. and Simons, Coleman & Co. produced 550 wagons
for the U.S. Army's Utah Expedition in about five weeks' time, which one
learned fellow computed to be "16 wagons per day, or a wagon in 45 minutes."[29] Wilson, Childs & Co. then averaged 178 workers, but even their
impressive operation would soon be dwarfed by a young upstart.[30] The
Indiana wagon-making concern of Studebaker Brothers, established in
South Bend in 1852, employed 130 men at its factory in 1867.[31] In 1872,
however, "the firm hired 325 men and built 6,950 vehicles. By 1874 they
employed 500 men and were turning out 11,050 vehicles."[32] Studebaker
Brothers became the leading wagon manufactory in the United States.[33]

Despite the great numbers of wagons being produced in the 1860s and
1870s by the large steam-powered factories, the demand for wagons was still
so great that numerous small shops were able to survive — for a time. In
1870, Jackson County, Missouri, had twenty-four carriage and wagon-
making establishments, employing a total of 109 hands with products valued at 150,255 dollars.[34] Only Oliver Case & Co. of Westport (probably

successors to Graham's factory) operated a steam-powered wagon factory in the county. Many of the small shops were likely turning out farm wagons for the local market, not freighters, and the industrial census reveals that usually half of their business was in repair work. Typical were F. & S. Weber, wagon makers of Kansas City, who operated with four hands and produced twenty-four wagons a year valued at 2,160 dollars. Their jobbing and repairing work, however, brought them five thousand dollars.[35] Weston & Strode of Independence employed seven men and had an annual product of twenty wagons valued at four thousand dollars, and also one hundred plows. The high value of the wagons, two hundred dollars apiece, suggests that the shop was still building at least some freighters.[36]

St. Louis County, Missouri, in 1870 counted 163 carriage and wagon-making establishments, employing 1,106 hands and turning out annual products valued at 2,044,547 dollars.[37] As the above figures indicate, the city of St. Louis was home to Missouri's largest wagon manufacturers, particularly Joseph Murphy, John Cook, Louis and Henry Espenschied, and Jacob Kern. It is noteworthy, however, that only one of these St. Louis manufacturers is listed in the 1870 industrial census as using steam power: Joseph Murphy. According to the census, the Espenschieds, Kern, and Cook all relied on "hand power" for their operations. Nevertheless, their factories were probably not that much different from Murphy's. Many of the special-purpose machines used in wagon factories, such as mortisers, tenoning machines, drills, and scroll saws, were also available in hand or foot-powered models (Fig. 5.8). And certainly the factory system of subdividing manufacturing operations could be followed with or without a power source.

As for the "hand-powered" shops' production, it appears that they were definitely holding their own. John Cook's wagon manufactory employed seventy-five men and produced 1,500 farm wagons in a year valued at 137,500 dollars (Fig. 5.9). Louis Espenschied, with forty-five workers, manufactured 650 wagons a year valued at 65,000 dollars. By comparison, Murphy, still operating with fifty men, turned out 1,049 wagons valued at 97,429 dollars.[38]

By the time steel rails reached Santa Fe in 1880, the wagon industry had been virtually taken over by a relatively small number of large manufacturers who were able to turn out massive quantities of wagons at incredibly low prices. The bigger firms usually operated branch outlets, employed sales agents in numerous locations across the country, and issued illustrated catalogs. Some mounted impressive advertising campaigns in newspapers in several states.[39] This situation is reflected in the decrease in wagon and carriage makers in some areas. In Jackson County, Missouri, the wagon and carriage establishments had shrunk to a total of five by 1880, employing

5.8.   Foot-operated scroll or jig saw. From *Scientific American*, August 27, 1859.

5.9.   John Cook's St. Louis wagon manufactory, from Richard Edwards and M. Hopewell, *Edwards's Great West . . .* (1860).

forty-four men (the Westport factory of Oliver Case & Co. had failed a few years before). In St. Louis, the number had dropped to thirty-nine (there were also fifty-two shops engaged in wheelwrighting, which at this time consisted largely of the business of repairing wheels).[40]

The predominance of the large manufactory is seen in the following examples. In St. Joseph County, Indiana, home of the Studebaker Brothers factory of South Bend, there were only five carriage or wagon manufacturers in 1880. Yet these five—and of these, Studebaker Brothers was the largest—accounted for 926 workers (including 5 women and 72 children) with products valued at 1,632,500 dollars, a figure greater than that for the entire city of St. Louis.[41] Leavenworth County, Kansas, in 1880, also counted five carriage and wagon-making establishments. The Kansas Manufacturing Company of Leavenworth, founded in 1874, employed 233 men, a little more than half of all the men engaged in the carriage and wagon-making business in the county.[42] The use of the word *employed*, however, is somewhat misleading, for approximately two hundred of these workers were convicts from the Kansas State Penitentiary. From 1874 to 1878, the company paid the state of Kansas a total of forty-five cents a day for each convict employed; from 1878 to 1880 it was fifty cents (in 1880, Joseph Murphy paid his "skilled" workers $1.85 a day; an "ordinary laborer" received $1.25).[43] With the help of a 250-horsepower steam engine and a large assortment of machinery, the workers of the Kansas Manufacturing Company turned out seven thousand wagons a year in 1880, or "thirty wagons per day, or one wagon every twenty-five minutes." The firm was proclaimed the "largest manufacturing concern" in the state of Kansas.[44]

The Kansas Manufacturing Company was one of two large wagon manufacturers using convict labor. The other was Austin, Tomlinson & Webster of Jackson, Michigan (the prison wagon shop in Jefferson City mentioned above apparently did not remain in business long). The use of convict labor by these factories had a significant impact on the wagon industry, and it affected both large and small concerns. The nature of this impact is revealed in the following proud claims made by the state penitentiary board of directors in their report for 1876:

> The Kansas Manufacturing Company . . . are making very superior wagons and selling them at from ten to twenty dollars below the price other wagons were selling for before they put theirs in the market, thus compelling other manufacturing companies to reduce their prices also, and making a net saving to the people of the state of at least ten dollars on every wagon sold within its border; and upon careful

inquiry we are satisfied that there are sold annually to our own people, at the very least, five thousand wagons, making a clear saving to the tax-payers of the state of not less than fifty thousand dollars, besides the hundreds of thousands of dollars sent here in payment for wagons and carriages from other states and territories.[45]

As the smaller shops were being displaced by the manufacturing might of the large factories, there was growth in another area of the wagon industry. This was the business of manufacturing wagon and carriage "materials;" that is, hubs, spokes, felloes, bows, axles, hardware, and so on. In short, almost every part of a wagon eventually came to be produced in bulk quantities in specialized factories. The manufacture of wagon and carriage materials as a separate enterprise had fairly early beginnings. In 1848, Jacob Woodburn and an associate left Newark, New Jersey, for the West, each with a spoke lathe. One gentleman settled in St. Louis and the other in Cincinnati. They supposedly "made the first spokes ever manufactured by machinery west of the Alleghany Mountains."[46] Spoke factories eventually became quite common. By 1866, New York alone boasted sixteen, which produced 1,115,500 spokes a year.[47] Woodburn, by the way, became the head of the Woodburn "Sarven Wheel" Company (the Sarven Wheel was a patent wheel design). In 1870, the company's St. Louis factory produced forty thousand sets of hubs a year valued at sixty thousand dollars.[48]

Early on, the large wagon factories are known to have produced all the parts for their wagons in-house, but it is evident that they came to rely more and more on the manufacturers of wagon materials, who could produce these parts at less cost.[49] In 1879, the Pittsburgh firm of Lewis, Oliver & Phillips employed seven hundred men in the production of wrought iron wagon hardware. The concern made the "necessary fittings for 90,000 wagons per annum." Their customers were the largest wagon manufacturers in the country, including Studebaker Brothers; Peter Schuttler of Chicago; Austin, Tomlinson & Webster of Jackson, Michigan; and the Kansas Manufacturing Company.[50] It would seem, then, that many of the freight wagons traveling the Santa Fe Trail in its last years were an assemblage of parts and materials from several states. For example, the Kansas Manufacturing Company obtained hardware from Pittsburgh, hubs from Wisconsin, felloes and spokes from Indiana and Ohio, and tongues, hounds, and lumber for bodies from Ohio, Indiana, and Michigan.[51]

The great revolution the wagon and carriage industry underwent in the nineteenth century had occurred quickly. It took place not only within the lifetime of the Santa Fe Trail, but also within the lifetimes of many of the

5.10.   *(Above left)* Wheelwright or carriage maker, from an extremely rare tintype dating to the 1860s. The workman is holding a brace with a hollow auger attached. This hollow auger would be used to cut the tenons on the ends of the wheel spokes pictured. The tools displayed behind the workman to the right are a circular saw blade, two hand saws (one a crosscut and the other a rip), a hammer, and a draw knife. The circular saw blade would have been used with a power-driven machine, probably a table saw. (© Mark L. Gardner Collection.)

5.11.   *(Above right)* Tintype of a wheelwright or carriage maker dating to the 1870s. Visible on the workbench behind the carriage wheel are a wood plane, a brace, and a hand saw. Note that the man is wearing sleeve protectors to prevent the soiling of his white shirt. He is holding a wrench in one hand and what may be a small paintbrush in the other. (© Mark L. Gardner Collection.)

5.12.   The large hub and spokes of the wheel in this 1880s tintype indicate that the two individuals pictured here are wagon makers. The man on the right stands behind the anvil holding a hammer and tongs clinching a piece of iron; he is obviously a blacksmith in the wagon shop or factory. The man behind the wagon wheel, which does not yet have its iron tire, is holding a hatchet, probably to signify that he is a woodworker. As in all occupational tintypes illustrating this chapter, this image was made in a photographer's studio. The limits of photography during this period made interior shots of factories and shops difficult. Thus, proud workers desiring a portrait generally had to haul their tools (including heavy anvils as seen here) and products to the closest studio. (© Mark L. Gardner Collection.)

wagon makers themselves. Writing on the changes in wheel making, one individual made these observations in 1891:

> There are carriage workmen now actively engaged in the business who can recall the days when they begun the wheel at the chopping block, hewing the spokes with a broad axe, then squaring up with a draw knife and plane, then tenoning and rounding up, all by hand. The hubs were turned but the boring and morticing was all handwork. So, too, all work upon the felloes, except the heavy sawing, and

in many shops even that, was performed by hand labor. Now all is changed, machinery everywhere.[52]

Makers like Joseph Murphy, the Espenchieds, and others had begun their careers when it was necessary to have the skills and knowledge to produce every individual part of a wagon. In other words, they were required to learn the "craft" of wagon making. These men eventually came to oversee factories, however, where their workers knew little beyond their department or the specific part assigned to them. The craft remained—it was simply absent the craftsman.[53]

Although this chapter has focused on the many changes in wagon manufacturing that occurred during the Santa Fe Trail's existence, there is still another important change that has not yet been discussed: the change in freight wagon design, a subject that will be taken up in the next chapter.

SIX

The Santa Fe Wagon, 1858–1880

In 1858 and 1860, two important articles were published by Missouri news-papers that provide us with the best contemporary descriptions of freight wagons used on the Santa Fe Trail on the eve of the Civil War. The first article appeared in the Kansas City *Western Journal of Commerce* of May 22, 1858.[1] The paper stated emphatically that the wagons used to traverse the plains and mountains "are not 'double wagons,' or 'lumber wagons,' or 'farm wagons,' or 'Chicago wagons,' or 'Concord wagons,'—they are 'prairie wagons,' or 'schooners,' as the boys call them, and as novel a sight to an Eastern man, as any Yankee institution is to a frontiersman." The *Journal* then proceeded to give the specifications for these freighters:

> A wagon weighs about four thousand pounds, the pole, or tongue, is thirteen feet long, and with all the "fixings" about it is as heavy as a light buggy. One of the hind wheels weighs three hundred pounds, and is sixty-four inches in diameter—the tire is four inches wide, the hub twelve inches through and eighteen inches deep, and the spokes are as large as a middle sized bed post.—Any one can conceive what an axletree for such a wheel must be. The body is three feet eight inches wide, thirteen feet long at the bottom and eighteen feet long at the top; with bows extending above the bed three feet high, and also extending fore and aft of the bed two feet and a half, so that the top of the wagons, measuring over the bows, is eighteen feet long—height of wagon from bottom of wheels to top of bows is ten feet. These bows are covered with three wagon sheets, made of the best quality of duck, and cost about $30.

This wagon, according to the *Journal*, "always carries from fifty-five to sixty hundred pounds of freight."

Two years later, the *Westport Border Star* published its take on the "prairie schooner": "A regular wagon of the first magnitude, capable of carrying 6,500 pounds is what we here call a 'Santa Fe wagon,' from the fact that so many trains of these wagons are continually leaving Westport and Kansas City for Santa Fe, New Mexico." Although the *Border Star*'s description of the "Santa Fe wagon" is not quite as thorough as that found in the *Western Journal of Commerce*, it is just as valuable:

> Some of the dimensions of these wagons would supprise [*sic*] an Eastern man. The diameter of the larger wheel is five feet two inches, and the tire weighs 105 pounds. The reach is eleven feet and the bed forty-six inches deep, twelve feet long on the bottom and fifteen feet on the top, and will carry 6,500 pounds across the plains and through the mountain passes.[2]

Despite what at first examination appears to be a great disparity between the vehicle specifications provided in the two papers, the *Western Journal of Commerce* and the *Westport Border Star* are actually describing the same freight wagon type. The "hind wheels" of the *Journal*'s wagon is only two inches larger in diameter than the one described in the *Border Star*. What seems to be a big difference in the weight of the rear wheels, 300 pounds versus 105, is explained by the fact that the *Journal* is stating the weight of the complete wheel with tire, whereas the *Border Star* provides the weight of just the iron tire alone. In regard to the wagon bodies, the *Journal* gives the length along the bottom of the bed, thirteen feet, and the *top* of the bows (from end bow to end bow), eighteen feet. The *Border Star* also provides a measurement for the length of the bed at the bottom, twelve feet, but its top measurement of fifteen feet is taken along the top of the bed, not the top of the bows. If we recall that the bows of the *Journal* wagon extended "fore and aft of the bed two feet and a half," that would make the length of the top of the bed of the *Journal* wagon exactly fifteen and a half feet, just a half-foot longer than the *Border Star* wagon.

The wagon described by the *Journal* and the *Border Star* is not the Conestoga-type wagon discussed in earlier chapters of this work. This wagon did not have the famous curved or downbowed body of the Conestoga; its bottom and top were straight (the *Journal* called the wagon "cumbrous and ugly," a description one would never associate with a Conestoga). And it lacked the complex joinery of rails and uprights characteristic of the Conestoga body. Yet, as the *Journal* and *Border Star*'s dimensions make obvious, this freighter did retain the outward-canted end gates, front and back, although the angle of the gates was not as extreme as those found on many Conestoga wagons. Because this new style of wagon was probably first proven on the Santa Fe Trail—and quickly became commonplace on that route—the appellation given it by the *Border Star*, "Santa Fe wagon," has been retained for this study.[3] However, the Santa Fe wagon did see service on other overland routes.

All of this brings up a most interesting question. Why the change from the Conestoga to the Santa Fe wagon? Large Conestogas could match the hauling capacity of the Santa Fe wagon, so this was not a factor. The body of the Santa Fe wagon, however, was simpler with regard to construction, so it may have been that the overwhelming demand for wagons caused wagon makers to simplify the design in order to speed up production. Still, with the introduction of machine tools and the division of labor, there is no reason why a basic Conestoga-type wagon could not also be produced in mass quantities. Perhaps, then, the change was an effort not only to produce greater numbers of wagons, but to produce them at lower costs. The wagon-making business could be highly competitive, after all. Or was the design change a response to certain needs identified by the contract freighters who were using the wagons out on the trail? Another possibility, which must be considered, is that this shift in styles may have represented the rejection of a vehicle that had come to be considered old fashioned or obsolete. In 1852, C. L. Fleischmann, writing for the benefit of Germans considering immigration to the United States, warned German wagon makers that they "must eschew all these silly and uncritical statements to the effect that the wagon or plow is better the way he learned to make it in Germany. He must bear in mind that everything Dutch is considered cumbersome and inefficient by the Americans."[4] Was the German influence in the Conestoga design well enough known in the nineteenth century to have contributed to the wagon's demise? J. Richards, writing in 1872, claimed that the "very same reasons that are adduced in England or on the Continent for continuing a plan of construction, are presented in America as a sufficient reason for changing it. In England it is said, a custom so old 'must be right;' in America, that a custom so old 'must be wrong,' and need revolution or change."[5] Perhaps it was a combination of all of the above that spawned the Santa Fe wagon. Unfortunately, in the absence of a primary source on this subject, we are left to speculate.

The Santa Fe wagon appears in the earliest-known photograph of Santa Fe Trail freight wagons, the now-famous view of the Elsberg & Amberg

6.1.   Elsberg & Amberg train of ox and mule wagons on the plaza in Santa Fe, New
Mexico, October 1861. (Courtesy of the Colorado State Historical Society, Neg.
No. 1532).

train on the plaza in Santa Fe in October 1861 (Fig. 6.1, especially the larger
wagon in this image). This wagon type is also seen in two photographs
depicting the warehouses of Otero & Seller at Hays City, Kansas, both
taken circa 1867 (Figs. 6.2 and 6.3). And the Santa Fe wagon is featured
quite dramatically in a photograph (Fig. 6.4) of the D. & B. Powers train
from Leavenworth corralled on a Denver street on June 20, 1868. Of these
images, the best for discerning details of the Santa Fe wagon's construction
is the photograph depicting the Otero & Sellar warehouse on the railroad
siding at Hays City (Fig. 6.3).[6]

A distinguishing characteristic that emerges in all of the images is the
triangular configuration of three wooden uprights on the wagon's side
panels. In the center of the panel, a wide upright runs vertically from the
bottom of the wagon side to near its top edge. On each side of this upright
are two more uprights running at an angle from the panel's bottom edge
until meeting at the top of the vertical upright, thus forming what looks like
two triangles. Additional uprights are sometimes found on the side panels
of these wagons, but they are narrower and do not emerge as distinctly in

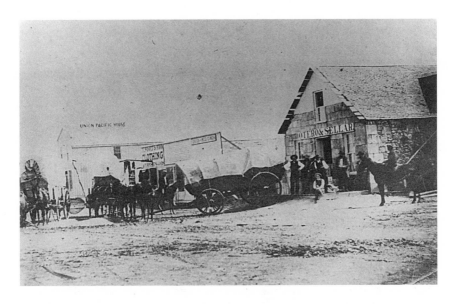

6.2.   One of the warehouses of Otero & Sellar at Hays City, Kansas, ca. 1867. (Courtesy of Daniel T. Kelly, Jr.)

6.3.   The second Otero & Sellar warehouse at Hays City, ca. 1867. (Courtesy of the Museum of New Mexico.)

6.4. D. & B. Powers train from Leavenworth corralled on a Denver street, June
20, 1868. (Courtesy of the Colorado State Historical Society.)

images as the triangular configuration, which provided extra strength to the
body as well as preventing the boards of the side panel from shifting.

Other features visible in the Otero & Sellar photograph (Fig. 6.3) are two
wide vertical uprights on the end gate; two horizontal iron box rods running across the end gate, connecting the wagon sides; seven bows, with
generally two bow staples per bow on a side; two stringers attached to bows
(the wagon to the right and behind the first vehicle has a single ridge pole
or stringer). The wagons in the Otero & Sellar image are not equipped with
brakes; however, what appears to be a brake lever is visible on the larger
wagon in the 1861 view of the Elsberg & Amberg train in Santa Fe. Brakes
are also clearly seen on some of the wagons of the D. & B. Powers train in
Denver in 1868. Brakes were no doubt an option for purchasers of wagons.
In an excellent engraving (Fig. 6.5) of a Santa Fe wagon, entitled "Ship of
the Plains at Anchor," from a sketch circa 1875, a drop tongue is clearly in
view. Drop tongues are also visible in an 1874 photograph of Santa Fe
wagons loaded with buffalo hides (Fig. 6.8). Both of these last two images
show ox yokes leaning against the wagons.

A Santa Fe wagon of the 1860s is shown in a modern photograph (Fig. 6.9)
taken at the now-defunct Pioneer Village Museum of Salt Lake City, Utah.

6.5. "Ship of the Plains at Anchor," from A. C. Wheeler, *The Iron Trail* (1876).

6.6. "Ship of the Plains in Dock," La Junta, Colorado, ca.1875, from A. C. Wheeler, *The Iron Trail* (1876).

6.7. "Ship of the Plains at Sea," from A. C. Wheeler, *The Iron Trail* (1876).

6.8.   Santa Fe wagons loaded with buffalo hides, 1874. (Courtesy of the Kansas State Historical Society.)

6.9.   A Santa Fe wagon once in the collections of the Pioneer Village Museum in Salt Lake City, Utah. Its current location is unknown. (Courtesy of the St. Joseph Museum, St. Joseph, Missouri.)

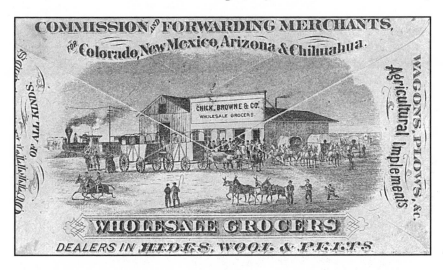

6.10.   Chick, Browne & Co. store and warehouse at Granada, Colorado, ca. 1873, from an envelope. (© Mark L. Gardner Collection.)

It appears that this wagon had a removable side board, a feature that is suggested in some contemporary images. The wagon has wooden axles with wheels that are secured by linchpins, and it is equipped with a brake. Note also that a number can be seen painted on the side of the wagon, which was important in matching bills of lading with the appropriate wagons. Unfortunately, the current location of this wagon, which would answer many questions in regard to freight wagon construction of this period, is unknown.[7]

The Santa Fe wagon seems to have changed relatively little during the last twenty years of the Trail's history. It is depicted in an engraving (Fig. 6.10) of the Chick, Browne & Co. store and warehouse at Granada, Colorado, circa 1873. It is clearly delineated in three engravings (Figs. 6.5, 6.6, and 6.7) in A. C. Wheeler's *The Iron Trail*, published in 1876 (one of these is the "Ship of the Plains at Anchor" mentioned above). And it is also visible in a view of Raton Pass made in 1879 (Fig. 6.11), just a year before the railroad reached Santa Fe.[8]

In later years, freighters began to use "trails" or "trailers": a second, smaller wagon, coupled to the rear of a regular freight wagon. Colonel Homer W. Wheeler, wagonmaster for several wagon trains freighting from the end of the Kansas Pacific railroad to Denver in 1869, recalled that these tandem rigs were drawn by ten and twelve yoke of oxen, and the "large wagons with their trails each held from ten to twelve thousand pounds of freight." In difficult terrain, the freighters "would cut off the 'trail' and

6.11.   Raton Pass, Colorado, after a sketch by Henry Worrall. From *Frank Leslie's Illustrated Newspaper*, August 23, 1879. (Courtesy of the Pueblo Library District.)

return for it after all the rough spots had been passed."[9] George Curry remembered a freighting trip made by his Uncle John Riney from the railhead at Granada, Colorado, to New Mexico in 1875: "Uncle John loaded thirty wagons, each with a trailer, and drawn by four-horse teams."[10]

Trailers are visible in the photograph of the Santa Fe wagons loaded with buffalo hides (Fig. 6.8) and also, apparently, in the engraving of Chick, Browne & Co.'s Granada store (Fig. 6.10). However, the available evidence seems to indicate that tandem rigs were less common than the individually drawn wagons, at least on the Santa Fe Trail.[11] Trailers became a mainstay, though, on other routes, especially during the last twenty-five years of the nineteenth century. The use of trailers led wagon manufacturers to reduce the overhang of wagon end gates—the last vestige of the rakish Conestoga style—until there was finally no overhang at all; the wagon beds became simple square boxes with high sides, which were better suited to close coupling (the triangulated uprights or bracing characteristic of the Santa Fe wagon's bed is lacking on many of these later square-box vehicles).[12] Some of these tall, square-box freight wagons saw use on the Santa Fe Trail, but without the overhanging end gates they must be classed as a different type or, in some cases, a variation of the "Santa Fe wagon" as described and illustrated in this chapter.

Makers

The *Border Star* noted that a "large portion of these [Santa Fe] wagons are manufactured at St. Louis and at establishments in Indiana and Illinois, and are forwarded here by water." On July 6, 1861, St. Louis wagon makers Louis Espenschied, Jacob Kern, Jacob Scheer, and John Cook wrote to the assistant quartermaster of the army at St. Louis, offering to furnish the army with

> 6 mule wagons 2½ inch Iron Axles 12 inch Box with substantial Wagon beds for the Sum of One hundred & twenty five Dollars each. These wagons are warranted to carry 5000 to 6000 lbs each and are used by the Freighters to New Mexico & Utah.[13]

In 1863, the St. Louis forwarding and commission firm of Glasgow & Brother purchased "*8 Carros completos para 10 Mulas*" (eight wagons completed for ten mules) of Louis Espenschied for New Mexico merchant Felipe Chaves. The cost was 140 dollars per wagon.[14] In 1880, the year rail lines reached Santa Fe, Espenschied employed twenty-seven men and three children in his factory. They worked ten-hour days and had an annual product valued at 22,500 dollars.[15] Louis Espenschied died seven years later, but the Espenschied name continued to appear on St. Louis–made wagons into the early 1930s.[16]

Joseph Murphy continued to be a leading St. Louis manufacturer of freight wagons, outlasting the Santa Fe Trail by several years. His annual product in 1880 was fifty-six thousand dollars.[17] He eventually retired from the wagon business in 1888, turning over his interest to his sons.[18] Murphy's freighters, probably no different in style from those of his competitors, were recalled by William F. "Buffalo Bill" Cody:

> The wagons used in those days by Russell, Majors & Waddell were known as the 'J. Murphy wagons,' made at St. Louis specially for the plains business. They were very large and were strongly built, being capable of carrying seven thousand pounds of freight each. The wagon-boxes [read "bodies"] were very commodious—being about as large as the rooms of an ordinary house—and were covered with two heavy canvas sheets to protect the merchandise from the rain. These wagons were sent out from Leavenworth, each loaded with six thousand pounds of freight, and each drawn by several yokes of oxen in charge of one driver.[19]

An 1870 chattel mortgage from Trinidad, Colorado, includes "two 'Murphy' wagons sometimes called 'sixty Hundred' wagons," additional evidence that the six-thousand-pound load was standard.[20]

On the western border of Missouri, Hiram Young's position as an important maker of the Santa Fe wagon was cut short by the outbreak of the Civil War, when the volatile conditions in Jackson County forced Young, a free black, to abandon his shop and home. As one contemporary later testified, Independence

> was a rather unsafe place for rich men like Hiram Young to live here at that time; [I] believe some of them [the townspeople] were prejudiced; I think he was in danger, think he had enemies on account of his trade; his enemies were whites, not the soldiers . . . [I] believe it was just the ordinary littleness of human nature, didn't like to see a man get rich.[21]

In December 1861, Young relocated with his family a safe distance away in the town of Leavenworth, Kansas, situated four miles from the major military post of the same name. There he continued to produce his popular wagons, presumably on a more limited scale. Young's name appears in several surviving Leavenworth city directories from the 1860s, although he is listed only once as a wagon maker.[22] Young returned to Independence about 1868, but it is not clear whether or not he ever resumed his wagonmaking operation there. Young is found in the 1870 industrial census not as a wagon maker but as a manufacturer of ox yokes. He and his nine employees turned out an estimated five thousand yokes a year valued at fifteen thousand dollars. Young owned real estate valued at three thousand dollars and had a personal estate estimated at nine hundred dollars. Ten years later, Young was operating a Jackson County sawmill.[23]

As noted in chapter 5, Minor T. Graham established his "Steam Wagon Factory" in Westport in 1860. He had actually started in the wagon business about two years earlier, in partnership with the Indiana wagon-making firm of A. Eberhart & Co., purchasing the Westport shops "formerly carried on by Messrs. Majors & Russell" and refitting them. These shops were apparently used primarily for repairing wagons, while orders for freight wagons were filled by the factory in Mishawaka, Indiana.[24] In a testimonial published in the *Westport Border Star* of December 31, 1858, Henry T. Chiles heaped high praise on M. T. Graham & Co.'s vehicles: "GENTLEMEN:—Having used your wagons last spring and summer on a trip across the plains to Salt Lake City, I take pleasure in saying to you and the public that they prove DECIDEDLY the best wagons I have ever used on the plains." It seems to have been the intent of M. T. Graham & Co. to set up a wagon factory at Westport from the very start. What A. Eberhart & Co.'s role in the new factory was to have been is not known. Their partnership with Minor T. Graham & Co., however, was dissolved by mutual consent in March of 1859. Minor T. Graham proceeded to construct the factory on his own, which was completed sometime before June, 1860.[25]

How long Graham remained in business is unclear. Three months after his impressive factory was described in the *Westport Border Star* of June 23, 1860, he mortgaged it, and he took out a second mortgage on the factory in January 1861.[26] The Civil War must have had some kind of impact on Graham's operation. Henry Crump, a wagon maker employed by Hiram Young, stated bluntly that the war stopped the wagon-making business in Jackson County: "It was at a time there was no one wanted to set up wagons when they expected them to be taken off by the army."[27] Minor T. Graham is not found in the 1870 industrial census for Jackson County. Yet there is a steam wagon factory listed in Westport operating under the name of Oliver Case & Co.[28] It is very likely that this factory had formerly been Graham's works.

Oliver Case & Co. had twenty thousand dollars invested in their wagon-making business and five thousand in the manufacture of agricultural instruments. The firm employed fifteen men and reported an annual product in 1870 of 100 wagons (valued at 10,000 dollars), 100 drills (4,500 dollars), 125 plows (800 dollars), and 100 cultivators (3,300 dollars).[29] A rare billhead dating from the 1870s (Fig. 6.12) states that Oliver Case & Co. manufactured both freight and farm wagons. This firm failed, an early Jackson County history informs us, "on account of the severe drouth and grasshoppers of 1872 devastating Kansas."[30]

Although the industrial census identifies other wagon makers in Jackson County during this period, it is difficult to determine with certainty which ones actually produced wagons or wagon work for the Santa Fe trade. In the case of two Jackson County craftsmen, both of whom died in 1866, the evidence of such involvement is found, interestingly, in their estate inventories. Among the unsettled accounts of Christian Glunz appear the names of several Trail merchants and freighters who had been his customers (and debtors): Samuel Watrous & Co., Charles W. Kitchen, Franz Huning & Co., Charles Raber & Co., and Epifanio Aguirre. The inventory also lists "10 New Ox Wagons" at Glunz's shop with a value of 160 dollars each. Additionally, Glunz had been the owner of an ox train. That train's twenty-four "Large Wagons with Sheets," used, are listed at one hundred dollars each.[31]

Frederick Klaber of Westport was the other Jackson County wagon maker to die in 1866. His unsettled accounts include the names of William W. Bent, Samuel Hays, Grecoria Mina (Gregorio Mena?), and Boggs & Ross. The values given for both new and used ("Second Hand") wagons in

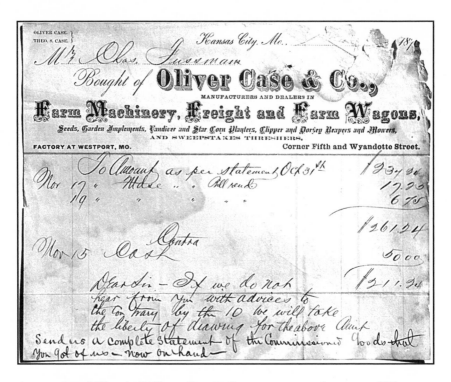

6.12. 1870s billhead of Oliver, Case & Co., wagon manufacturers of Westport, Missouri. (© Mark L. Gardner Collection.)

6.12a. The Studebaker Brothers carriage and wagon factory as it appeared in the late 1860s. From *Turner's Guide from the Lakes to the Rocky Mountains . . .* (1868).

his estate are the same as those found in Glunz's estate inventory, 160 dollars and 100 dollars respectively. In 1860, Klaber's wagon-making operation employed eight men and cranked out an annual product of seventy-two wagons worth 8,400 dollars.[32]

As the *Westport Border Star* noted above, many Santa Fe wagons came from other states, particularly Indiana and Illinois. South Bend, Indiana's Michigan Street was the location of the now-famous Studebaker Brothers Manufacturing Company (Fig. 6.12a), discussed in chapter 5. By 1867 this firm had established a branch house in St. Joseph, Missouri, and counted seventeen agents in seven states.[33] The Denver *Rocky Mountain News* announced on March 18, 1874, that D. K. Wall, "who has an extensive wagon and blacksmithing establishment on Fifteenth Street," had made arrangements with Studebaker Brothers "to sell their wagons and buggies in the territory of Colorado." The news item reveals that wagon makers were still trying to cope with an age-old problem:

> Mr. Wall's long residence in this western country has taught him that it is necessary to construct woodwork in a peculiar manner in order to make it withstand the climactic influences. In view of this he prevailed upon the Studebaker company to construct their wagons in the future so that they will stand our climate perfectly. This is a great point gained and gives this wagon a great superiority over many others made east and sold here.

The *News* went on to comment that "the factory at which these wagons are made is probably the largest of its kind in the United States."

A rare 1876 price list for Studebaker Brothers contains an engraving (Fig. 6.13) of their freight wagon intended "for Western, Southwestern and Northwestern States and Territories."[34] The wagon pictured has the triangulated uprights typical of the Santa Fe wagon (and additional bracing), although it is very nearly a square-box wagon. The top of the bed, however, does appear to be slightly longer than the bottom. The 1876 price list provides valuable specifications for this vehicle. Because the entire page featuring the Studebaker freight wagon is reproduced in this chapter, only a summary of the information will be given here. Four varieties of thimble skein wagons were offered, ranging from four-inch axles to five-inch, the larger the axle the greater the hauling capacity. The four-inch thimble skein wagon had a bed twelve feet long (bottom measurement), three feet eight inches wide, and thirty-eight inches deep. The tire was two inches wide and was available in a seven-eighths or one-inch thickness. The capacity for this wagon was six thousand pounds; price, 165 dollars. The five-inch wagon had

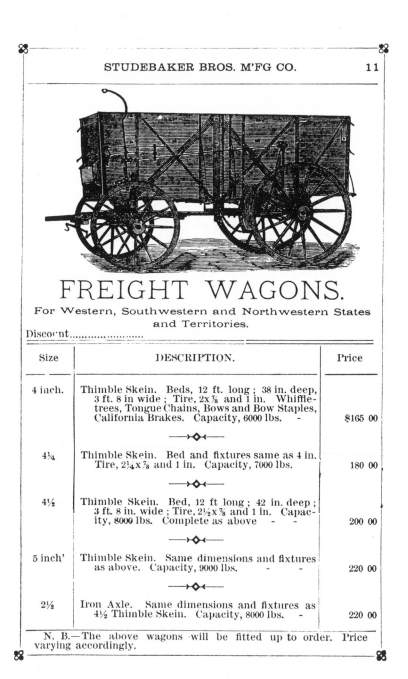

FREIGHT WAGONS.

For Western, Southwestern and Northwestern States and Territories.

Discount.......................

Size	DESCRIPTION.	Price
4 inch.	Thimble Skein. Beds, 12 ft. long ; 38 in. deep, 3 ft. 8 in wide ; Tire, 2x⅞ and 1 in. Whiffle-trees, Tongue Chains, Bows and Bow Staples, California Brakes. Capacity, 6000 lbs. -	$165 00
4¼	Thimble Skein. Bed and fixtures same as 4 in. Tire, 2¼x⅞ and 1 in. Capacity, 7000 lbs.	180 00
4½	Thimble Skein. Bed, 12 ft long ; 42 in. deep ; 3 ft. 8 in. wide ; Tire, 2½x⅞ and 1 in. Capacity, 8000 lbs. Complete as above - -	200 00
5 inch'	Thimble Skein. Same dimensions and fixtures as above. Capacity, 9000 lbs. - -	220 00
2½	Iron Axle. Same dimensions and fixtures as 4½ Thimble Skein. Capacity, 8000 lbs. -	220 00

N. B.—The above wagons will be fitted up to order. Price varying accordingly.

6.13. A page from the 1876 price list of Studebaker Brothers, wagon manufacturers located in South Bend, Indiana. (© Mark L. Gardner Collection.)

a slightly taller body, a two and one-half inch tire width, and a capacity of nine thousand pounds. This wagon cost 220 dollars. The one iron axle wagon listed with the above freighters had a two and one-half inch axle and could haul eight thousand pounds. It was priced the same as the five-inch thimble skein wagon.

The thimble skein, described in chapter 4, became more and more common on freight wagons through the 1860s. Eugene F. Ware remembered that the freighters he observed on the Central Overland Route in 1864 had wooden axles and were

> what they called the thimble-skein variety. On the end of the heavy wooden axle was the iron thimble which revolved in another iron thimble [axle-box] in the hub . . . the axle [wheel] was held on by a linch-pin made by a blacksmith. The thimble-skein was lubricated with tar, and the tar bucket hung on the rear axle. At every ranch were lift-jacks, so that these wheels could be raised, taken off, and the axles lubricated. The wind and whirling sand and dust made it necessary for this to be frequently done.[35]

As the Studebaker price list indicates, freight wagons were available that could haul much more than the "sixty hundred" load. However, even those wagons intended for a six-thousand-pound cargo could, and did, carry heavier loads. Gerhard Stulken, a Wisconsin volunteer who served along the Santa Fe Trail during the Civil War, explained that the freight wagons "were made so heavy that it was impossible to overload them or to break down on the way, for there was no chance to repair it when started on its long journey from Kansas City to Albuquerque or other places."[36] While the "sixty hundred" load did remain the standard on the Santa Fe Trail, heavier per-wagon loads do seem to have became more common in the Trail's later years. In 1872, a St. Louis–bound Mr. Coffin "met no less than two hundred wagons, each carrying about nine thousand four hundred pounds of freight, general merchandise, going from Kit Carson [Colorado] to New Mexico. Each wagon was drawn by twelve mules."[37] Richens Lacy ("Uncle Dick") Wootton claimed that to "put six or eight thousand pounds on a wagon was not loading uncommonly heavy, and frequently we put as high as ten thousand pounds on a wagon."[38] Yet one does wonder about the accuracy of many estimates of the weight of loaded wagons — there were no weigh stations on the Santa Fe Trail.

The fame of Studebaker Brothers has overshadowed another large Indiana wagon-making firm, George Milburn & Co., which was situated just

6.13a.   The Peter Schuttler wagon shop in 1843. (© Mark L. Gardner Collection.)

a few miles from the Studebaker factory in Mishawaka. It appears that George Milburn & Co. was the successor to A. Eberhart & Co., which, as noted above, had sold wagons at Westport, Missouri, through M. T. Graham and Co. in the late 1850s. In 1867, George Milburn & Co. employed approximately one hundred hands. The "mammoth" factory's power source was the St. Joseph River. Nearly 150,000 dollars worth of carriages and wagons were produced a year, and they were "sold all the way from lake Erie to the Rio Grande."[39]

Many of the Illinois wagons that the *Border Star* reported were shipped to the Missouri border for use in the Santa Fe trade were undoubtedly Peter Schuttler wagons. A native German, Schuttler set up shop in Chicago in 1843 (Fig. 6.13a); fourteen years later, his shop had grown into a factory with one hundred hands turning out 120 wagons a month. The Schuttler freighter saw heavy usage on various overland routes.[40] Schuttler advertised his "Waggons for the Plains" in a Colorado gold rush guidebook published in Chicago in 1859.[41] And he had another advertisement for his Chicago Wagon Manufactory in the *Illinois State Business Directory, 1860*, proclaiming he had "the largest and best stock of Wagons in the West." More importantly, this latter ad listed some of the sizes of wagons available: wagons with iron axles, either 2 or 1¾ inches; thimble skein wagons with 3¾- or 3½-inch boxes; nut skein wagons with 3½- or 3¾-inch boxes; and washer linchpin wagons with 3¾-inch box.[42] The Pueblo, Colorado, wagon shop of

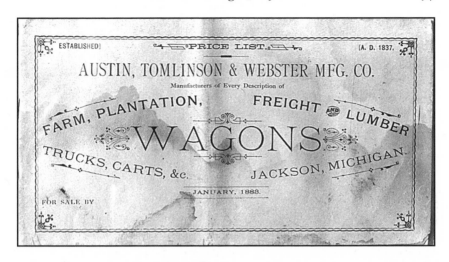

6.14.   1883 price list of Austin, Tomlinson & Webster Manufacturing Co., Jackson, Michigan. (© Mark L. Gardner Collection.)

Hyde & Kretschmer carried Schuttler wagons in 1872.[43] By 1877, Schuttler's freight wagons were of the large square-box variety.[44]

About 1861, a visitor to Kansas City toured the "camping ground of the immense caravans of Russell, Majors & Co." He found

> several acres covered with the enormous wagons that are used in the prairie trade.. . . It was to me something of a sight to see such a number of *land ships*. They will carry from seven to ten thousand pounds, and are drawn by from three to six yokes of oxen. They are covered when loaded, so as to protect the goods from the rains. I examined them, and found them made many hundreds of miles to the east. I saw a large number which came from Michigan. They are strong, heavily ironed and massive wagons.[45]

The Michigan wagons were made by Austin & Tomlinson of Jackson, Michigan. This firm had been in the wagon business since 1837. In 1852 its name was Davis, Austin & Co., becoming Austin & Tomlinson in 1856. Sometime later it became Austin, Tomlinson & Webster (Fig. 6.14). This wagon factory in Jackson was one of two in the country that are known to have used prison labor, employing 120 convicts in 1872.[46]

On January 12, 1861, The Denver *Rocky Mountain News* carried an advertisement for the" Michigan Waggon Depot" of St. Joseph, Missouri, the western outlet for Austin & Tomlinson. The ad called particular attention "to our

Iron Axle Waggons, which we think are unsurpassed for durability and light-ness of draught." The editor of the *News*, always glad to welcome new adver-tisers, commented in another column "These wagons are justly celebrated for their strength and durability, and as they have been extensively used by Alex. Majors, Train & Co., and other heavy freighters in the Pike's Peak trade, there can be no doubt of their excellence and adaptation to the trials of a trip across the Plains." The *Leavenworth Daily Times* of March 26, 1862, featured an ad-vertisement offering "Three Four Mule Teams, with Jackson, Michigan, built wagons, and harness all complete and entirely new last December, and all in perfect order for freighting to Denver."

William Henry Jackson, who later became famous for his western pho-tographs, remembered that the wagons used in the freight outfit he hired onto in 1866 were "50 'Jackson Wagons' coupled in pairs — 'back actions' in current vernacular — making 25 teams, each one requiring six yoke, or twelve oxen as motive power."[47] The freighters were destined for Salt Lake City. In 1870, Jackson wagons were being offered for sale by Leavenworth wagon dealer A. Woodworth at his "Great Western Wagon Depot."[48] How long Austin, Tomlinson & Webster remained in business has yet to be de-termined; they are known to have manufactured wagons into the 1890s.[49]

The Kansas Manufacturing Company of Leavenworth, the other wagon manufacturer to utilize convict labor (see chapter 5), was a relatively late starter in the wagon trade. Established in 1874, its low-priced wagons quickly gained a good share of the market. In an 1875 newspaper advertise-ment, the Leavenworth firm claimed that because its wagons were "Manu-factured in the Dry Atmosphere of Kansas," its vehicles were "Much Better Adapted to the Climate of the West than those Manufactured in the Damp Climate of Indiana, Wisconsin and other Eastern Points." This claim was complete balderdash, as any visit to eastern Kansas in summer will attest. Nevertheless, the company was very successful, selling thirty thousand ve-hicles by 1880. It also succeeded in obtaining several U.S. Quartermaster's Department contracts: from 1876 to 1880, the Kansas Manufacturing Com-pany supplied the army with two hundred six-mule army wagons, two hun-dred two-horse and four-horse or mule wagons, fifty ambulance wagons (army pattern), and twenty-five Dougherty spring wagons.[50] It is unknown whether or not the Kansas Manufacturing Company produced any Santa Fe–style freight wagons. An 1880 description of the factory states that they manufactured the "famous Rocky Mountain freight wagon, the Leadville quartz wagon, and a line of ponderous timber wagons, employed in the construction of the Atchison, Topeka & Santa Fe road."[51]

One additional item should be mentioned in regard to the Kansas Manufacturing Company, although it is more in the form of an aside. One of the firm's non-convict employees, the general agent of the company, was a man by the name of Cyrus Townsend. Townsend was described as "an accomplished gentleman, full of energy and ability, and one of the most efficient of wagon men." He should have been, for as it turns out, this Cyrus Townsend was the son of Cyrus Townsend of Pittsburgh, who manufactured numerous wagons for the Santa Fe Trade in the 1830s and 1840s (discussed in chapter 2).[52]

An interesting assessment of various makes of wagons at the close of the Santa Fe Trail era is found in an 1880 report written by an Indian Department inspector. Although the inspector's observations appear to pertain mostly to farm wagons, not freighters, his comments may very well be applicable to other vehicles in a company's line. This inspector, E. L. Cooper, claimed to have spent forty-five years in the hardware business and had closely examined wagons of the following brands: Studebaker, Milburn, Moline, Kansas, Jackson (Austin, Tomlinson & Webster), Mitchell, La Belle, Fish Bros., Schuttler, Whitewater, Lukin, Espenschied, Gestring & Becker, Weber & Damme, Luedinghaus, Murphy, and Shaw & Backus. In some cases, he had even been in the wagon factories, taking note of their raw materials and manufacturing techniques.[53]

In regard to St. Louis wagons, and these would include those made by Joseph Murphy, Louis Espenscheid, Henry Luedinghaus, Gestring & Becker, and Weber & Damme, Cooper advised the department to "drop them . . . on account of timber, mode of workmanship, and [the] fitting [of] the parts [of] their wheels and not oiling the same, and above all from the fact of the parts not being interchangeable." He considered the wagon made by the Kansas Manufacturing Company "a fair wagon, but they were made in prison by convict labor," thus

> the work was not likely to be as good as free labor, for a convict had a certain task to perform, and as long as he performed said task, there was no interest at stake with him to do better work when complained of, whereas the free workman has his position and support and the support of his family dependent upon his work being good at all times.

Cooper felt the same way about the Jackson wagons of Austin, Tomlinson & Webster, also made with convict labor. However, although he did not consider Austin, Tomlinson & Webster "among the best makers," he did rate the Jackson wagon higher than the St. Louis wagons and those made

by the Kansas Manufacturing Company. Studebaker Brothers "made a good
wagon, but there was a rumor that they made two grades of wagons, which
I knew that his wagons had failed in use by the department; if he offered in
his bid his standard western wagon it was as good as any."[54]

In addition to his own opinions, Cooper also offered something of a survey
of popular opinion gathered from those individuals actually using the wagons,
although these again appear to have been primarily farmers. "I learn a great deal
about the different make of wagons through conversation with farmers and
others who use plows, wagons, &c.," Cooper wrote in his report.

> I make it a point to converse with such, as I travel about, in order to
> obtain an idea as to which is the best makes, and from all that I can
> learn Sputler [Schuttler], Bain, Cooper are placed first, then comes
> Milburn, Mitchell, Moline, Jackson, Studebaker, and the Saint Louis
> makers, and the Kansas do not rank with any of the other makes.[55]

The wagon-making business continued for many years after freighting
days ended on the Santa Fe Trail, even into the twentieth century, although
the market for large freighters shrank dramatically and finally disappeared
as railroads and then auto highways penetrated the farthest reaches of the
American West. Before closing this chapter, however, a brief discussion
follows on two wagon types utilized on routes other than the Santa Fe. They
are noted here not only for purposes of comparison, but also to prevent their
being confused with the wagon types employed on the Santa Fe Trail.

The Chihuahua Wagon

The Chihuahua wagon was larger and heavier than the Santa Fe wagon. An
1899 encyclopedia states that "'Chihuahua wagons' are known to this day,
for their enormous capacity and carrying power."[56] The wagon was used
primarily on the route between San Antonio, Texas, and Chihuahua, Mexico. Wilson, Childs & Co. of Philadelphia seems to have made a specialty
of the Chihuahua wagon, selling the vehicle through their agent, August
Staacke of San Antonio, Texas. In the San Antonio Express of September 29,
1868, Staacke advertised that he kept "constantly on hand and dayly [sic]
arriving direct from the Main Factory" wagons, drays, and ox cart wheels.
Staacke then had in stock 162 mule wagons. They were all equipped with
iron axles, ranging in size from three inches down to one and one-half. He
also advertised the running gears for eighteen ox wagons; these featured

iron axles of two and one-half inches. All of the above wagons, Staacke noted, came with "heavy tire."

Additional features of the Chihuahua wagon were recalled by freighter August Santleben:

> The hind wheels measured five feet, ten inches in height, and the tire was six inches wide and one inch thick; the front wheels were built like them, but they were twelve inches lower. The axles were of solid iron, with spindles three inches in diameter, and all the running gear was built in proportion for hard service. The wagon-bed was twenty-four feet long, four and a half feet wide and the sides were five and a half feet high. Wagon-bows were attached to each, and over them two heavy tarpaulins were stretched, which hung down around the sides, that thoroughly protected the freight. On these covers the train-owner's name was painted, and beneath, a number, from one upwards, to distinguish the wagons, in which freight was loaded as it was entered on memorandum. The woodwork of these wagons was painted blue and the iron-work black.
>
> Every wagon was furnished with a powerful brake which was used to regulate the speed when going down steep hills, and two heavy chains were provided that were attached to the wagon-body for use in cases of necessity. Occasionally accidents happened to a brake and the heavily loaded wagon would become uncontrollable, with the result that mules and driver were often crushed to death under the wheels.
>
> The beam that constituted the brake was seven feet in length, six by eight inches square, and it was made out of choice hickory timber. It was placed beneath the wagon-box, before the hind wheels, in two heavy iron stirrups that were secured to the frame on each side by heavy braces or bolts, and a block of wood was fastened near each end which pressed against the wheels when the lever was manipulated by the driver in his seat. He could control the motion of the wagon according to the grade by forcing the brake against the wheels until they ceased to revolve, when necessary, or check them at will with a motion of his hand as easily as a motorman controls his car.
>
> An average load for such wagons was about seven thousand pounds, but generally, with ten small mules attached, sixteen bales of cotton was a load, because it could be transported with more ease.[57]

Santleben's diameter measurement of the Chihuahua wagon's rear wheels is six inches larger than that for the Santa Fe wagon described in the

6.15. "Large Mule Team Going Out Of Stockton [California], Often Called 'Prairie Schooners.'" From *Hutchings' California Magazine* (February 1860).

Kansas City *Western Journal of Commerce* above. Also, the length of the Chihuahua wagon's bed is eight and a half feet longer than the Santa Fe wagon. Additionally, Santleben's description indicates that the Chihuahua wagon had a seat for the driver. Santa Fe wagons had no such seat. Teamsters rode the near wheeler with mule-drawn wagons and walked alongside those drawn by oxen. No image of a Chihuahua wagon has definitely been identified.[58]

The Stockton Wagon

The February 1860 issue of *Hutchings' California Magazine* contains a very interesting engraving titled a "Large Mule Team Going Out of Stockton, Often Called 'Prairie Schooners'" (Fig. 6.15). It depicts a very large wagon with a trail attached. The lead wagon has curved lines and outward-canted end gates reminiscent of the Conestoga. This same lead wagon is equipped with a brake. A tool box is mounted to the front end gate, and what appears to be a feedbox is suspended from the front of the trail wagon. The wagons are drawn by six pairs of mules. According to the accompanying article on Stockton, California, "One of the principal features connected with the commerce of this city, is the number of large freight wagons, laden for the mines; these have, not inappropriately, been denominated 'Prairie Schooners,' and 'Steamboats of the Plains.' Some of these have carried as high as 32,000 pounds of freight."[59]

Little is known of this wagon. However, a wagon identical in appearance to the lead freighter in the *Hutchings* engraving is the subject of an 1894 photograph in the collections of the National Museum of American History (Fig. 6.16). A plaque on the side of the wagon reads "A Prairie Schooner of the 50s." In addition to the very high bed with Conestoga-type lines, the photograph clearly reveals a stiff tongue, patent wheels, and a brake mechanism with a long brake lever. The vehicle is heavily ironed and was

6.16.   Large California freight wagon; photograph taken in 1894. (Courtesy of the Library of Congress.)

probably equipped with iron axles. According to a note on the reverse of this photograph, the wagon was exhibited at the Mid-Winter Fair in San Francisco in 1894.[60] This very same wagon is also shown in something of a museum setting, possibly an old mission, in two postcards in the author's collection that date to the early 1900s. The current location of this vehicle is unknown. Very similar wagons may be seen in action in the 1931 Paramount movie *Fighting Caravans*, which was filmed in California.

Artist Nick Eggenhofer depicted this same vehicle type in a drawing that appeared in his 1961 book *Wagons, Mules and Men*. The drawing is captioned "Freight wagon of the '40s and '50s, showing Conestoga influence."[61] Eggenhofer provides no additional information on this vehicle in the text of his work. It seems likely, however, that he based his drawing, in part, on a stereoview in his private collection picturing freight wagons at "Websters Station Sugar Loaf Mountain" dated 1865.[62] From the available evidence, it would appear that this type of wagon, which for the want of a better name is here classified as the Stockton wagon, did not see service on the Santa Fe Trail.

SEVEN

Wagon Remnants

No documented Santa Fe Trail wagons are known to survive today. However, various bits, pieces, and accessories can be found in museums and private collections. Numerous iron wagon parts were recovered from archeological excavations at Bent's Old Fort National Historic Site, on the Raton Route of the Santa Fe Trail, in the 1960s. This private Indian trading post, owned and operated by Bent, St. Vrain & Co., was active from 1833 to 1849; it subsequently served as a stage station in the 1860s and early 1870s. A blacksmith shop was a prominent fixture of both the trading post and stage station. Here the freight wagons of Bent, St. Vrain & Co., and passing trains of Santa Fe traders, underwent needed repairs. During the stage station period, farrier work and repairs to coaches were probably ongoing.

The room identified by archaeologists as the blacksmith shop (Room S5) displayed the highest concentration of iron wagon parts of all the rooms dating to the Bent period (Fig. 7.1).[1] Most of the items recovered in this room were wagon hub bands and axle-boxes, pieces probably saved from damaged wheels for use with other vehicles or simply as scrap. Three of these axle-boxes examined by the author measured from $5^3/_8$ inches to $4^3/_8$ inches in diameter, exclusive of the teeth; the length was $2^1/_2$ to $2^3/_4$ inches (Fig. 7.2). The objects were heavily corroded, however, making exact measurements difficult.[2] Also uncovered within the fort were several long axle-boxes known as pipe boxes. Pipe boxes were used with both thimble-skein and iron-axle wagons and also coaches. Many of these pipe boxes appear to have been found at the level dating to the stage station period.[3]

On display in the Arrow Rock State Historic Site Visitor Center, Missouri, is a hub and axle-arm said to have been part of a wagon that traveled

7.1.   Wagon axle-boxes and hub bands found during archaeological excavations at Bent's Old Fort. These artifacts are shown in situ in Room S5, believed to have been the fort's blacksmith shop. (Courtesy of Bent's Old Fort National Historic Site.)

7.2.   One of numerous wagon axle-boxes unearthed during archaeological excavations at Bent's Old Fort. (© Mark L. Gardner Collection.)

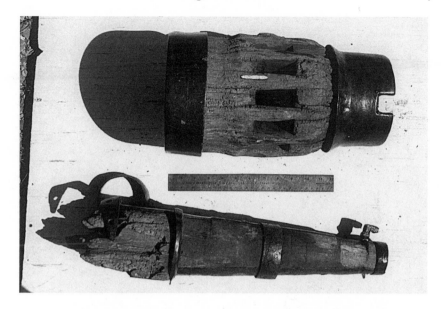

7.3. This hub (top) and axle-arm are all that are left of a wagon that is supposed to have traveled the Santa Fe Trail. Note the axle-arm's thin iron skeins and linchpin. (© Mark L. Gardner Collection.)

the Santa Fe Trail (Fig. 7.3).[4] The axle-arm is approximately fifteen inches long, and its hand-forged top and bottom skeins and other ironwork are typical of early wagons. The hub and axle-arm are a linchpin assembly.

The remnants of a freight wagon running gear are on display in the Fort Garland Museum, Colorado (Fig. 7.4). An exhibit label, which was at one time tacked to the running gear but is now missing, claimed that the wagon was "used in the early days of the San Luis Valley by the grandfather of Alexander Russell, of Russell, Majors and Wadell [Waddell] Freighting Co." There are many problems with this statement. It was not Alexander Russell, for instance, but William Hepburn Russell. His grandfather, Benjamin Russell, came to Vermont from England about 1783! If the label refers instead to the grandfather of Alexander Majors, it is just as impossible: Alexander Majors's grandfather was a farmer who settled in Kentucky about 1800.[5] The wagon's connection with Russell, Majors & Waddell, if any, is probably much more direct, for this firm did have the government contract to freight military supplies to New Mexico during the first few years of Fort Garland's existence. It is possible, then, that this wagon was once the property of these contractors. But it could just as easily have belonged to some

7.4. The remains of a freight wagon running gear on display at the Fort Garland Museum, Fort Garland, Colorado.(Photograph by Kathryn Davis Gardner.)

other freighting outfit. No additional information on the running gear is provided in the museum's catalog records.

Regardless of who owned the wagon, measurements taken from the running gear compare favorably with the known dimensions of Santa Fe Trail freight wagons. The diameter of the one surviving iron tire is sixty inches. It is approximately 2½ inches in width and a half-inch thick. In order to determine the width of the wagon's missing bed, a measurement was taken on the rear bolster between the mortises for the two bolster stakes. This measurement is 43⅞ inches. As will be recalled from the previous chapter, the width of the bed of the Santa Fe wagon described by the *Western Journal of Commerce* was "three feet eight inches wide," which equals forty-four inches. The axle-arms are equipped with top and bottom skeins and the wheels are secured to the axle-arm with linchpins. It appears that the wagon may also have featured a drop tongue.[6]

A pseudo-freight wagon (Fig. 7.5) may be found in the collections of Fort Leavenworth's Frontier Army Museum. The vehicle's running gear is sup-

7.5.   Reproduction freight wagon in the collections of the Fort Leavenworth Frontier Army Museum. (Courtesy of the Frontier Army Museum.)

posed to have been constructed from parts "salvaged from Russell, Majors and Waddell wagon shops in the corral area originally used by the R, M and W Government Freighting Contractors."[7] The "reproduction" was built for the museum by John and William McGlinn about 1937. It is not known how the McGlinns determined the style or design of the wagon simply from the running gear "parts." Nor is it known exactly which parts were the originals found in the "corral." The body is built to resemble the raved body of a Conestoga wagon, but it is far from true Conestoga construction. Simply put, this is an extremely questionable vehicle that is only mentioned here so as to prevent scholars and others from misconstruing it as an authentic Santa Fe Trail freighter.

A large freight wagon supposed to date to 1849 is housed at the Yolo County fairgrounds in Woodland, California. The author has not personally examined this vehicle, but has gleaned the following information from a 1998 article on California emigrant wagons. The wagon is known as the Bemmerly wagon for its original owner, John Bemmerly, who is believed to have brought it over the Oregon Trail and finally to California, where he used it for freighting in the 1850s. Unfortunately, the wagon was restored or "refitted" at least twice in the 1930s, leaving us unsure as to the wagon's original appearance or construction. A photograph of the restored wagon shows it to have a tall, flat bed with overhanging end gates. The sides are absent the triangulated uprights or bracing common to many post-Conestoga freight wagons. The axles are iron, and the rear wheels are 64 inches in diameter with a tire width of 2⅝ inches. The wagon has a stiff tongue and is equipped with a brake; the brake shoes are unusually large.[8] This vehicle may very well be of the type described in the previous chapter as the Stockton wagon, with the more complicated construction of the Stockton wagon's bed having been abandoned during the restorations. Until more is learned of the extent of this restoration work on the Bemmerly wagon, the vehicle must remain a question mark.

At least three possible freight wagons, perhaps dating to the 1860s or 1870s, are in the collections of the Lagoon Corporation's Pioneer Village at Farmington, Utah. Their condition is said to be poor and their provenance is unknown. The author has been unable to examine these wagons, either in person or through photographs. However, any true freight wagon of the nineteenth century is rare, and on the chance that these wagons may prove worthwhile for future research, they are noted here.

Two provision or tool boxes survive which were used with plains freight wagons. One is in the collections of the Weston Historical Museum in Weston, Missouri, and is supposed to have belonged to freighter Benjamin Holladay (Fig. 7.6). The box has a hinged lid, which once had a hasp. It is 45⅞ inches long (slightly longer on the top), 15⅝ inches tall at the back and tapering to 12 inches in the front. The box's bottom side is 13 inches wide. The lumber used to construct the box appears to be pine and is seveneighths of an inch in thickness. Hand-forged hooks are found mounted on each side by which the box was suspended from the wagon with chains. The exterior of the box is painted a shade of blue or blue-green and the ends are reinforced with iron strips. The most interesting feature of this box is the name of the maker stenciled in red on the front panel. It reads "H. ESPENSCHIED & Co./No. 148 Broadway/ST. LOUIS, MO." The firm of Henry Espenschied & Company is first listed in the St. Louis city directory of 1866, which is a good indication that the box dates to 1866 or after.[9]

The other provision box (Fig. 7.7) is in the collections of the Coronado-Quivira Museum in Lyons, Kansas, and it has a very intriguing history. According to family tradition, it was once attached to a wagon belonging to merchant Antonio José Chávez, and it was holding some of Chávez's money intended for eastern purchases when he was robbed and murdered on the Trail in 1843.[10] This story may very well be true, but without supporting documentation, it is also possible that the box dates to a later period. The Chávez box is very simi-

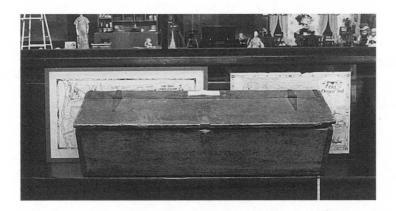

7.6. Wagon provision or tool box, ca. 1866, in the collections of the Weston Historical Museum, Weston, Missouri. The box was made at the St. Louis wagon factory of Henry Espenschied, a brother of wagon maker Louis Espenschied. (© Mark L. Gardner Collection.)

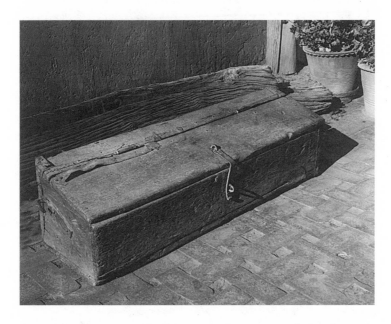

7.7. A provision box supposed to have come from a wagon belonging to Antonio José Chávez, ca. 1843. Now in the collections of the Coronado-Quivira Museum, Lyons, Kansas. (Photograph by Marc Simmons.)

lar in size and construction to the Holladay box. It is painted a "brick red," but because this paint also covers a later tin repair to the box, it is readily apparent that this is not the original paint. What the original paint was, if it indeed had an original coat, is uncertain without a closer inspection.

Curiously, provision boxes like the Holladay and Chávez boxes are not distinguishable in contemporary illustrations and photographs. However, Sir Richard F. Burton, writing in 1862, states: "A long covered wooden box hangs behind [the wagon]: on the road it carries fuel; at the halt it becomes a trough, being preferred to nose-bags, which prevent the animals breathing comfortably; and in the hut, where every part of the wagon is utilized, it acts as a chest for valuables."[11] Wagon maker Frederick Klaber's estate inventory of 1866 includes "9 Provision Boxes for Wagons" valued at $2.50 each.[12] In contrast to the provision box, feedboxes (almost always known without a lid or cover) are readily apparent in many contemporary images. Ox driver D. M. Draper remembered that his train in 1861 had a "tool box" which "was a feed box at the end of one of the wagons, and as the bottom of this happened to be loose we lost nearly all our tools the first day."[13]

The loss of a few tools on an eight-hundred-mile journey is understandable. But time has lost to us every single freight wagon that traveled the Santa Fe Trail—and there were literally thousands. The relics noted above, while by no means an exhaustive list, offer the last tangible connection to those great vehicles.

EIGHT

Dearborns, Personal Vehicles, and Provision Wagons

When the 1824 caravan set out for Santa Fe, it contained "2 road waggons, 20 dearborns, 2 carts and one small piece of cannon."[1] This is one of numerous references in the Trail literature to Dearborns; detailed specifications for the vehicle, however, are more difficult to come by. John Russell Bartlett, in his famous *Dictionary of Americanisms*, defined the vehicle simply as "a kind of light covered waggon, so named from its inventor."[2] More informative is transportation historian Don Berkebile's description: "A light SQUARE-BOX WAGON having two seat-boards and a standing top.. . . This carriage was developed early in the nineteenth century, and is said to have acquired its name because General Henry Dearborn used one in the field" (Fig. 8.1).[3] Dearborn carriages were advertised by St. Louis wagon makers James D. Earl and Andrew Light in 1821.[4] Unlike the freight wagons of the period, though, the Dearborn was equipped with springs (the elliptic spring was invented in England in 1804). Berkebile also suggests that the Dearborns of the early nineteenth century were of "slightly heavier build than the later types."[5]

During the first decade or so of the trade, Dearborns, pulled by two horses or mules, were used to carry both a prospective merchant and his merchandise, so a vehicle of heavier construction would certainly make sense. Colonel John Glover met returning Santa Fe trader Simeon Switzler in Saline County, Missouri, in 1826, and reported that his "cargo" had been "a dearbourn and $300 worth of domestic cottons."[6] A sturdy vehicle was also desirable because of the stress of the overland journey itself. Trader Meredith Miles Marmaduke, in a letter written from New Mexico in 1824, bragged that his Dearborn "held out well" on the Santa Fe Trail trip. "Not

8.1.   A Dearborn wagon of 1878, from Don H. Berkebile, *American Carriages, Sleighs, Sulkies, and Carts* (1977).

a wheel or axle tree gave way, and I yesterday refused 4 mules for it, notwithstanding it has been capsized twice."[7] As the Conestoga freighters came into general use, the Dearborn's role changed from cargo carrier to that of personal vehicle for traders and health and adventure seekers.

A problem inherent in a discussion of Dearborn wagons is the fact that several other names were used by Trail travelers to describe what was often the same or a very similar standing top wagon, including "Jersey wagon," "Carryall," and "dug out." John Russell Bartlett defined the carryall in 1848 as "a four-wheeled pleasure carriage, capable of holding several persons, or a family; hence the term, *carryall*."[8] In 1839, Matt Field and four companions embarked upon the Trail with a "carryall" pulled by mules and packed with trunks, carpet bags, cigar boxes, pistols, fishing rods, blankets, and other items. They had purchased the vehicle in Independence.[9] George W. Kendall traveled to New Mexico in 1841, as a member of the Texan-Santa Fe Expedition, in "a neat Jersey waggon, drawn by two mules, and covered so as to protect us from the sun and rain during the long marches." But he also refers to his vehicle as a "Jersey carryall."[10] In 1852, the U.S. mail was transported over the Santa Fe Trail in "a heavy Jersey wagon."[11]

When amateur scientist Frederick Adolphus Wislizenus left for a trip down the Santa Fe and Chihuahua trails in 1846, he took with him a "small wagon on springs, to carry my baggage and instruments, and [to serve] as a comfortable retreat in bad weather."[12] That same year, merchant William Henry Glasgow described his personal vehicle as a "'dug out' or carriage." On May 24, he wrote a letter to his sister while sitting in the carriage, "with the seat upon my knees for a table."[13] Two other merchants on the Trail that spring, Samuel Owens and James Aull, had purchased from Cyrus Townsend of Pittsburgh five "Sleeping Wagons" at 120 dollars each.[14] Were these Dearborns or another vehicle type? Obviously, a great deal of variation could exist between personal vehicles, even of the same style. After all, Dearborns and similar carriages were often made to order and could thus incorporate any custom work desired by the buyer.

A duly impressed volunteer/correspondent in the Army of the West reported that trader James Magoffin reached Bent's Fort in 1846 "in a buggy! Think of that—in a buggy!"[15] Bartlett's 1848 definition of a buggy is "a light waggon for one horse."[16] A party of topographical engineers traveled to New Mexico in 1846 "in a carriage, altering the same to make it suitable for the conveyance of their instruments." The same correspondent mentioned above described the vehicle as "a handsome spring car, with four mules harnessed to it."[17] In 1851, New Mexico-bound John Greiner acquired in St. Louis "a good light carriage at the cost of $105.00, and two very fine gentle mules for $100.00." He had been encouraged to purchase his personal vehicle in St. Louis because "it would be almost impossible to procure a carriage made of seasoned timber" farther west.[18]

Susan Magoffin, in her famous diary of 1846–1847, mentions that the personal vehicle employed by herself and husband, Samuel, was a "little Rockaway carriage" drawn by two mules and that her servant, Jane, traveled in a Dearborn, which indicates that there was then a difference between these vehicle types.[19] There were two types of Rockaways, however: the Rockaway and the Germantown Rockaway. The first was developed by a Jamaica, Long Island, carriage maker about 1830. The second was created in 1816 in Germantown, Pennsylvania, and was first known simply as a *Germantown* but supposedly acquired the additional term *Rockaway* because of the similarities between the two vehicles.[20] Here is an 1859 description of Rockaways:

A Rockaway proper, has a plain square or straight body, with standing top and leather curtains, to roll up; for either four or six persons;

8.2.   A Rockaway of 1845. From Ezra M. Stratton, *The World on Wheels; or Carriages, with their Historical Associations from the Earliest to the Present Time* (1878).

all seats on a level. Of late years, all vehicles with standing top and seats on a level are called Rockaways.... The following styles of Rockaways are in general use:

The square four-seat Rockaway, for one horse. Weight about 500 lbs. Cost, from $200 to $300.

The same for six persons and two horses. Weight, about 700 lbs. Price, $350 to $400.

The six-seat Germantown Rockaway has the body slightly curved. Weight, say 800 lbs. Cost, $450.

The Coupé Rockaway, for four persons, with a partition; having windows to divide the front and back seats; body curved, with windows or curtains in sides. Weight, about 700 lbs. Price, from $350 to $500.[21]

An illustration of an 1845 Rockaway (Fig. 8.2) shows the vehicle with a square body, two seats, and roll-up sides or curtains that could be let out and fastened in inclement weather (the roll-up curtains were a feature common

8.3. A Germantown Rockaway of 1847. From Ezra M. Stratton, *The World on Wheels; or Carriages, with their Historical Associations from the Earliest to the Present Time* (1878).

to Dearborns as well).[22] This is probably the vehicle described above as intended for one horse. Because Susan Magoffin specifically mentions that her Rockaway was pulled by two mules, her vehicle may have been either the square, six-seat Rockaway or the six-seat Germantown Rockaway. An illustration of an 1847 Germantown Rockaway (Fig. 8.3) shows it to be longer with an awning or storm hood for the driver.[23] The Germantown Rockaway resembles a Dearborn wagon. And it is interesting to note that according to the above 1859 account, a Dearborn could be referred to as a Rockaway, for a Dearborn was a standing top wagon with seats on a level. It is evident that there was much "borrowing" between styles, which explains many of the similarities often found in these light spring wagons (See Fig. 8.4).

Personal vehicles were also used by Mexicans on the Trail. George W. Kendall noted the arrival of a caravan at San Miguel, in 1841, "direct from St. Louis, owned by one of the Chavez family, a rich and powerful connection in New Mexico. Chavez himself, in a neat buggy waggon, accompanied his men."[24] In 1846, George A. F. Ruxton encountered Manuel Armijo on the Chihuahua Trail; the New Mexican governor was riding in an "American dearborn."[25]

8.4.   Jump Seat Top Wagon, from *G. & D. Cook & Co.'s Illustrated Catalogue of Carriages* (1860). Note the similarities between this vehicle and the Dearborn wagon (Fig. 8.1).

A few contemporary images depict Dearborns, carryalls, or Jersey wagons in the Southwest. The engraving from *Commerce of the Prairies*, entitled "March of the Caravan" (Fig. 2.4), depicts two light square-box wagons. Although quite small in the engraving, thin supports for the flat, standing top can be discerned. The sides are open, which would be the case when the curtains were rolled up and tied. Still, the engraving leaves much to be desired. A lithograph (Fig. 8.5) depicting Kendall's Jersey wagon appears in his *Narrative of the Texan Santa Fe Expedition* (1844). However, the artist, J. W. Casilear, was not a member of the expedition. The curtains of the wagon seem much too billowy, the wheels are not correctly proportioned, and other details do not ring true, although it is apparent that Casilear, like the artist for Gregg's work, was attempting to draw the same type of light, square-box wagon. Three Jersey wagons manufactured in New Jersey are pictured in an 1853 engraving (Fig. 8.6) that features several carriages. It is not known, however, if western Jersey wagons were identical to these.

Among the better images that show personal vehicles on the Trail are the sketches made by William J. Hinchey, who traveled to Santa Fe with Bishop

8.5. "Incident on the Prairies," a lithograph from George W. Kendall, *Narrative of the Texan Santa Fe Expedition* (1844). This is an artist's conception of Kendall's 1841 Jersey wagon. (Courtesy of Special Collections, Tutt Library, Colorado College.)

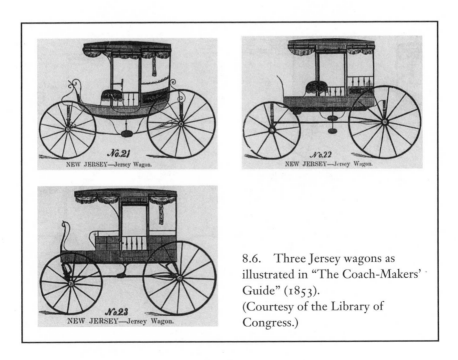

8.6. Three Jersey wagons as illustrated in "The Coach-Makers' Guide" (1853). (Courtesy of the Library of Congress.)

8.7. Sketch of a carriage on the Santa Fe Trail, 1854, by William J. Hinchey. (Courtesy of Elizabeth Holloman.)

8.8. Light Rockaway of 1860. Originally published in *The Carriage Builders and Harness Makers' Art Journal* (July 1860).

Jean Baptiste Lamy in 1854 and returned eastward in 1855.[26] One of these sketches depicts a moonlight scene of a parked carriage (Fig. 8.7) Clearly visible on the carriage is an unrolled curtain over the center door. Note also the storm hood and the body's curved sill or bottomside. The outline of this carriage resembles very much a light Rockaway (Fig. 8.8) as illustrated in an 1860 article on American carriages originally published in England.[27]

Another personal vehicle, one that developed later than the Dearborn, was the civilian ambulance. Although it took its name from the vehicle intended for sick and wounded, it was actually another type of standing top wagon with springs designed to transport several people on extended overland journeys. William Woods Averell remembered a military train on the Santa Fe Trail in 1857 in which there were "a dozen married officers who had private ambulances for their wives. These ambulances were marvels of strength and perfect in appliances and adaptations to the uses of a family. They were thoroughly weatherproof and could be converted into sleeping chambers in rough weather."[28]

A seat which could be converted into a bed was one of the distinguishing characteristics of the civilian ambulance.[29] Julius Froebel noted two "traveling-carriages" in the caravan he accompanied in 1857, which "could be closed up and the seats converted into a couch."[30] The ambulance Mamie Bernard Aguirre and her family traveled the Santa Fe Trail with in 1863 left a vivid impression:

> We rode in ambulances which were as comfortable as carriages, costing $500 apiece and built so they could be turned into beds at night just as a 'sleeper' seat is arranged on trains nowadays. They had boxes in the back seat for clothes, pockets on the sides in the doors which opened as hack doors do; in these pockets were brushes, combs and a looking glass. Under the front seat was another and there were two seats facing each other inside so that six people could be comfortably seated.[31]

Richens Lacy "Uncle Dick" Wootton recalled that in his caravans "we always had an ambulance in which we carried some of our provisions, and had room for a teamster, or any one else traveling with the train, who might happen to get sick along the road."[32]

Like the other personal vehicles already discussed, certain features of an ambulance could vary depending upon the particular needs of the customer. In 1860, carriage maker William U. Wiley of Kansas City advertised several vehicles, including Rockaways and "Ambulances for the Plains," that were "Manufactured to order of all kinds."[33]

One St. Louis carriage manufacturer built a type of ambulance that was apparently so distinctive or popular that the vehicle acquired his name. That manufacturer was Robert Dougherty. In 1850, Dougherty was a partner in the carriage manufactory of Osborne & Dougherty. The thirty men employed by the firm turned out an annual product of 20 carriages, 250 Rockaways, and 150 buggies valued at thirty-one thousand dollars.[34] By 1852, Dougherty had joined with carriage maker Alexander Finley. Health-seeker James Ross Larkin traveled the Santa Fe Trail in 1856 in a Finley ambulance. Cost: 202 dollars.[35] That year of 1856 saw Robert Dougherty on his own. The number of employees working at Dougherty's carriage manufactory in 1860 was thirty-five, and they produced one hundred wagons and one hundred buggies worth forty-three thousand dollars.[36] The wagons were probably the famous Dougherty wagon. By 1866, the name of the firm had changed to Robert Dougherty & Brother. The 1870 industrial census shows an increase in the number of employees and annual production for the firm. The workers now numbered forty-five. Only 5 carriages were manufactured, but the number of wagons made had grown to 350. The value of the annual product, including a large amount of job work, was estimated at 73,800 dollars.[37]

The Dougherty wagon had a standing top with roll-down curtains and a storm hood, three seats that folded down into a bed, side doors, and a rack for luggage hanging on the rear. The body rested upon four elliptic springs (Fig. 8.9).[38] William Hinchey depicts a standing top carriage in one of his 1855 sketches in which can be discerned a hanging luggage rack and an open side door.[39] This may be an early style of Dougherty wagon or another variety of ambulance. The Dougherty wagon was adopted by the U. S. Army as early as the 1870s, and an "improved" version was still being used by the army in the early 1900s.[40]

Some personal vehicles were simply small covered wagons. Two small wagons with striped canvas covers are visible in an 1840 sketch by William Fairholme (Fig. 2.6). These wagons and one without a cover and bows were acquired in St. Louis by British sportsmen and used along the Trail. Small covered wagons also appear in several sketches by William J. Hinchey made during the Lamy trip of 1854 (Fig. 8.10). They are definitely not large freighters. Some of Lamy's wagons may have been constructed by Joseph Murphy; in Murphy's day book is a transaction of July 10, 1852, with "Revd Bishop of Santa fee." The bishop purchased three four-mule wagons with double covers for a total price of 290 dollars.[41]

Regular freight caravans also might travel with small-sized wagons, intended for the clothing and bedrolls of the teamsters, food and mess kits,

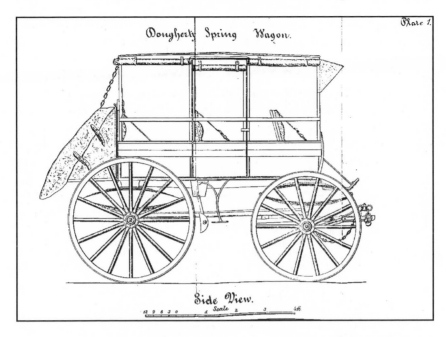

8.9.   Dougherty spring wagon as illustrated in *Specifications for Means of Transportation*, 1882. (Courtesy of the U.S. Army Quartermaster Museum.)

8.10.   "Making a Crib for the Mules," a Santa Fe Trail sketch by William J. Hinchey, 1854. (Courtesy of the late Kathryn Hinchey Cochran.)

and other personal items. An 1846 report on the number of vehicles that had traveled to Santa Fe that year included twelve "kitchen wagons" in the statistics.[42] The Magoffin caravan of that same year included what Susan called simply "a baggage wagon."[43] It was also possible for one freight train to have several types of personal vehicles represented. Charles G. Parker's train, which passed through Council Grove on March 17, 1860, consisted of "twenty wagons, two carriages, one buggy, one ambulance, 240 mules and some thirty men."[44]

In conclusion, when it comes to personal vehicles, it is readily apparent that they could be as different as the people who used them. This fact is aptly conveyed in the *Missouri Intelligencer*'s comment regarding the 1825 Santa Fe Trail caravan: "the wagons and carriages, of almost every description are numerous."[45]

NINE

To Sail Upon the Prairie Sea

The most famous Santa Fe Trail wagon was built by a man named William Thomas before the Civil War. This wagon, ironically, never went to Santa Fe. Exactly what it looked like has been anybody's guess, and, indeed, many artists have been happy to provide their guesses over the years. Some believe that Thomas's wagon belongs more to folklore than to history. And as for the mysterious Thomas himself, where he belongs depends upon whom you consult: was he a visionary or a simple quack? His wagon, of course, was the windwagon—not just any windwagon, mind you, but *the* windwagon. For it is Thomas's wagon that has been the subject of countless articles, an *Atlantic Monthly* short story, children's books, and even a Disney animated short film.[1] And why not? The image of a wagon topped with sails and rigging—a bonafide "prairie schooner"—rolling across the plains at breakneck speed is the stuff of romance and adventure. The very idea captures the imagination now just as it did then. What makes this story even better, though, is that it is absolutely true. Following are the facts, along with contemporary drawings of the celebrated vehicle published here for the first time.

William Thomas seems to have made two major attempts at developing a windwagon. The first was during 1846 to 1847, in the midst of the Mexican War. The second came twelve years later in 1859, during the gold rush to Colorado. Thomas did continue to tinker with his idea during those intervening years, but there are no contemporary newspaper accounts of an actual wagon except for those made in 1846–47 and 1859. Westport merchant William R. Bernard told the story of Windwagon Thomas to a *Kansas City Star* reporter in 1905, giving 1853 as the year of Thomas's second attempt, but it is clear from the contemporary sources and others that the events Bernard relates took place in 1859.[2] Unfortunately, later writers accepted Bernard's mistaken date, adding more confusion to the already confusing windwagon history.

Before getting into the wagons themselves, however, let us piece together what little is known about Thomas himself. Bernard remembered that Thomas "had been a sailor." Bernard is the earliest known source for this information; none of the contemporary newspaper accounts consulted mention anything about Thomas's background. The sailor aspect may fall into the "too good to be true" category, but it certainly makes sense that a man well versed with sails, spars, and rigging would be amply qualified to adapt sailboat technology to a wagon. In any event, this feature of Thomas's history has become an integral part of the windwagon legend.

A search of census records reveals that the name William Thomas was quite common, even on the frontier, and it is difficult to point to one man as *the* Windwagon Thomas. If only Thomas had given his occupation as "inventor," how much easier all this would be. But he did not, so the search must be directed elsewhere for pertinent clues. In Thomas's patent petition for his windwagon, dated January 29, 1859, he gave his residence as Benton County, Arkansas, yet the petition is dated and signed at Westport, Missouri. Accompanying the petition was a letter of the same date from Thomas to the commissioner requesting that all letters to Thomas be directed to him at Westport.[3] A search of the Arkansas census records for Benton County failed to turn up a likely candidate for Windwagon Thomas. How long Thomas was a resident of Arkansas is not known, but the available evidence suggests that it was only for a short time.

One important Jackson County, Missouri, deed record associated with William Thomas provides additional clues. In 1853 Thomas and Allen T. Ward, builder of the first water-powered gristmill in Westport, purchased two acres of land on the western border of Missouri, south of Westport, from Richard and John B. Wornall. The price paid was forty dollars, but there was a very specific condition attached to the deed. Thomas and Ward, the deed stated, had "undertaken to erect, build and set up a Wind-Mill" upon the property in question. If the new owners completed the windmill, and it proved "of use and benefit to the community," then the deed would remain final. If the windmill did not pan out as promised, however, the property was to be reconveyed to the original owners. The property was in fact reconveyed to John B. Wornall five years later, which suggests that the windmill project failed in some way.[4] But, a newspaper report on Thomas and his windwagon, dated Westport, April 14, 1859, states that Thomas "has long been the proprietor of a windmill, on the border not far distant."[5] This would indicate that the mill on the Wornall property had indeed been built. And this, in turn, leads us to a particular William Thomas in the 1860 census for Jackson County.

Of the several William Thomases living in Jackson County in 1860, there was only one whose occupation was listed in the census as "mill wright." This Thomas resided in the Westport township. His age was fifty-eight and he was born in New York. He had personal property valued at two hundred dollars and real estate valued at the same amount. There is no way of knowing how long this Thomas lived in New York after his birth, but one wonders if he did not indeed spend a few years at sea before going west. Living in the Thomas household were six children. Their mother may have been deceased, for she is not listed in the census. The three oldest children, ranging in age from fourteen to nineteen, were all born in Iowa, indicating that William Thomas lived there from roughly 1841 to 1846. The three youngest, with ages from six to thirteen, were born in Missouri, placing Thomas in that state at least from around 1847 to 1854.[6] Of course, this does not mean that the Thomas family resided in these states continuously during the above periods, just that his children were born there sometime during those specific years. Although none of the children were born in Arkansas, the above time frames do allow for Thomas to have moved to Arkansas at some point during or after 1854 and then to have returned to Missouri by January of 1859.

One of Thomas's children is worth special notice. He was thirteen years old, born in Missouri, and his given name was Rocky. Rocky is an extremely unusual nineteenth-century first name, to say the least. Even more intriguing is Rocky's middle initial as provided in the census: "M."[7] Did William Thomas name his son for the Rocky Mountains? Although confirmation is still being sought, the name does seem to fit well, considering that Rocky Mountains Thomas was born in 1847, the same year that William Thomas was experimenting with his first windwagon, his goal to reach the other Rocky Mountains.[8]

William Thomas is again listed in the 1870 census, living alone in the Westport township. He was sixty-seven years old with a personal estate valued at only one hundred dollars. His occupation is listed as "miller." His birthplace, however, is given in this census as New Jersey.[9] In 1859, one observer referred to Thomas as "the old captain," and his age in that year, fifty-six or fifty-seven, is not out of line with that description.[10]

Although Thomas has often been portrayed as a comical dreamer and even a shyster, his involvement with a windmill and the serious effort he put into his windwagon, particularly as revealed in his detailed patent application, suggest that he was quite earnest about the potential of wind power. The *Westport Border Star* reported in 1859 that "for years and years, he has been working, planning, studying, and maturing his [windwagon] idea." Bolstered by the granting of a patent for his wagon, Thomas projected that "the time is not far distant when all the commerce of the plains and all the travel between the western boundaries of the States and the gold regions of upper Kansas and Nebraska, will be carried on by means of Wind-carriages."[11] That time has yet to come, but the potential of wind power for the generation of electricity continues to be tested. Thomas would probably have loved today's wind turbines.

William Thomas's first windwagon received good coverage in the press. The source for most of the contemporary reports was the Independence *Western Expositor*, the only newspaper near the area of Thomas's experiments. Unfortunately, only a few stray issues of the *Western Expositor* have survived, and none of these cover the windwagon period. Yet several other papers, fascinated by the novelty of Thomas's windwagon, picked up the *Western Expositor*'s reports and ran them on their pages.

The earliest extant newspaper notice of the windwagon is dated October 24, 1846. Thomas was then in the process of building the wagon.[12] A later report recounted the following colorful episode connected with the wagon's construction:

> During the completion of the prairie ship, while it was still on the stocks, some twenty miles from Independence, and on the borders of the great north western prairies, a beautiful specimen of the field lark, the *Expositor* says, was in the habit of perching regularly every day on the mast head, and singing, while Mr. Thomas would be engaged at his work, regardless of the noise and bustle beneath him. No matter how many persons were assembled, the lark pursued his song with vigor, to the delight of both spectators and workmen. Martins also took their station on the rigging and added their sweet voices to that of the first visitor.[13]

It is significant that this account mentions "workmen," for the wagon that Thomas built would have been a very difficult and time-consuming project for one man.

After October 24, the next report on the windwagon appeared a month later, on November 30, 1846, in both the St. Louis *Weekly Reveille* and the St. Louis *Missouri Republican*. Both newspapers got their information from the "last Independence Expositor," but only the *Missouri Republican* published a detailed account based on the *Expositor*'s report. The *Missouri Republican* article is important enough to reproduce here in its entirety:

The Wind-Wagon.—We learn from the *Independence Expositor*, that Mr. Thomas, who has been at work on a Wind-Wagon, has got the machine completed, and has given it such a trial as to make its success certain. He run up and down across the plains, found that he could overcome a steep with gentle ascent without difficulty, and that the mole-hills, so numerous on the plains, were no bar to his progress. The construction of the wagon is very simple. It is a frame made of plank, well braced and placed edgewise on four axle trees—four wheels to each side—these wheels to be twelve feet or more in diameter and one foot broad—the forward axles, which can be turned just as the forward axle of any wagon with a tongue, by their movement turns the course of the whole concern—two tongues are joined together forward of the wagon and by ropes coming to the wheel similar to the pilot wheel of a steamboat—the wagon is steered by a pilot. The sails are like the sails and rigging of a ship, each wagon carries its own supply of sail—underneath, a foot or so from the deck of each wagon, the cast iron boxes, &c., will be suspended as ballast.
Mr. Thomas expects to convey freight and passengers, and will now engage and bind himself to take freight to Bent's Fort or to Santa Fe, in a reasonable time, at $6 per hundred lbs.
He is to have a depot at Bent's Fort, and thence across the other side of the Arkansas he will run another car within 60 miles of Santa Fe. A gentleman who rode on the wagon says that, with only one sail and a light breeze, it went at the rate of eight miles an hour. Properly rigged, its speed will be about 20 miles an hour.[14]

The article indicates that Thomas was well aware of the impossibility of "sailing" his wagon over the Raton Mountains southwest of Bent's Fort on the Raton Route of the Santa Fe Trail and also the Sangre de Cristo Mountains through which the Trail wound east of Santa Fe. Thus, the "car" he planned to run on the "other" or south side of the Arkansas no doubt was intended for the Cimarron Route of the Trail, which avoided the Raton Range. By this latter route Thomas probably imagined that he could reach the vicinity of Las Vegas, a little over sixty miles from the New Mexican capital. Thomas also envisioned running a line of windwagons on the Oregon Trail as far as South Pass.[15]

Interestingly, Allen T. Ward, Thomas's partner in the windmill venture of 1853, wrote about Thomas's first windwagon in a letter to his family of March 19, 1847. Ward was then a teacher and steam gristmill operator at the Shawnee Methodist Mission (in present-day Fairway, Kansas), situated on a branch of the Santa Fe Trail just a short distance from Westport. Presumably, Ward had not yet made Thomas's acquaintance, and it is unclear whether or not he actually saw the windwagon in person. Nevertheless, his description does agree with the account in the *Missouri Republican*. Something that could "only be seen in our almost boundless prairies," Thomas informed his family, was "the wind wagon or prairie schooner, booming along at the rate of 15 or 20 miles pr hour. The inventor has yet tried but one, which run on eight wheels with a platform of 20 by 40 feet for passengers, the Mast upwards of 40 ft high." Ward was told that Thomas surmised he could make the trip to Santa Fe and back in "20 days & carry 100 tons of freight." Ward thought his future partner's efforts rather dubious, however: "I think it will never be any thing more than a wind machine and should not be disappointed if it would all blow over."[16]

A news item from April 1847 stated that Thomas was "soon to make an experimental trip on the plains with his newly invented 'wind ship.'"[17] By this was surely meant an extended test, for Thomas had already been experimenting with his vehicle for some time. And indeed, it was reported on July 17 that Thomas had "just returned from a trip of 12 days on the prairies with his Wind Ship." He was now "willing to make a tour to the buffalo country if a sufficient number can be raised to justify him in making the expedition." As protection against hostile Indians, Thomas was going to travel with a six-pounder cannon. He also had a "beautiful stand of colors, tents, &c.," and planned to "start in a company."[18] A letter from Westport dated July 23, and published in the St. Louis *Daily Reveille*, stated: "Our enterprising citizen, Mr. Wm. Thomas, will positively start in a few days for Council Grove, with his *wind ship*. It works *well*! — he has been out twenty miles on a trial trip."[19]

Did William Thomas and his windwagon reach Council Grove? No further notice of such a trip has been found in the newspapers from 1847. However, one old-timer by the name of L. H. Dyer claimed that he was in Council Grove when, "to the astonishment of the Kaw Indians and the few settlers at the old trading post," a windwagon appeared. "I did not see the wagon cross the Neosho River," Dyer said, "but I visited it several times while it stood in the corral of Seth M. Hays, the old Indian trader."[20] The captain of the wagon had made the trip from Westport in about twenty-four hours. Unfortunately, no date was given for this intriguing episode. Seth

Hays had just started trading in Council Grove in the spring of 1847, so Thomas's visit could very well have taken place that year, but Hays was still running a store in Council Grove in 1860, when the *Council Grove Press* reported the arrival of a windwagon from Westport in its issue of July 23. It seems likely, then, that Dyer is referring to this later event. According to a *Westport Border Star* article of 1859, the "first public experiment made by Mr. Thomas with a Wind-wagon was (we believe) about the year 1847, when he actually succeeded in propelling it eighty miles, at a rate of speed about equal to the average speed of European Railroad cars."[21] This eighty-mile excursion would place Thomas far short of Council Grove, which is roughly 120 miles from Westport. If Thomas had indeed successfully sailed to Council Grove prior to 1859, it is curious that the *Border Star* makes no mention of it.

Regardless of how far Thomas got with his first windwagon, it appears that his vehicle was not quite the success claimed at the time. The *Border Star* commented that Thomas's 1847 overland trip had been made in spite of "defective machinery and faulty proportions of parts which became evident to him so soon as constructed."[22] This statement is supported by the fact that Thomas's 1859 wagon was very different in design from his first vehicle. After July of 1847, Thomas and his windwagon suddenly disappear from notice in the newspapers of the day. It was apparently back to the drawing board, then—for another twelve years.

William Thomas's patent petition was signed and dated at Westport, Missouri, on January 29, 1859. In the application, he stated that he had "invented a new and improved mode of land conveyance by means of the wind, which he verily believes has not been known or used prior to the invention thereof by your petitioner." The signatures of two witnesses appear on the application: Henry Sager and James T. Swartz. Swartz has not been identified. Sager, however, was one of several Westport citizens who were supposed to have invested in Thomas's windwagon.[23] In a 1905 interview, William R. Bernard stated that Sager, Dr. James W. Parker, Benjamin Newson, John J. Mastin, Thomas M. Adams, and William Thomas formed the Westport and Santa Fe Overland Navigation Company after Thomas demonstrated the merits of his windwagon project by successfully sailing a "trial model" from Westport to Council Grove and back.[24] Contemporary sources are silent on this trial model, and, as remarked above, a successful trip to Council Grove before 1860 cannot be confirmed. Bernard was probably confused; his error with regard to the date of Thomas's second attempt has already been noted.

John S. Hough, also a resident of Westport during the windwagon excitement of 1859, recalled in 1920 that

> before the Civil War, the exact date I do not recall, a man Thomas, came to Westport telling the people he had an invention that would revolutionize the carrying of the mails and express matter across the plains, but lacked the means in which to carry it out. The Westporters came to his aid and furnished the means for the building of the first Wind Wagon.[25]

The Hough account again demonstrates the problem with reminiscences, for Hough is incorrect in referring to the 1859 wagon as "the first Wind Wagon." However, he is in agreement with Bernard regarding the Westport investors, and a newspaper correspondent who visited Thomas and his windwagon on April 18, 1859, provides additional evidence on this point. He wrote that the wagon had been completed "at a cost of $800, through the liberality of some of the citizens of Westport."[26] Whether or not they actually formed an enterprise called the Westport and Santa Fe Overland Navigation Company is not known. Articles of incorporation for a company by that name are not found in Missouri state records.

By April of 1859, Thomas's windwagon was nearly complete. Local histories claim that the wagon was constructed by the Independence foundry and machine works of Robinson, Crooks & Co., established in 1852 (Fig. 9.1).[27] This may be true, for there are certain features of the wagon, particularly the unusual wheels and axles, which would have benefited from the services of such an establishment. But before getting into the actual details of the wagon as revealed in Thomas's patent application, following are the few contemporary descriptions of the 1859 windwagon.

A correspondent of the St. Louis *Missouri Republican* visited the wagon on April 13 and reported:

> It is a queer looking affair, and I was forcibly struck with the picture it presented.. . . The affair is on wheels which are mammoth concerns, about twenty feet in circumference, and the arrangements for passengers is built somewhat after the style of an omnibus-body. It is to be propelled by the wind, through the means of sails. As to the wheels it looks like an overgrown omnibus; and as to the spars and sails, it looks like a diminutive schooner. It will seat about twenty-four passengers.[28]

Another writer, known only by his nom de plume "Jefferson," inspected the wagon on April 18 and found it to be

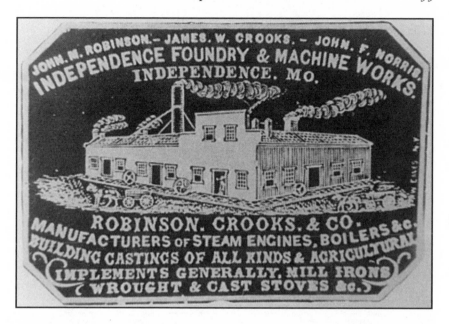

9.1. The Independence Foundry and Machine Works is supposed to have assisted in the construction of the 1859 windwagon. (Courtesy of the Jackson County Historical Society.)

a large, nondescript sort of a machine, with a body like a small sloop with both bow and stem cut off, suspended on four double spoked wheels, about eight feet in height, with hollow hubs about the size and appearance of one of Wagoner's beer barrels, with steering apparatus, &c. The whole is surmounted by a mast, some twenty-five feet high, upon which will be suspended two sails, cut yacht fashion.[29]

Diarist Charles C. Post, on his way to the Colorado gold fields via the Santa Fe Trail, wrote the following under the date of May 13:

We overtook today a curiosity in the shape of a wind wagon. It is a four wheeled vehicle, about nine feet across schooner rigged a very large sail. The whole weighs three thousand pounds.[30]

These eyewitness descriptions, although brief, indicate that Thomas did follow the plans and specifications for his windwagon as submitted to the patent office. The first panel (Fig. 9.2) of the set of drawings Thomas

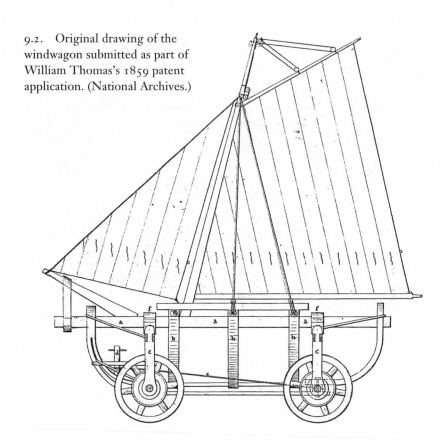

9.2. Original drawing of the windwagon submitted as part of William Thomas's 1859 patent application. (National Archives.)

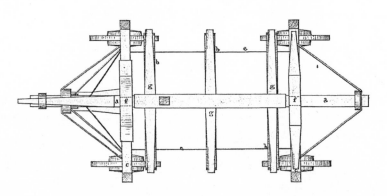

9.4. Top view of windwagon, 1859. (National Archives.)

William Thomas, Sail Wagon, Patented March 13, 1859

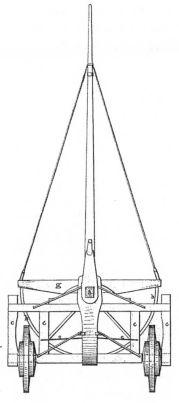

9.3. Front view of windwagon, 1859. (National Archives.)

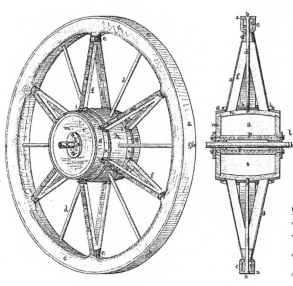

9.5. The "barrel-hub" wheel invented by Thomas for use with his windwagon. (National Archives.)

included with his application shows the windwagon with a bowsprit and single mast carrying two sails: a jib and a fore-and-aft mainsail. This arrangement is indeed common to sloops. The cargo-box frame in this same drawing is represented by the letter "b." This area would have been enclosed. What is unclear is whether or not the enclosure extended over the framework to the front and rear of the vehicle. Because the "pilot wheel and shaft," labeled "d," is located in the forward part of the wagon, one would assume that this area remained open for visibility. And the absence of framing in the rear of the wagon may indicate that this area was open as well.

The above eyewitnesses described the vehicle's body as "somewhat after the style of an omnibus-body" and "like a small sloop with both bow and stem cut off." A later reminiscence also spoke of the wagon as having "a body of a very large omnibus."[31] An omnibus was a "public street vehicle intended to carry a large number of persons."[32] It had paneled sides, a door in the rear, and large drop windows, usually across all four sides. Because the vehicle was intended to carry several passengers, its body was longer than a typical stagecoach, in order to accommodate the extra seats. According to transportation historian Don H. Berkebile, most omnibuses were designed for twelve to fifteen people, although there were larger ones.[33] One eyewitness stated that the windwagon could seat about twenty-four passengers, but the *Westport Border Star* reported that it had "comfortable quarters for about fifteen men."[34] This latter estimate is probably more correct, as the vehicle was supposedly intended for freight as well.

Thomas explained in his patent application that the framing of the cargo-box was attached to the crossbeams, labeled "g," which in turn were secured to a "longitudinal rocking shaft," marked "a." Also mounted to the rocking shaft were the mast and bowsprit (see Figs. 9.2, 9.3, and 9.4). This rocking-shaft assembly, one of just two important features Thomas claimed as his sole invention, lowered the vehicle's center of gravity; and because it was designed to "vibrate" or give laterally, it allowed the vehicle's sails to "yield to violent gusts of thwart wind, receiving their force gradually, and spilling it more and more as they decline."[35] At least that was the idea.

The other feature of the windwagon Thomas claimed exclusively as his invention was the hollow hubs of the wheels, which he "called the barrel-hub, to be used for purposes of freight, thereby relieving the axle, avoiding friction, and adding to the power of the vehicle to stand up safely against strong cross-winds" (Fig. 9.5). As quoted above, one correspondent thought the hubs to be "about the size and appearance of one of Wagoner's beer barrels." John W. Parker, a son of windwagon investor Dr. James W. Parker, stated in 1931 that the hubs were "actually intended to hold much of the water supply needed in crossing the desert."[36] This seems doubtful; Thomas specifically states that the hubs were intended for "part of the freightage." A manhole, he wrote, was "made in the head of this barrel-hub through which to receive and discharge the wheel freight."[37] One does wonder, however, what types of freight could stand the constant turning of the wheels on an eight-hundred-mile trip to Santa Fe.

The wheels themselves, according to one eyewitness, were eight feet in diameter. In addition to the hollow hub, they featured six splayed or double spokes, to reinforce the wheel against lateral thrusts, as well as six metal suspension rods. Another unique feature was that the felloes were entirely enclosed within a "metallic casing," and the outside surfaces of the spokes, which were square, were also clad with iron plates. Each wheel had its own iron axle upon which it turned, and the wheel and axle were mounted within the vehicle's wooden axle frames (Figs. 9.5 and 9.3).[38]

A comparison of the 1859 windwagon with what is known of its predecessor of 1846–47 reveals that there were significant differences between the two. The first model, for instance, had a total of eight wheels, four to a side, while the 1859 vehicle had just four. Another change can be found in the steering operation. On the first model, the two forward axles could be turned "just as the forward axle of any wagon with a tongue."[39] The patented wagon, however, was designed so that the rear axle frame was the one to swivel. "To this frame," Thomas wrote, "the tiller-ropes *e* are attached, and connect with the pilot wheel and shaft *d*, thus completing the apparatus for steerage" (Fig. 9.2).[40] With this arrangement, the rear axle frame performed much like the rudder on a boat.

It should be noted that Thomas did not attempt to patent his windwagon as a whole, just the "combination of the spars and cargo-box on the rocking shaft" and the "hollow wheel-hub." "I do not claim the application of sails and steering apparatus to vehicles for transportation by land," Thomas explained in his application, "neither do I claim the splayed spokes and suspension rods used in the strengthening of the wheel; they are well known." Thomas's patent, officially number 23277, was issued on March 15, 1859, one of 4,314 patents granted by the U. S. Patent Office that year.[41]

On Tuesday, April 19, the great windwagon rolled out of Westport to the chosen testing ground on the prairie. Although the wagon was finished, the masts, spars, and rigging could not be assembled within the confines of the town, so Thomas relied on "animal power" to pull his wagon the few miles down the Santa Fe Trail. According to the *Westport Border Star*, hundreds of people came into town that day to get a glimpse of the wondrous vehicle. "Among the visitors," the *Border Star* reported, "we observed several citizens of Independence, Kansas City, Shawnee and Olathe." The windwagon was "accompanied beyond the limits of the town by a concourse of the citizens and friends of the enterprising inventor, Mr. Thomas, who occupied a prominent position at the pilot wheel, and seemed evidently gratified at the cheers and hurras [*sic*] of the crowd."[42] On April 21, a Kansas City newspaper published information received from "a gentleman down from Westport last evening [April 20]." He related that on the windwagon's "passage out of port, a sudden gust of wind caused it to keel to larboard, thereby bringing it in contact with a boy's head, cutting him severely—after which it proceeded on its course for about three miles, when it again came to anchor. Wind and weather permitting, we understand it will leave to-day."[43] It did not leave that day, for the *Border Star* reported on April 22 that the windwagon was then "a few miles from town, receiving the last touches in the way of dressing and rigging, and a choice set of adventurous spirits are getting ready to go out in her."[44]

Thomas seems to have still been working on those "last touches" as of May 13. Charles C. Post came upon Thomas and his wagon on that date just a few miles over the Missouri/Kansas border. "It plowed right through the mud," Charles penned in his diary, "but cast anchor in a deep ravine where the wind failed to fill the sail and she stopped, the old captain . . . says when he gets it perfected he will bet ten thousand dollars he can get to the Rocky mountains in six days."[45] But it soon became apparent that Thomas's windwagon would never be perfected. One newspaper referred to "several discouraging failures" in connection with the vehicle."[46]

On June 4, *The Weekly Western Argus* of Wyandotte City, Kansas, published a poem that gleefully poked fun at both the wagon and the boosterism of the *Border Star*'s editor. After noting that the wagon was still standing on the plain, the poet asked: "Why do not the ponderous wheels revolve? / And why idly flappeth the sail? / For surely you've furnished it WIND enough— / What need of a stronger gale?"[47] If this was not adequately painful, a Kansas City newspaper printed a facetious article on August 30 that reported the arrival of the windwagon in Westport straight from Chihuahua, Mexico, which place it supposedly departed on August 19! The lengthy article, which gave several particulars of the trip and the excitement generated in Westport by the wagon's return, ended this way:

LATER—We stop the press to announce that we have been grossly imposed upon by the aforesaid messenger. That we took the trouble to visit Westport after the above was in type for the purpose of obtaining the minutia of the great trip, and to our great astonishment *learned that the* only machine in that town, that is known to be propelled by wind, gas, chloroform and "busthead" was the sanctum machinery of the *Border Star*.[48]

Several reminiscences relate how the dreams of Thomas and his investors burst suddenly during an important trial run, although the exact date of this unfortunate episode is not known. William R. Bernard, in the same 1905 interview cited above, tells us that the trial began magnificently. All the investors were on board the windwagon except for Dr. James W. Parker, who followed along on his mule, and the "way the cumbersome looking rig scooted over gullies and small hillocks was surprising." Then, Bernard continues, Thomas "began a course of fancy sailing not in the catalogue of prairie navigation." When he attempted to run the wagon in the face of the wind, the

> wagon came around all right, but the sudden veering of the wind brought on a catastrophe. The big sail, catching the wind suddenly, sent the wagon backward at a speed never attained before, and in some manner the steering apparatus became deranged. Faster and faster went the wind wagon, propelled by a rising wind and guided only by whimsical fancy.. . . [T]he wagon revolved in a circle of about a mile in diameter with the terror-stricken faces of the stockholders and prominent citizens looking longingly at mother earth.

Soon Thomas's important passengers began to abandon ship, eventually leaving him all alone on the three-thousand-pound juggernaut. "The inventor stayed until another vagrant zephyr, stronger than the rest, wafted the entire outfit into a ten-rail stake and rider fence near Turkey creek, and there the wind wagon collapsed." Dr. Parker, briefly quoted in the same 1905 article as Bernard, remembered the event as "one of the most laughable things I ever saw. But that wagon could go! I had one of the best saddle mules in the country, and he could not hold a candle to that wagon."[49]

Bernard's "reminiscence" ends like a classic folktale: "[W]hen the next easterly wind appeared in Westport, Thomas mounted his original wind-propelled vehicle and disappeared. Where he went I don't know. Some persons say that his wind wagon is still circling about the plains." Such "yarn spinning," evident throughout the 1905 article, makes one seriously wonder how much of Bernard's story is truly Bernard's and how much belongs to the unknown interviewer.

In 1931, John W. Parker, son of windwagon investor James W. Parker, told the story of the windwagon to a reporter for the *Kansas City Journal-*

Post. Parker, or the reporter, almost certainly consulted Bernard's 1905 interview, evidenced by the fact that some of Parker's phrasing matches that of Bernard. And the 1931 article also furnishes the same incorrect date for the second windwagon as Bernard. Parker, interestingly, gives his father partial credit for coming up with the idea of a windwagon. In Parker's account of the disastrous final moments of the wagon's trial run, he states that the passengers began to bail after observing how quickly they were distancing Dr. Parker and his mule:

> one by one they dropped off and hit rolling; yes, sir, the last one of those fellows rolled off and left Thomas there with that sail spread full out and the wind blowing nearly a gale. Thomas didn't know it; he couldn't see; he kept shouting for them to draw in the sail not knowing they had deserted him. Dad got left clear out of sight.
>
> Well, we don't just know what happened; some say it headed straight into a ravine and some that Thomas turned it sidewise and the wind turned it around and run it backwards.
>
> Anyway, it went into a ditch, a good big ditch.

As for the ultimate fate of the wagon, Parker claims that it "lay in that ravine for years and years and years. Then little by little it was carted off. Why only a few years ago Al Doershuk drove his car out there and got the last souvenir pieces of that old wind wagon. He's got a part of the old sideboards down in his drug store yet."[50]

A simpler and less colorful account of the windwagon's final run exists in the 1920 recollections of John S. Hough. Hough's story did not come from the pen of a newspaper reporter, for he wrote it himself for an organization named the Daughters of Old Westport. Hough says that after the wagon was completed,

> a trial was made, starting on the Prairie some three or four miles out and of course all the stockholders and many more being on hand to witness the trial, the wind being favorable, Wind Wagon, vessel or air-ship, whatever it might be called, started off at a railroad speed. Persons on horseback being unable to keep up, but unfortunately in crossing the first deep arroya (gully) the machine was wrecked and no further attempt was made for repairs.[51]

George A. Storz happened upon the abandoned windwagon while on his way to New Mexico in 1859. "The first uncommon thing we met," he recalled years later, "was a prairie schooner, now the appelation [*sic*] given to a bull wagon, but this was something else, a real one, . . . a real windwagon. Whether it ever ran I could not find out as the poor thing couldn't talk and having been left to a lonesome existence by its former owners."[52]

The *Westport Border Star* admitted to the failure of the windwagon experiment in its issue of September 2, 1859, and it was a good sport about it. A "slight mistake" had been made in regard to the "proper motive power to work this architectural leviathan," the *Border Star* stated tongue-in-cheek, and it was "willing to concede that it cannot be successfully propelled by *wind*." However, the *Border Star* suggested that if the sails were taken off and twenty or thirty yoke of good oxen hitched to the vehicle, it would "go over any ordinary road in any kind of weather" at "a rate of speed equal to the best wind[?]-tread wagon of any country."

All of the above would indicate that Windwagon Thomas's sailing days were over. But as previously noted, the *Council Grove Press* of July 23, 1860, reported the arrival of a windwagon from Westport, "propeled [*sic*] all the way by wind." The *Press* expected "soon to see this wagon making regular trips between this place and Westport. Running time 48 hours." What was almost certainly this same wagon was spotted along the Santa Fe Trail on its return journey the next month. It had traveled the seven miles between the town of Burlingame and 110 Mile Creek in half an hour.[53] And here the record ends once again. Had Thomas salvaged his giant windwagon? Or did he come up with another vehicle? And if he did use another vehicle, what became of it? Could the 1860 windwagon have been the product of another local inventor? It is hoped that further research will answer these questions.

Additional windwagons have been documented on the Oregon-California Trail. The two most famous came out of the town of Oskaloosa, Kansas, in 1860. The first, created by Andrew J. Dawson, made it all the way to Denver, Colorado. The second, built by Samuel Peppard, came within sixty miles of Denver when it had an unfortunate encounter with a prairie whirlwind, scuttling the craft. The success, albeit limited, of these vehicles came from the fact that they were small, relatively simple affairs, nothing like the huge craft Thomas created.[54]

Another attempt to do away with animal power was a steam wagon invented by a Kansan named Thomas L. Fortune. It was built in St. Louis and shipped to Atchison, Kansas, by steamboat in 1860. The heavy wheels were eight feet in diameter with a tread twelve inches wide. Hundreds witnessed the first trial of the steam contraption, which took place on July 4. The pilot, however, promptly crashed the machine into a store building. A second pilot extracted the vehicle from the damaged structure and got the wagon up to eight miles per hour. Unfortunately, when the steam wagon was stopped, its great weight caused the wheels to sink in soft ground. This, and presumably other problems, led the inventor to conclude the vehicle a failure. Fortune's steam wagon never left the town of Atchison.[55]

The revolution in prairie transportation imagined by these inventors was not to be found in windwagons or steam wagons. It came when steel rails and locomotives crossed the Missouri River and snaked quickly westward following the Civil War. As fate would have it, the golden dreams of Thomas and his companions were to be realized instead by railroad magnates, who measured their success with golden spikes.

Mountain and Prairie Trains and Commerce

The following article appeared in the June 24, 1858, issue of the *Freemen's Champion*, Prairie City, Kansas. It originally appeared in the Kansas City *Western Journal of Commerce* of May 22.

Mountain and Prairie Trains and Commerce

It is estimated by our warehouse and commission merchants, that including the wagons loading for the Utah Expedition, destined for Salt Lake, and the various Forts in the mountains, there will be ten thousand full loaded and fully equipped wagons leave Kanzas City this season to cross the plains—none of these make a shorter trip than six hundred miles, and many of them to go full eleven hundred miles.

A wagon that takes merchandise over the plains and into the mountains, is by no means, such a wagon as people unaccustomed to prairie countries are in the habit of seeing. They are not "double wagons," or "lumber wagons," or "farm wagons," or "Chicago wagons," or "Concord wagons"—they are "prairie wagons," or "schooners," as the boys call them, and as novel a sight to an Eastern man, as any Yankee institution is to a frontiersman, or as the railroad will be to most of the Jackson county people *when it gets here*. A wagon weighs about four thousand pounds, the pole, or tongue, is thirteen feet long, and with all the "fixings" about it is as heavy as a light buggy. One of the hind wheels weighs three hundred pounds, and is sixty-four inches in diameter—the tire is four inches wide, the hub twelve inches through and eighteen inches deep, and the spokes are as large as a middle sized bed post.— Any one can conceive what an axletree for such a wheel must be. The body is three feet eight inches wide, thirteen feet long at the bottom and eighteen feet long at the top; with bows extending above the bed three feet high, and also extending fore and aft of the bed two feet and a half, so that the top of the wagons, measuring over the bows, is eighteen feet long—height of wagon from bottom of wheels to top of bows is ten feet. These bows are covered with three wagon sheets, made of the best quality of duck, and cost about $30.

These details will give one an idea of a prairie wagon, which always carries from fifty-five to sixty hundred pounds of freight, and transports it never less than six hundred miles. Now for the team. The team or the motive power of these cumbrous and ugly wagons, consists of six yoke of oxen, or "steers," as they are called by old freighters, or five span of mules. A driver with a ragged flannel shirt, a pair of buckskin, "jeans" or "store" pants, with pockets made or breaking out almost any where, a pair of brogans, an old hat and whip, the stock of which is generally a hickory sapling ten or fifteen feet long, the lash about the same length made out of undressed raw hide, an inch and a half thick in the "belly," the whole weighing five pounds and a half, and when brought upon the aforesaid steer, crack, crack, crack, it goes with reports loud as a navy pistol.

Such are, in brief, the details of one of these mountain wagons, ten thousand of which will leave Kanzas City for the forts and trading posts in the mountains this season. A wagon and team hitched up and ready for travel is about one hundred feet long, and they travel on the average about one hundred feet apart. Now if all these wagons were to leave in one train, they would stretch out over the prairie *three hundred and seventy nine miles*! Some team, that. When "corraled," or encamped, they would make an encampment of over one hundred and fifty thousand head of stock, about twenty thousand and five hundred men—no women—and if in the mountains they would probably be surrounded by ten thousand "Ingins." The wagons would contain sixty-five million pounds of merchandise, worth in Kanzas City twenty million dollars, and in the mountains, twenty-four millions and a half.

Here, then, are the figures of the great commerce of the prairies, which is centered in Kanzas City, as we compute it when gathered together in one grand encampment:

Men, ... 20,500
Wagons, ... 10,000
Cattle and mules, ... 150,000
Lbs of merchandise, ... 65,000,000
Value of merchandise in the mountains, ... $24,500,000

Rolling Stock of the Plains

Following is the complete article on Santa Fe wagons that appeared in the *Westport Border Star* (Westport, Missouri), June 23, 1860, p. 2, cols. 1 and 2.

Rolling Stock of the Plains

Facts Respecting Western Commerce

In our issue of the 2nd ult., we referred somewhat at length to a particular branch of trade incident to the commerce of the plains and the mountains — the ready made clothing outfit of men engaged therein — and showed with statistics computed from authentic sources, that the amount of ready made clothing purchased annually by men who follow the plains for a livelihood amounted to $270,000.In further considering the details of this commerce, we now purpose [*sic*] to furnish our readers with an abstract of the grandest feature of this overland traffic — the rolling stock of the prairies; and as this term, when applied to railways embraces the motive power, or their iron horses, we know no good reason why we should not use it in its most extended signification when applied to our over-land transportation and include the motive power, horses, oxen, and mules.

It will be reccollected [*sic*] that our estimate of the number of wagons employed in hauling the merchandise yearly sent forward over the plains was five thousand, though as we said before, there are a number of old freighters who think this number far too small. But as we wish to be within bounds in any statements we may make, calculated to attract the attention of business men, and perhaps enlist their capatal, [*sic*] we give the number of wagons engaged in the transportation of freight across these plains to Mexico, the Forts, the Mountains and Utah, at *five thousand*, with a tonage equal to 32,500,000 pounds. What this merchandise consists of, where purchased, and by whom sold and consumed will constitute the subject matter of another article, our object now being to give all the information possible about the rolling stock, and to so prepare that information as to enable our readers east or elsewhere, who may not be familiar with the plains and the mode of transport, to understand the subject.

A regular wagon of the first magnitude, capable of carrying 6,500 pounds is what we here call a "Santa Fe wagon," from the fact that so many trains of these wagons are continually leaving Westport and Kansas City for Santa Fe, New Mexico. During the spring and summer and part of the fall months we see hundreds of them every day, but as yet, have never attempted to furnish an accurate description of either wagon or train.

A large portion of these wagons are manufactured at St. Louis and at establishments in Indiana and Illinois, and are forwarded here by water. Within the year, however, a factory has been erected in our own city, under the immediate control and proprietorship of Mr. M. T. Graham, from whom we gather the following information concerning the construction of these "prairie schooners."—In this establishment there are four departments, employing in all thirty-five men, and turning out fifty-three wagons per month. The expense of keeping a concern of this character in "full blast" would be about $200 per diem, or $65,000 per year.

The material for the construction of a wagon is obtained mostly in the counties of Clay and Jackson, Missouri, Wyandotte county, Kansas, and Indiana, and is consumed into "shaped lumber" at the factory, when it then undergoes a seasoning process before being worked up. As in factories for the construction of locomotives, every thing is reduced to a system—as it is in these "shops," and in the various departments, machine shops, painting room, furnishing and trimming room, and lathe room, we find men engaged on some particular part of a wagon.

In looking through the shops we find a series of machines, that with the human hand and an arm of steam do all the work upon a wagon, the mortices, tenents, felloes, grooves, scrolls, etc., etc., and in addition to this a gang of knives that work in one of Daniel's planers give the finishing touch to all the axles, bolsters, tongues, and other heavy timber about a wagon.—These machines consist of a morticer that in eighteen minutes make all the mortices for a set of hubs—a job that would occupy a man all day and even then he could not do the work with near the niceity and exactness that the machine does. Then comes the planer, spoke lath, upright drill, tenenting machine, the knives of which revolve three thousand times a minute cutting tenants of any size, felloe saws, scrolls saws, a swinging saw that cuts the lumber crosswise, and which is a most ingenious contrivance, four circular saws, grind-stones, and other machinery for finishing work. All of these machines are new and of the latest and best patterns, and after once witnessing the amount of labor they perform in a time that you can compute in minutes, one no longer wonders at the rapidity with which the steam machines turn out the strong and unwieldy looking wagons. Some of the dimensions of these wagons would supprise [sic] an Eastern man. The diameter of the larger wheel is five feet two inches, and the tire weighs

105 pounds. The reach is eleven feet and the bed forty-six inches deep, twelve feet long on the bottom and fifteen feet on the top, and will carry 6,500 pounds across the plains and through the mountain passes. When ready for a voyage a wagon has an amount of rigging equal to many small water crafts. This consists of bows, yokes, ox bows, sheets, chains, ropes, extra spars in the shape of tongues, axles and bolsters, kegs, bolts, nuts and a number of tools.

Such in brief is a prairie wagon—one of the freight cars in the valley stock equipment of overland commerce. When merchandise is forwarded in these cars they go out in trains of from eighteen to thirty-three, and sometimes fifty wagons, and are propelled by a team of six yoke of strong and heavy cattle—stock that is accustomed to the plains, many trains, however, use mules and we can safely estimate this motive power at *seventy thousand* head of live stock—all mules and oxen. The value of the rolling stock is no less than $3,000,000! More than equal to the rolling stock of some of the longest and best railroads in the Union. To keep this stock moving requires about six thousand men, including wagon-masters, teamsters, agents, &c., at a cost of $180,000 a month, or $2,160,000 a year.

These, then are some of the features and figures of a branch of business in the West, that is done over the great thoroughfares of the plains, creating a commerce that would be enhanced a hundredfold by railway facilities.

Wilson, Childs & Co.'s
Wagon Manufactory

The following description of Wilson, Childs & Co.'s Philadelphia wagon works was written by Edward Young and appeared in Edwin T. Freedley's *Philadelphia and its Manufactures . . . in 1857* (Philadelphia: Edward Young, 1858), 447–48.

Wilson, Childs & Co.'s Wagon Manufactory

The largest Wagon-making establishment in Philadelphia, and perhaps in the country, is that of D. G. Wilson, J. Childs & Co., whose office is at the corner of St. John and Buttonwood streets. Messrs. Wilson & Childs formed a copartnership in 1829, and commenced business on the premises now occupied by them, which fronts on three streets—Third, Buttonwood, and St. John—extending 230 feet on Buttonwood, and 113 on St. John. A four-story brick building, 86 by 45 feet, has recently been erected on the St. John street front. Their increased business requiring more room, they purchased, in 1850, a manufactory erected by Mr. Simons, also the adjoining property—comprising in all a square on Second street, and Lehigh Avenue; the whole containing 260,000 square feet, or over 6 acres. The square on the East side of Second street is 500 by 248 feet, and is used as a Lumber Yard, in which are piled plank and boards of various thicknesses, from one to five inches; also spokes and hubs. These are left to season from one to five years; one year being required for every inch in thickness. Spokes in the rough are also piled and seasoned. Timber for hubs is made chiefly from black locust trees of different sizes, sawed into suitable lengths, and before being stowed away to season, have the bark removed, and a hole bored in the centre, to facilitate the seasoning process. On the western side of Second street—the lot being 500 feet by 273, and containing over three acres—the various workshops are situated. The principal buildings are one brick Wheel and Body Shop, 100 by 45 feet, and three stories high; one brick Blacksmith Shop, 200 by 35 feet; the Saw-Mill, Engine House, and Machine Shop, 80 by 45 feet, and three stories high; Running-gear Shops, 100 by 45 feet; Paint Shop, Office, Stables, Sheds, &c.; the Boiler House is a separate building.

The variety and extent of the business may be learned by an inspection of the different successive operations required to make a wagon. Plank of three or four inches of thickness, for felloes and shafts, spokes, hubs of proper sizes—all sufficiently seasoned—are selected from the lumber yard, and removed into the saw-mill. Here there are two Upright and six Circular Saws; a machine for boring holes in the centre of the hub; another for boring holes for the spokes; four Drills (self-feeding) for drilling iron. In other shops there are a Planing Machine, a Mortising Machine, two machines for turning Spokes, machines for driving in the Spokes and for shaping the Felloes, and finishing them complete, and a machine for boring Hubs so as to put the boxes in properly, and to ensure accuracy and a solid bearing. The planks, after being marked, are sawed into shafts, and into felloes. Hubs are turned in a lathe, and both ends sawed at once by circular saws. They are then conveyed to other shops, where the wheels and running-gears are completed. The bodies are made by a number of men, each having his particular work assigned him; and, by such subdivision of labor, greater excellence and celerity is attained. In the Engine and Machine Shop the Iron Axles are turned, Screws cut, and a number of other operations performed. The Blacksmith's Shop, a new brick building, is one of the best arranged I have ever seen. It is very high, and thoroughly ventilated, the gas being carried off, rendering it healthy and pleasant for the men; it has twenty-four fires, a machine for Punching, for making Bolts, Rivets, &c. Of course, all the Hoops or Bands, Tires, Straps, Bolts, Rivets, Staples—in short, all the iron-work for the wagon is made here. The upper story of the Body-shop, and also a separate building, are used as Paint Shops. Previous to this finishing operation, however, and when every defect can easily be discovered, the Wagons for the Government are minutely examined by an inspector, whose keen eyes are not easily blinded: and when passed by him their excellence and durability may be relied on.

To give an idea of the extent of business carried on in one of these great establishments, and of the large capital required, the stock on hand a few months since may be stated, viz.:—1,500,000 feet of hard-wood plank and boards, 30,000 hubs, 472,000 spokes, and 150 tons of iron. At the period of my visit, the second story of a building 273 by 23 feet, except twenty feet of one end, was filled with wheels; there must have been several thousands. The lower floor of the same building was filled with cart and wagon bodies. The number of hands employed averages 178.

The old establishment on St. John, Buttonwood, and Third streets, is still used by this firm, but it is eclipsed by the larger one above described. They also own the warehouse, 70 Carondelet street, New Orleans; and have an agency in Mobile.

Notes

CHAPTER 1

1. *Missouri Intelligencer* (Franklin, Mo.), Apr. 22, 1823.

2. Ibid.

3. Ibid. In the *Missouri Intelligencer* of Feb. 13, 1823, the editor states that only "*one waggon has ever gone from this state to Santa Fe, and that was taken by Capt. Wm. Becknell.*" Despite the fact that the editor claims to have obtained this information directly from Becknell, he is contradicted by both Becknell's journal, published in the same paper just two months later, and other accounts. Larry M. Beachum, *William Becknell: Father of the Santa Fe Trade*, Southwestern Studies Monograph No. 68 (El Paso: Texas Western Press, 1982), 38.

4. Alphonso Wetmore wrote in 1824 that "Mr. Becknal . . . took with him a wagon, as did also two or three of his associates." Augustus Storrs and Alphonso Wetmore, *Santa Fe Trail First Reports: 1825* (Houston, Tex.: Stagecoach Press, 1960), 61.

5. *Missouri Intelligencer*, Feb. 13, 1823, as quoted in Beachum, *William Becknell*, 38.

6. Meredith Miles Marmaduke, "Santa Fe Trail: M. M. Marmaduke Journal," ed. Francis A. Sampson, *Missouri Historical Review* 6 (October 1911): 3.

7. U.S. Congress, Senate, *Answers of Augustus Storrs, of Missouri, to Certain Queries upon the Origin, Present State, and Future Prospect, of Trade and Intercourse between Missouri and the Internal Provinces of Mexico, Propounded by the Hon. Mr. Benton*, Sen. Doc. 7, 18th Cong., 2d sess., 1825 (Serial 108), 3.

8. Don H. Berkebile, *Carriage Terminology: An Historical Dictionary* (Washington, D.C.: Smithsonian Institution Press, 1978), 239.

9. "We had fourteen road-wagons, half drawn by mules, the others by oxen (eight of each to the team); besides a carriage and a Jersey wagon." Josiah Gregg, *Commerce of the Prairies*, ed. Max L. Moorhead (Norman: University of Oklahoma Press, 1954), 229. The term *road wagon* is also used in an early Pittsburgh newspaper to

describe freight wagons arriving at that place from Philadelphia in 1835; and Thomas B. Searight, who grew up along the National Road in the nineteenth century, uses the term *road wagon* for the large Conestoga wagons that operated on that famous thoroughfare. See Catherine Elizabeth Reiser, *Pittsburgh's Commercial Development, 1800–1850* (Harrisburg: Pennsylvania Historical and Museum Commission, 1951), 77 n. 33; and Thomas B. Searight, *The Old Pike: A History of the National Road* (Uniontown, Pa.: T. B. Searight, 1894), 119.

10. John A. Paxton, *The St. Louis Directory and Register* (St. Louis: John A. Paxton, 1821).

11. Louise Barry, *The Beginning of the West: Annals of the Kansas Gateway to the American West, 1540–1854* (Topeka: Kansas State Historical Society, 1972), 119; and *Missouri Intelligencer*, June 19, 1825. Josiah Gregg gives the number of wagons on the Trail that year as thirty-seven. Gregg, *Commerce of the Prairies*, 332.

12. Kate L. Gregg, ed., *The Road to Santa Fe: The Journal and Diaries of George Champlin Sibley* (Albuquerque: University of New Mexico Press, 1952), 30, 176, and 217–18.

13. Gregg, *Commerce of the Prairies*, 332.

14. Susan Calafate Boyle, *Commerciantes, Arrieros, y Peones: The Hispanos and the Santa Fe Trade*, Southwest Cultural Resources Center Professional Papers No. 54 (Santa Fe, N.M.: National Park Service, 1994), 68.

15. *Missouri Intelligencer*, May 22, 1830.

16. Storrs and Wetmore, *Santa Fe Trail First Reports*, 68.

17. Gregg, *Commerce of the Prairies*, 24.

18. Leo E. Oliva, *Soldiers on the Santa Fe Trail* (Norman: University of Oklahoma Press, 1967), 28.

19. Gregg, *Commerce of the Prairies*, 24–25.

20. Ibid., 25.

21. Randolph B. Marcy, *The Prairie Traveler: A Hand-Book for Overland Expeditions* (New York: Harper & Brothers, 1859), 27–28.

22. "Used Both Mules and Oxen," undated clipping from the *Kansas City Star*, 1905. James Brice spent the period of 1858 to 1868 on the Trail; see his *Reminiscences of Ten Years Experience on the Western Plains: How the United States Mails Were Carried Before Railroads Reached the Santa Fe Trail* (Kansas City, c. 1906).

23. James F. Meline, *Two Thousand Miles on Horseback* (1868; repr. ed., Albuquerque: Horn & Wallace, 1966), 3.

24. See D. M. Draper, "The Santa Fe Trail in '61: Personal reminisences [*sic*] of a 'train' conductor before the railroads came," Denver Public Library, Western History Collection; and William Henry Jackson, *The Diaries of William Henry Jackson, Frontier Photographer*, ed. LeRoy R. Hafen and Ann W. Hafen, The Far West and the Rockies Historical Series, vol. 10 (Glendale, Calif.: The Arthur H. Clark Co., 1959).

25. George Shumway and Howard C. Frey, *Conestoga Wagon, 1750–1850: Freight Carrier for 100 Years of America's Westward Expansion* (York, Pa.: George Shumway,

1968), 142; and Berkebile, *Carriage Terminology*, 342 and 388. The spreader bar is also known as a "stretcher bar." See Michael H. Piatt, "Hauling Freight into the 20th Century by Jerk Line," *Journal of the West* 36 (January 1997): 84.

26. Arthur Woodward, *Ox Carts and Covered Wagons* (Los Angeles County Museum, 1951), 5; and Jackson, *Diaries of William Henry Jackson*, 35–36.

CHAPTER 2

1. Thomas J. Farnham, *Travels in the Great Western Prairies, the Anahuac and Rocky Mountains, and in the Oregon Territory* (New York: Greeley & McElrath, 1843), 44

2. *Pittsburgh Morning Chronicle*, Mar. 5, 1842; and *Weekly Mercury and Manufacturer* (Pittsburgh, Pa.), July 22, 1843. See also Catherine Elizabeth Reiser, *Pittsburgh's Commercial Development, 1800–1850* (Harrisburg: Pennsylvania Historical and Museum Commission, 1951), 122–23; and Louise Barry, *The Beginning of the West: Annals of the Kansas Gateway to the American West, 1540–1854* (Topeka: Kansas State Historical Society, 1972), 449.

3. Josiah Gregg, *Commerce of the Prairies*, ed. Max L. Moorhead (Norman: University of Oklahoma Press, 1954), 24. In 1883, merchant Reuben Gentry was interviewed by a Santa Fe newspaper concerning his many years in the Mexican trade. In regard to an 1843 trading expedition of Gentry's, the article stated: "The goods occupied twelve 'prairie schooners,' or Pittsburgh freight wagons, as they were sometimes called, from the place where the wagons were purchased." "An Old Timer: Reuben Gentry a Pioneer Pays a Visit to the Scenes of his Youth," *Santa Fe New Mexican Review*, Sept. 27, 1883 (repr. in *Wagon Tracks* [Quarterly of the Santa Fe Trail Association], 5 [February 1991]: 24–25).

4. See Reiser, *Pittsburgh's Commercial Development*, 3–4; and Lewis E. Atherton, *The Frontier Merchant in Mid-America* (Columbia: University of Missouri Press, 1971), 85–86.

5. Wagons could be disassembled for shipping (sometimes referred to as shipping in "knock-down" fashion). However, Francis Parkman's description of Santa Fe wagons on the steamboat *Radnor* in 1846 suggests that he saw wagons that were largely intact: "Her upper-deck was covered with large wagons of a peculiar form, for the Santa Fé trade, and her hold was crammed with goods for the same destination." Francis Parkman, *The Oregon Trail*, ed. E. N. Feltskog (Madison: University of Wisconsin Press, 1969), 2.

6. *Pittsburgh Morning Chronicle*, Mar. 5, 1842.

7. Don H. Berkebile, *Carriage Terminology: An Historical Dictionary* (Washington, D.C.: Smithsonian Institution Press, 1978), 106; George Shumway and Howard C. Frey, *Conestoga Wagon, 1750–1850: Freight Carrier for 100 Years of America's Westward Expansion* (York, Pa.: George Shumway, 1968), 14.

8. J. Geraint Jenkins, *The English Farm Wagon, Origins and Structure* (Newton Abbot, England: David & Charles, 1981), 57 n. 9.

9. Seymour Dunbar, *A History of Travel in America* (New York: Tudor Publishing Company, 1937), 203.

10. Berkebile, *Carriage Terminology*, 110 and 375. In addition to Shumway and Frey, already cited, see John Omwake, *The Conestoga Six-Horse Bell Teams of Eastern Pennsylvania* (Cincinnati: The Ebbert & Richardson Co., 1930); Arthur L. Reist, *Conestoga Wagon: Masterpiece of the Blacksmith* (Lancaster, Pa.: Forry and Hacker, 1975); and Ron Vineyard, *Virginia Freight Waggons, 1750–1850*, Colonial Williamsburg Foundation Library Research Report Series no. 345 (Williamsburg, Va.: Colonial Williamsburg Foundation Library, 1994).

11. Reiser, *Pittsburgh's Commercial Development*, 77.

12. Vineyard, *Virginia Freight Waggons*, 141 and 190–91.

13. Today, the name *Conestoga* is commonly applied to almost any old covered wagon. However, it is evident that this generic use of the term was not prevalent in the first half of the nineteenth century. *Conestoga* or *Conestoga wagon* does not appear in the first edition of John Russell Bartlett's *Dictionary of Americanisms*, published in 1848. A second edition of this famous work was published in 1859 and a third in 1860. I did not have access to the second edition, but the third does contain entries for both "Conestoga Horse" and "Conestoga Waggon." Bartlett associates both the horse and wagon with Pennsylvania; the latter was a "a huge white-topped waggon . . . first made in Conestoga, a township of Lancaster county, Pennsylvania." Bartlett, *Dictionary of Americanisms* (Boston: Little, Brown and Company, 1860), 94.

While the majority of nineteenth-century observers were hardly transportation scholars, the available evidence, particularly the 1846 description of Conestogas provided by Frank Edwards (see below), and the several artists' renderings reproduced in this study, indicates that the term *Conestoga wagon* was being used correctly at the time. On a similar note, the term *Pennsylvania wagon* may not have referred simply to the wagon's place of origin. It is possible that the term may have been used to indicate any Conestoga-type wagon, which was in widespread use in Pennsylvania during this period.

14. Farnham, *Travels in the Great Western Prairies*, 15.

15. Lewis Garrard, *Wah-to-Yah and the Taos Trail* (1850; repr. ed., Norman: University of Oklahoma Press, 1955), 12. Thomas B. Searight uses wording very close to Farnham and Garrard to describe the bodies of the freight wagons that he frequently saw on the National Road in the nineteenth century: "long and deep, bending upward at the bottom in front and rear." Thomas B. Searight, *The Old Pike: A History of the National Road* (Uniontown, Pa.: T. B. Searight, 1894), 119.

16. Rufus Sage, *Scenes in the Rocky Mountains*, ed. LeRoy R. Hafen and Ann W. Hafen, The Far West and the Rockies Historical Series, vols. 4 and 5 (Glendale, Calif.: Arthur H. Clark Co., 1956), 4:125.

17. Lieut. James W. Abert, *Abert's New Mexico Report, 1846–'47* (Albuquerque: Horn & Wallace, 1962), 120.

18. [Charles Hallock], "The Seige of Fort Atkinson," *Harper's New Monthly Magazine* 15 (October 1857): 641; and Barry, *The Beginning of the West*, 1106.

19. George A. F. Ruxton, *Life in the Far West* (New York: Harper & Brothers, 1855), 66.

20. Frank S. Edwards, *A Campaign in New Mexico with Colonel Doniphan* (Philadelphia: Carey and Hart, 1847), 79–80.

21. See Josiah Gregg, *Diary and Letters of Josiah Gregg*, ed. Maurice Fulton, 2 vols. (Norman: University of Oklahoma Press, 1941 and 1944), 1:133–45. For a discussion of the artists who created the illustrations for *Commerce of the Prairies*, see David J. Weber, *Richard H. Kern: Expeditionary Artist in the Far Southwest, 1848–1853* (Albuquerque: University of New Mexico Press, 1985), 7 and 291 n. 12.

22. Even if the artists for *Commerce of the Prairies* based their engravings on the work of others, it is clear from statements left by John Bigelow, who was hired by Gregg to edit his manuscript for publication, that the Santa Fe trader/author, if not a perfectionist, was at the least a stickler for accuracy. Gregg "always had the critics of the plains before his eyes," wrote Bigelow, "and would sooner have broken up the plates and reprinted the whole book than have permitted the most trifling error to creep into his description of the loading of his mules or the marshaling of one of his caravans." Judging from the following extract of a review which appeared in the *Independence* [Missouri] *Journal*, it seems that Gregg ably satisfied the "critics" he most respected: "Perhaps one of the highest encomiums which could be passed upon this work, is the universal commendation which it receives from all those who have visited Santa Fe, and who have had opportunities of becoming acquainted with Mexican manners, prairie life, and the Indians of the plains; and there are many such here." Gregg, *Diary and Letters*, 1:142, n. 33, and illustration opposite 188.

23. Pauline Fowler to Mark L. Gardner, Independence, Missouri, Feb. 20, 1989.

24. See David Boutros, "The West Illustrated: Meyer's Views of Missouri River Towns," *Missouri Historical Review* 80 (April 1986):304–20.

25. See Benjamin Franklin Taylor, ed., *Short Ravelings from a Long Yarn, or Camp March Sketches of the Santa Fe Trail; from the Notes of Richard L. Wilson* (Chicago: Geer & Wilson, Daily Journal Office, 1847); and William H. Richardson, *Journal of William H. Richardson, a Private Soldier in Col. Doniphan's Command* (Baltimore, J. W. Woods, printer, 1848).

26. Fairholme's journal and sketches have been published as *Journal of an Expedition to the Grand Prairies of the Missouri, 1840*, ed. Jack B. Tykal (Spokane, Wash.: The Arthur H. Clark Co., 1996). The original journal belongs to the Huntington Library, San Marino, California.

27. Ibid., 51, 54, 67, and 74–75.

28. M. Rondé, "Voyage Dans L'Etat de Chihuahua, (Mexique)," *Le Tour Du Monde* 4 (1861): 147.

29. It is perhaps worth noting here that for many years the provenance of this important engraving has been a mystery. It has previously been known only as a curious illustration in an 1888 work of fiction entitled *Great Grandmother's Girls in New Mexico* by Elizabeth Champney (the engraving appeared with just enough of the image cropped on the bottom to leave off the names of the engraver and artist). I speculated about the illustration's significance in an article on Conestoga wagons published in 1989, but it was not until pursuing my research for this study that I discovered, quite by chance, Rondé's account with its excellent engravings buried in the bound volumes of *Le Tour Du Monde*.

30. Edward Kern Diary, 1851 (HM 4276), Huntington Library, San Marino, California.

31. S. Jones, *Pittsburgh in the Year Eighteen Hundred and Twenty-Six* (Pittsburgh: Johnston & Stockton, 1826), 78.

32. Isaac Harris, *Harris' Pittsburgh Business Directory, for the Year 1837* (Pittsburgh: Isaac Harris, 1837).

33. Isaac Harris, *Harris' Pittsburgh & Allegheny Directory* (Pittsburgh: A. A. Anderson, 1839).

34. Isaac Harris, *Harris' Business Directory of the Cities of Pittsburgh and Allegheny* (Pittsburgh: A. A. Anderson, 1844); Samuel Fahnestock, *Fahnestock's Pittsburgh Directory for 1850* (Pittsburgh: Geo. Parkin & Co. Book and Job Printers, 1850); and *Pittsburgh Business Directory and Merchants and Travelers' Guide* (Pittsburgh: Jones & Co., 1854).

35. "Pittsburgh: Her Manufactures, Commerce, and Railroad Position," *Merchants' Magazine and Commercial Review* 30 (June 1854): 691.

36. Julius Froebel, *Seven Years' Travel in Central America, Northern Mexico, and the Far West of the United States* (London: Richard Bentley, 1859), 431.

37. *Weekly Mercury and Manufacturer* (Pittsburgh, Pa.), July 22, 1843.

38. Invoice Book (Owens & Aull), Feb. 14, 1846–1847, p. 36, in James Aull Business Records, 1825–1851, Coll. no. 3001 (microfilm), Western Historical Manuscript Collection, Columbia, Missouri.

39. John G. O'Brien, *O'Brien's Philadelphia Business Directory . . . for the Year 1844* (Philadelphia: King & Baird, Printers, 1844), 113–15.

40. J. Leander Bishop, *A History of American Manufactures from 1608 to 1860*, 2 vols. (Philadelphia: Edward Young & Co., 1864), 2:564.

41. Percival G. Lowe, *Five Years a Dragoon ('49 to '54) and Other Adventures on the Great Plains* (1906; repr. ed., Norman: University of Oklahoma Press, 1965), 243.

42. August Santleben, *A Texas Pioneer: Early Staging and Overland Freighting Days on the Frontiers of Texas and Mexico*, ed. I. D. Affleck (New York: The Neal Publishing Company, 1910), 64 and 109; and A. Staacke advertisement, *San Antonio Express*, Sept. 29, 1868.

43. Shumway and Frey, *Conestoga Wagon, 1750–1850*, 180.

44. *San Antonio Express*, Sept. 29, 1868.

45. Santleben, *A Texas Pioneer*, 109. The exact dimensions of these Chihuahua wagons, as remembered by Santleben, will be provided elsewhere in this study. See also Roy L. Swift and Leavitt Corning, Jr., *Three Roads to Chihuahua: The Great Wagon Roads that Opened the Southwest, 1823–1883* (Austin, Tex.: Eakin Press, 1988).

46. The Kansas City *Western Journal of Commerce* noted on July 3, 1858, that of over twelve hundred wagons that had departed thus far that season for the West, the majority had been purchased in St. Louis, Chicago, Springfield, and Pittsburgh.

47. Septimus Scholl to Rodney M. Hinde, Jackson County, Mo., Apr. 23, 1848, in Isabel Stebbins Giulvezan, ed., *A Collection of Letters Written by the Scholl Family and Their Kin, 1836–1897* (St. Louis, 1959), 26.

48. Isaac Jones Wistar, *Autobiography of Isaac Jones Wistar, 1827–1905* (Philadelphia: The Wistar Institute of Anatomy and Biology, 1937), 45.

49. *Western Journal of Commerce*, June 19, 1858.

CHAPTER 3

1. "William H. Eisele—Trinidad, 1874–1888," *Chronicle-News* (Trinidad, Colo.), Nov. 8, 1931.

2. Independence *Journal*, Sept. 19, 1844, as quoted in *The Merchants' Magazine and Commercial Review* 11 (November 1844): 475. It is not clear if these wagons were all freight wagons.

3. W. & J. McCoy to Massey & James, Independence, Mo., Mar. 20, 1846, Lucy Wortham James Collection, Western Historical Manuscript Collection, Columbia, Missouri.

4. St. Louis *Missouri Republican*, Mar. 27, 1850.

5. Julius Froebel, *Seven Years' Travel in Central America, Northern Mexico, and the Far West of the United States* (London: Richard Bentley, 1859), 216.

6. Pearl Wilcox, *Jackson County Pioneers* (1975; repr. ed., Independence, Mo.: Jackson County Historical Society, 1990), 170; Louise Barry, *The Beginning of the West: Annals of the Kansas Gateway to the American West, 1540–1854* (Topeka: Kansas State Historical Society, 1972), 221, 245, 300, 317, and 574; and *History of the Arkansas Valley, Colorado* (Chicago: O. L. Baskin & Co., 1881), 663–64.

7. *The History of Jackson County, Missouri* (1881; repr. ed., Cape Girardeau, Mo.: Ramfre Press, 1966), 170 and 646; "The Santa Fe Trail," Kansas City *Journal*, Mar. 5, 1905; Wilcox, *Jackson County Pioneers*, 171–73 and 276; and *The Western Expositor* (Independence, Mo.), Jan. 31 and July 18, 1846.

8. *The Western Expositor*, Jan. 31, 1846. Modie, incidentally, was the brother-in-law of fellow craftsman Robert Weston. See Will of Samuel Weston, Record of Wills, Vol. L, p. 88, Jackson County Probate Court, Independence, Missouri.

9. *The Western Expositor*, July 18, 1846.

10. James Josiah Webb, *Adventures in the Santa Fe Trade, 1844–1847*, ed. Ralph P. Bieber, Southwest Historical Series, vol. 1 (Glendale, Calif.: Arthur H. Clark Co., 1931), 179, 281, and 300.

11. *U.S. Census: Products of Industry*, 1850, Jackson County, Missouri, 96–101 (microfilm), State Historical Society of Missouri, Columbia. The industrial census does not identify every individual wagon maker in Jackson County; only those businesses with products purported to amount to five hundred dollars or more per year were enumerated. Also, the occupation designation for some individuals is somewhat questionable. For example, David Vance is listed as a wagon maker, yet his annual product is listed solely as six hundred yokes, no wagons. Additionally, Robert Weston is listed only as a blacksmith (with six individuals employed), but his operation is shown as having an annual product that included twelve wagons valued at twelve hundred dollars. For an abstract of the above census, see Joanne Chiles

Eakin, *Farmers and Merchants Census, 1850, 1860, and 1870, Jackson County, Missouri* (Independence, Mo., 1992), 113–14.

12. H. David Condron, "The Knapheide Wagon Company, 1848–1943," *The Journal of Economic History* 3 (May 1943): 34–35.

13. *U.S. Census: Products of Industry*, 1850, Jackson County, Missouri, 96. It appears that the making of ox yokes and wagon bows at this time fell largely to "mechanics" (this term was defined in the nineteenth century as "artisan"). Nelson Low is listed in the industrial census as a mechanic with an annual product of twenty-five hundred wagon bows valued at five hundred dollars. Another mechanic, Thomas M. Burgess, is enumerated with an annual product that included twelve hundred ox yokes (value: twelve hundred dollars) and twenty-four hundred ox bows (value: two hundred dollars), in addition to fifty wheels and two hundred chairs.

14. William Patrick O'Brien, "Hiram Young: Pioneering Black Wagon Maker for the Santa Fe Trade," *Gateway Heritage* 14 (Summer 1993), 57; Hattie E. Poppino, ed., *Census of 1850, Jackson County, Missouri* (Kansas City, Mo.: Mrs. Hattie E. Poppino, 1959), 140; and Missouri vol. 16, p. 510, R. G. Dun & Co. Coll., Baker Library, Harvard University Graduate School of Business Administration.

15. James Thomas, *From Tennessee Slave to St. Louis Entrepreneur: The Autobiography of James Thomas*, ed. Loren Schweninger (Columbia: University of Missouri Press, 1984), 99.

16. Percival G. Lowe, *Five Years a Dragoon ('49 to '54) and Other Adventures on the Great Plains* (1906; repr. ed., Norman: University of Oklahoma Press, 1965), 255.

17. W. B. Napton, *The Santa Fe Trail, 1857* (1905; repr. ed., Arrow Rock, Mo.: The Friends of Arrow Rock, 1991), 6.

18. *U.S. Census: Products of Industry*, 1860, Jackson County, Missouri, City of Independence, 1.

19. See the discussion of the wagons for the 1825 government survey in chapter 1 of this study.

20. Emily Ann O'Neil Bott, "Joseph Murphy's Contribution to the Development of the West," *Missouri Historical Review* 47 (October 1952), 19; James Cox, *Old and New St. Louis: A Concise History of the Metropolis of the West and Southwest, with a Review of its Present Greatness and Immediate Prospects* (St. Louis: Central Biographical Publishing Co., 1894), 490–91; and Account Book, 1825–1836, p. 1, Joseph Murphy Collection (microfilm), Missouri Historical Society, St. Louis (hereafter cited as JMC).

21. See Account Book, 1825–1836, JMC.

22. Ibid., 18. An additional account for Jarrett is found on p. 21.

23. The sum of 27 dollars is far too low for the purchase of a wagon at this time. Recall from chapter 1 that William Becknell's wagon is said to have cost 150 dollars in Missouri in 1822.

24. Day Book, 1847–1853, p. 159, JMC.

25. For example, an 1850 entry records the sale of twelve large ox wagons "to go to Santafee." Yet wagons purchased by freighter F. X. Aubry the following year, obviously for use on the Santa Fe Trail, were not identified as such in the accounts.

26. *Missouri Historical Review* 47 (October 1952): 18–28.

27. Bott, "Joseph Murphy's Contribution," 22. The quotation is from a monograph entitled *Joseph Murphy*, which was privately printed by Anselm. I have not examined this monograph. W. Earl Givens, who has conducted much research on Murphy and his wagons, provided me with the 1938 date of publication.

28. Josiah Gregg, *Commerce of the Prairies*, ed. Max L. Moorhead (Norman: University of Oklahoma Press, 1954), 79–80.

29. David H. Coyner, *The Lost Trappers*, ed. David J. Weber (Albuquerque: University of New Mexico Press, 1970), 150.

30. James W. Abert, *Through the Country of the Comanche Indians in the Fall of the Year 1845*, ed. John Galvin (San Francisco: John Howell, 1970), 21.

31. Wide-wheeled wagons have also been associated with freighter Benjamin Holladay. According to Holladay biographer Ellis Lucia, the Missouri freighter *personally* made wheels for his wagons with iron tires ten and twelve inches wide. Historian Henry Pickering Walker speculates that these wagons "were probably built by Murphy and carried five tons each." These wagons, the story goes, enabled Holladay "to make three trips a season, breaking all records for the Santa Fe Trail." The author has been unable to locate any primary sources that substantiate this account, and Ellis's book is absent of footnotes. See Ellis Lucia, *The Saga of Ben Holladay: Giant of the Old West* (New York: Hastings House, 1959), 31–32; and Henry Pickering Walker, *The Wagonmasters: High Plains Freighting from the Earliest Days of the Santa Fe Trail to 1880* (Norman: University of Oklahoma Press, 1966), 96–97.

32. Dale Morgan, ed., *Overland in 1846: Diaries and Letters of the California-Oregon Trail*, 2 vols. (1963; repr. ed., Lincoln: University of Nebraska Press, 1993), 2:474.

33. Thomas B. Searight, *The Old Pike: A History of the National Road* (Uniontown, Pa.: T. B. Searight, 1894), 118. Shumway and Frey provide tire widths for sixteen existing Conestoga wagons of various sizes, and none exceed four inches. George Shumway and Howard C. Frey, *Conestoga Wagon, 1750–1850: Freight Carrier for 100 Years of America's Westward Expansion* (York, Pa.: George Shumway, 1968), 191–92.

34. Transportation historian W. Earl Givens came to a similar conclusion, believing that if a "monster" Murphy wagon actually did exist, only a very few were ever made, "and they had little or no use on the Santa Fe Trail." Correspondence of W. E. Givens with Marc Simmons, Doug Thamert, Charles Bennett, and Mark Gardner, 1991. Copies provided courtesy of Mr. Givens. In a 1989 article, the author suggested that Anselm's description might be applied to the Murphy wagons of another period, say the late 1850s, yet it is clear that his dimensions do not agree with what is known of these wagons as well. Suffice it to say, we will probably never know what Anselm Murphy was talking about. See Mark L. Gardner, "Conestogas on the Santa Fe Trail," in Gardner, ed., *The Mexican Road: Trade, Travel, and Confrontation on the Santa Fe Trail* (Manhattan, Kans.: Sunflower University Press, 1989): 96 n. 22.

35. There are examples of huge freight wagons, even what could be considered "monster wagons," that were built and used on routes other than the Santa Fe Trail,

although these vehicles date to a later period than the period discussed here. In 1876, a wagon built by Studebaker Brothers to be used in the mountains west of Denver was proclaimed the largest freight wagon in Colorado. It featured wheels six feet in diameter with hubs fourteen inches in diameter. The wagon weighed thirty-seven hundred pounds and was guaranteed to haul five tons but could support eight. An amazingly large wagon built for one of the mining districts in Mexico in the late 1870s had front wheels of seven feet in diameter and rear wheels of twelve feet. The width of the tread was twelve inches. The tires for the rear wheels weighed 1,250 pounds each! *The Daily Tribune* (Denver), Apr. 18, 1876; and Don Peloubet, *Wheelmaking: Wooden Wheel Design and Construction* (Mendham, N.J.: Astragal Press, 1996), 31. The largest wagon to travel the Santa Fe Trail was probably William Thomas's 1859 windwagon (discussed in chapter 9 of this book). See also the discussion of the Chihuahua wagon and the Stockton wagon in chapter 6.

36. Walker, *The Wagonmasters*, 97. Walker's sole source of information on Murphy is Bott's article, "Joseph Murphy's Contribution."

37. William Clark Breckenridge, "Freighters' Wagons Commonly Called Conestoga Wagons," in James Malcolm Breckenridge, *William Clark Breckenridge: Historical Research Writer and Bibliographer of Missouriana; His Life, Lineage and Writings* (St.Louis: J. M. Breckenridge, 1932), 233.

38. St. Louis *Missouri Republican*, Sept. 28, 1850, as quoted in Walker D. Wyman, "Freighting: A Big Business on the Santa Fe Trail," *The Kansas Historical Quarterly* 1 (November 1931): 20.

39. Jane Lenz Elder and David J. Weber, eds., *Trading in Santa Fe: John M. Kingsbury's Correspondence with James Josiah Webb, 1853–1861* (Dallas: Southern Methodist University Press, 1996), 33.

40. *U.S. Census: Products of Industry*, Fifth Ward, City of St. Louis, St. Louis County, Missouri, 1850, 284.

41. James Cox, *Old and New St. Louis*, 491.

42. James Green, *The Saint Louis Business Directory for the Year of Our Lord 1850* (St. Louis: M'Kee Printer, 1850), 94.

43. "The Trade and Commerce of St. Louis in 1850," *Merchants' Magazine and Commercial Review* 24 (March 1851): 316.

44. *U.S. Census: Products of Industry*, 1850, Third Ward, City of St. Louis, Missouri, 268, and Second Ward, City of St. Louis, 245.

45. Lloyd Espenschied, "Louis Espenschied and His Family," *Bulletin of the Missouri Historical Society* 18 (January 1962): 89 and 93–94; and Lowe, *Five Years a Dragoon*, 255.

46. The ten-thousand-pound hauling capacity, if correct, was probably achieved through overloading. Judge W. L. Kuykendall, *Frontier Days: A True Narrative of Striking Events on the Western Frontier* (N.p. [probably Denver]: J. M. and H. L. Kuykendall, 1917), 63.

47. Espenschied, "Louis Espenschied and His Family," 96–98.

48. Taylor & Crooks, *Sketch Book of Saint Louis* (St. Louis, Mo.: George Knapp & Co., 1858), 251–52; and Espenschied, "Louis Espenschied and His Family," 96.

49. Gregg, *Commerce of the Prairies*, 146–47.

50. William Watts Hart Davis, *El Gringo; or, New Mexico and Her People* (1857; repr. ed., Lincoln: University of Nebraska Press, 1982), 212.

51. H. Bailey Carroll and J. Villasana Haggard, eds. and trans., *Three New Mexico Chronicles* . . . (1942; repr. ed.; New York: Arno Press, 1967), 39.

52. Lewis E. Atherton, "Business Techniques in the Santa Fe Trade," *Missouri Historical Review* 34 (April 1940): 340.

53. "Official Roster of Kansas, 1854–1925," *Collections of the Kansas State Historical Society* 16 (1923–1925): 724–25 and 728; and Barry, *The Beginning of the West*, 183 and 220.

54. Jackson County Deed Record, vol. L, p. 340, Jackson County Clerk's Office, Independence, Missouri.

55. There is a James M. Pool listed as a private in the muster rolls of the Jackson County company of the First Regiment Missouri Volunteers, which was accepted into the service at Fort Leavenworth on June 6, 1846. However, would James Pool, blacksmith, have volunteered for a twelve-month stint when he had a promissory note that would come due before the end of that period? William Elsey Connelley, ed., *War with Mexico, 1846–1847: Doniphan's Expedition and the Conquest of New Mexico and California* (Kansas City: Bryant & Douglas Book and Stationery Co., 1907), 530 and 533.

56. James Pool vs. St. Vrain & McCarty, Case File no. 275a, District Court Records (1850), Santa Fe County, New Mexico State Records Center and Archives, Santa Fe.

57. Seventh U.S. Census, Santa Fe County, New Mexico, 347.

58. *The Missouri Magazine* 7 (January 1935): 11.

59. Francis, or Frank, Hahn is not among the significant Missouri wagon makers. A native of Germany, he first appears in the 1860 U.S. population schedules for Jackson County, where he is listed as a twenty-six-year-old wagon maker. His real estate was valued at five hundred dollars and his personal estate at fifty dollars, which explains why he was not listed in the industrial census for that same year (only individuals or firms with an annual product of five hundred dollars or more were enumerated). Hahn is found in the 1870 industrial census for Jackson County; his annual product at that time was valued at one thousand dollars. Hattie E. Poppino, ed., *Census of 1860, Population Schedules for Jackson County, Missouri* (Kansas City, Mo.: Mrs. Hattie E. Poppino, 1964); and *U.S. Census: Products of Industry*, 1870, Westport, First Ward, Jackson County, Missouri, 1.

60. "The Cover," *Bulletin of the Missouri Historical Society* 8 (April 1952): 225.

61. See Ron Vineyard's excellent study, *Virginia Freight Waggons, 1750–1850*, Colonial Williamsburg Foundation Library Research Report Series no. 345 (Williamsburg, Va.: Colonial Williamsburg Foundation Library, 1994); and Shumway and Frey, *Conestoga Wagon, 1750–1850*, 12–13.

62. My source was Poppino, *Census of 1850, Jackson County, Missouri*. Poppino claims to have found a total of forty-three wagon makers and wheelwrights in the 1850 census. Although her book was examined page by page, it is quite possible that

five individuals could have been missed, which is the difference between our two figures.

63. I corrected one entry, that of Jacob Leader, a wagon maker who was born in Pennsylvania. He is incorrectly given in the census as a native of Illinois. Not included in the list are five carriage makers (three born in Pennsylvania, two in Virginia) and one coach maker (born in Virginia).

64. Seventh U.S. Census, City of St. Louis, Missouri, Fifth ward, 214 and 215.

65. *The History of Jackson County, Missouri*, 874–75; Marilyn Ruth Crosswhite McLaughlin, "Independence, Jackson County, Missouri, c. 1827–1844: With Emphasis on Independence as Staging Area for Westward Commercial Movements" (Master's thesis, University of Washington, 1971), 149; and Wilcox, *Jackson County Pioneers*, 171 and 173.

CHAPTER 4

1. George Shumway and Howard C. Frey, *Conestoga Wagon, 1750–1850: Freight Carrier for 100 Years of America's Westward Expansion* (York, Pa.: George Shumway, 1968), 11–12; and Ron Vineyard, *Virginia Freight Waggons, 1750–1850*, Colonial Williamsburg Foundation Library Research Report Series no. 345 (Williamsburg, Va.: Colonial Williamsburg Foundation Library, 1994), 138–39.

2. Don H. Berkebile, *Carriage Terminology: An Historical Dictionary* (Washington, D.C.: Smithsonian Institution Press, 1978), 110; and Shumway and Frey, *Conestoga Wagon, 1750–1850*, 189.

3. William H. Richardson's *Journal of William H. Richardson, a Private Soldier in Col. Doniphan's Command* (Baltimore, 1848) contains a woodcut picturing Colonel Alexander Doniphan's army of Missouri Volunteers marching across the Jornada del Muerto of New Mexico. One of the wagons pictured in the scene, a Conestoga, features a tool box on the left side of the body.

4. Dimensions are given for a wagon in Joseph Murphy's earliest account book, in an undated entry that falls between accounts of 1826 and 1828, although there is no evidence that the wagon was ever intended for the Santa Fe trade. The vehicle was presumably ordered by a Mr. Rider, and the "whole length of the bottom sides" of the wagon was to be nine feet six inches and the width, three feet five inches. It was to have a "lose tongue" eleven feet long. The height of the rear wheels was to be four feet ten inches and the front wheels, three feet eight inches. The tread was to be one and a half inches wide. Because the wagon was to have a double tree, it is clear that it was intended for use with horses or mules. Unfortunately, such detailed dimensions as those provided for Mr. Rider's wagon (of which the above is only a summary) are an aberration in the Murphy account books. Joseph Murphy's order books, which were the proper place for recording the dimensions of wagons ordered, have not survived. See Account Book, 1825–1836, p. 6, Joseph Murphy Collection (microfilm), Missouri Historical Society, St. Louis (hereafter cited as JMC).

5. Frank S. Edwards, *A Campaign in New Mexico with Colonel Doniphan* (Philadelphia: Carey and Hart, 1847), 79–80.

6. Berkebile, *Carriage Terminology*, 110.

7. See Shumway and Frey, *Conestoga Wagon, 1750–1850*, 191–92.

8. John Omwake, *The Conestoga Six-Horse Bell Teams of Eastern Pennsylvania* (Cincinnati: The Ebbert & Richardson Co., 1930), 72; Shumway and Frey, *Conestoga Wagon, 1750–1850*, 182 and 188; and taped comments of Doug Thamert, Apr. 10, 1996, in the author's collection.

9. Berkebile, *Carriage Terminology*, 110.

10. Omwake, *The Conestoga Six-Horse Bell Teams*, 75.

11. Thomas J. Farnham, *Travels in the Great Western Prairies, the Anahuac and Rocky Mountains, and in the Oregon Territory* (New York: Greeley & McElrath, 1843), 15.

12. Julius Froebel, *Seven Years' Travel in Central America, Northern Mexico, and the Far West of the United States* (London: Richard Bentley, 1859), 239.

13. Josiah Gregg, *Commerce of the Prairies*, ed. Max L. Moorhead (Norman: University of Oklahoma Press, 1954), 27.

14. Martin Hardingham, *The Fabric Catalog* (New York: Pocket Books, 1978), 65.

15. A sale of seven pieces of "Hickory Axletree stuff" is found in one of Joseph Murphy's 1847 Day Book entries. Day Book, 1847–1853, p. 12, JMC.

16. Day Book, 1847–1853, pp. 22, 189, and 508, JMC.

17. Thamert comments, Apr. 10, 1996.

18. Invoice Book (Owens & Aull), Feb. 14, 1846–1847, p. 36, in James Aull Business Records, 1825–1851, Coll. no. 3001 (microfilm), Western Historical Manuscript Collection, Columbia, Missouri (hereafter cited as JABR).

19. James Pool vs. St. Vrain & McCarty, Case File no. 275a, District Court Records (1850), Santa Fe County, New Mexico State Records Center and Archives, Santa Fe.

20. See advertisement for P. Schuttler's Chicago Wagon Manufactory in Smith & DuMoulin, *Illinois State Business Directory, 1860* (Chicago: J. C. W. Bailey & Co., 1860), 460.

21. James Josiah Webb, *Adventures in the Santa Fe Trade, 1844–1847*, ed. Ralph P. Bieber, Southwest Historical Series, vol. 1 (Glendale, Calif.: Arthur H. Clark Co., 1931), 129–30. Webb contradicts himself later in his account, p. 300, when he states: "No iron axles were run on the prairie for carrying freight until 1848."

22. Day Book, 1847–1853, pp. 417 and 418, JMC.

23. Percival G. Lowe, *Five Years a Dragoon ('49 to '54) and Other Adventures on the Great Plains* (1906; repr. ed., Norman: University of Oklahoma Press, 1965), 255.

24. Thamert comments, Apr. 10, 1996.

25. W. B. Napton, *The Santa Fe Trail, 1857* (1905; repr. ed., Arrow Rock, Mo.: The Friends of Arrow Rock, 1991), 6.

26. Berkebile, *Carriage Terminology*, 110.

27. *Youatt's History, Treatment, and Diseases of the Horse . . . with a Treatise on Draught* (Philadelphia: J. B. Lippincott & Co., 1874), 436.

28. Shumway and Frey, *Conestoga Wagon, 1750–1850*, 206; and J. Geraint

Jenkins, *The English Farm Wagon, Origins and Structure* (Newton Abbot, England: David & Charles, 1981), 27–28.

29. John S. Foggett, "The Manufacture of Carriage Wheels," *Carriage Journal* 15 (Summer 1977): 236–38; and Thamert comments, Apr. 10, 1996.

30. Randolph B. Marcy, *The Prairie Traveler: A Hand-Book for Overland Expeditions* (New York: Harper & Brothers, 1859), 26.

31. Gregg, *Commerce of the Prairies*, 73.

32. Froebel, *Seven Years' Travel in Central America*, 226.

33. Gregg, *Commerce of the Prairies*, 73.

34. James A. Little, *What I Saw on the Old Santa Fe Trail* (Plainfield, Ind.: The Friends Press, 1904), 19. Marcy provides additional prairie repair methods. See his *The Prairie Traveler*, 71–74.

35. Day Book, 1847–1853, p. 13, JMC; and Invoice Book (Owens & Aull), Feb. 14, 1846–1847, p. 36, JABR.

36. Dale Morgan, ed., *Overland in 1846: Diaries and Letters of the California-Oregon Trail*, 2 vols. (1963; repr. ed., Lincoln: University of Nebraska Press, 1993), 2:474.

37. James Pool vs. St. Vrain & McCarty, Case File no. 275a, District Court Records (1850), Santa Fe County, New Mexico State Records Center and Archives, Santa Fe.

38. Day Book, 1847–1853, pp. 13, 88, 159, 417, and 418, JMC.

39. Jackson County Deed Record, vol. Y, pp. 106–9, Jackson County Clerk's Office, Independence, Missouri.

40. Max L. Moorhead, "Spanish Transportation in the Southwest, 1540–1846," *New Mexico Historical Review* 32 (April 1957): 119.

41. Berkebile, *Carriage Terminology*, 110.

42. Ibid., 339, 359, and 385; and Nick Eggenhofer, *Wagons, Mules and Men: How the Frontier Moved West* (New York: Hastings House, 1961), 42–44.

43. Berkebile, *Carriage Terminology*, 352.

44. A drop tongue was able to pivot because it was affixed to a second set of hounds mounted within the front hounds. See Berkebile, *Carriage Terminology*, 340 and 352. Eggenhofer illustrates a drop tongue in his *Wagons, Mules and Men*, 112.

45. Marcy, *The Prairie Traveler*, 26.

46. Day Book, 1847–1853, p. 249, JMC.

47. See Shumway and Frey, *Conestoga Wagon, 1750–1850*, 12.

48. Berkebile, *Carriage Terminology*, 110.

49. John W. Reps, *Saint Louis Illustrated: Nineteenth-Century Engravings and Lithographs of a Mississippi River Metropolis* (Columbia: University of Missouri Press, 1989), 34.

50. William Ellis vs. Phineas Skinner, Case File Drawer "1848/March," Circuit Court Records, Platte County Courthouse, Platte City, Missouri.

51. Froebel, *Seven Years' Travel in Central America*, 216.

52. Testimony of Mary Baxter and John Douglas, in Thomas J. Seehorn, Admin-

istrator of Hiram Young vs. U.S., Cong. Jurisdiction Case File no. 7320, Records of the United States Court of Claims (Record Group 123), National Archives.

53. See chapter 7 of this study, where the provision box is discussed; and Mark L. Gardner, "Discovered: Rare Independence-made Ox Yoke," *Wagon Tracks* (Quarterly of the Santa Fe Trail Association) 6 (May 1992): 16–17.

54. J. Everts Greene, *The Santa Fe Trade: Its Route and Character* (Worcester, Mass.: Press of Charles Hamilton, 1893), 17. One word of caution when examining primary accounts that include estimates of tonnage. In the mid-nineteenth century, a ton could equal either 2,000 pounds ("short ton") or 2,240 pounds ("long ton"), depending on the state or region. See Delos W. Beadle, *The American Lawyer, and Business-Man's Form-Book* (New York: Phelps, Fanning & Co., 1853), 355.

55. James Hall, *Letters from the West; Containing Sketches of Scenery, Manners, and Customs; and Anecdotes Connected with the First Settlements of the Western Sections of the United States* (1828; repr. ed.; Gainesville, Fla.: Scholars' Facsimiles & Reprints, 1967), 35.

56. Mathew C. Field, *Matt Field on the Santa Fe Trail*, ed. John E. Sunder, collected by Clyde and Mae Reed Porter (Norman: University of Oklahoma Press, 1960), 161.

57. Gregg, *Commerce of the Prairies*, 24.

58. James W. Abert, *Through the Country of the Comanche Indians in the Fall of the Year 1845*, ed. John Galvin (San Francisco: John Howell, 1970), 21.

59. Morgan, *Overland in 1846*, 2:474.

60. See *Report of the Quartermaster General* in H. R. Ex. Doc. 2, 32d Cong., 1st sess., 1851 (Serial 634), p. 296. I am indebted to Harry Myers for bringing this document to my attention.

61. Froebel, *Seven Years' Travel in Central America*, 225.

62. John Russell Bartlett, *Personal Narrative of Explorations and Incidents in Texas, New Mexico, California, Sonora, and Chihuahua . . .* , 2 vols. (1854; repr. ed., Chicago: The Rio Grande Press, 1965), 2:436.

63. Lowe, *Five Years a Dragoon*, 255.

64. Napton, *The Santa Fe Trail, 1857*, 6.

65. Invoice Book (Owens & Aull), Feb. 14, 1846–1847, p. 36, JABR.

66. Day Book, 1847–1853, pp. 86 and 288, JMC.

67. Bartlett, *Personal Narrative*, 2:436.

68. U.S. Congress, House, *Thomas S. J. Johnson. Mr. Ready, from the Committee of Claims, made the following Report*, H. R. Rep. 85, 33d Cong., 1st sess., 1854 (Serial 742), 5.

CHAPTER 5

1. Taylor & Crooks, *Sketch Book of Saint Louis* (St. Louis, Mo.: George Knapp & Co., 1858), 251–52.

2. *G. & D. Cook & Co.'s Illustrated Catalogue of Carriages and Special Business Advertiser* (New Haven, Conn.: G. & D. Cook & Co., 1860), 226.

3. Ibid.

4. Edwin T. Freedley, *Philadelphia and its Manufactures: A Hand-Book Exhibiting the Development, Variety, and Statistics of the Manufacturing Industry of Philadelphia in 1857* (Philadelphia: Edward Young, 1858), 448.

5. *Westport Border Star*, June 23, 1860.

6. Edwin T. Freedley, *A Treatise on the Principal Trades and Manufactures of the United States* (1856; repr. ed., New York: Garland Publishing, 1974), 119; and *Eighty Years' Progress of the United States: A Family Record of American Industry, Energy and Enterprise*, 2 vols. (Hartford, Conn.: L. Stebbins, 1867). 1:264.

7. Isaac Harris, *Harris' Pittsburgh & Allegheny Directory* (Pittsburgh: A. A. Anderson, 1839), 209.

8. Freedley, *A Treatise on the Principal Trades and Manufactures of the United States*, 560.

9. *U.S. Census: Products of Industry*, 1850, Cole County, Missouri, 50, State Historical Society of Missouri, Columbia, Missouri (microfilm). In 1856, C. W. Stuart, the factor at the Missouri Penitentiary, ran the following advertisement in the *Kansas City Enterprise* for several weeks beginning February 16: "The undersigned has on hand two hundred Wagons manufactured expressly for the Salt Lake, Santa Fe and California trade, which he will sell lower than they can be bought at any other establishment in the State. Emigrants and Traders will find it to their interest to examine his Wagons, at the Penitentiary in Jefferson City, before buying elsewhere."

10. *U.S. Census: Products of Industry*, 1860, City of St. Louis, Ninth Ward, 1, and Fifth Ward, 1, and Jackson County, Westport Division 35, 3.

11. The states with the highest number of carriage or wagon establishments using a waterwheel were New York (88), followed by Vermont (74) and Maine (47). Francis A. Walker, comp., *Ninth Census—Volume III: The Statistics of the Wealth and Industry of the United States . . . from the Original Returns of the Ninth Census . . .* (Washington, D. C.: Government Printing Office, 1872), 424.

12. *Westport Border Star*, Dec. 31, 1858, and May 20, 1859.

13. See John M. Peterson, "The Lawrence Windmill," *Kansas History* 3 (Autumn 1980): 147–64.

14. *U.S. Census: Products of Industry*, 1860, Jackson County, Missouri, City of Independence, 1; and *U.S. Census: Products of Industry*, 1870, Jackson County, Missouri, City of Independence, 1.

15. Inventories, Sale & Appraise Bills, Book B, 199, Jackson County Probate Records, Independence, Missouri.

16. *Scientific American*, Sept. 10, 1864.

17. Freedley, *Philadelphia and its Manufactures . . . in 1857*, 448.

18. M. T. Graham Mortgage Deed, Jackson County Deed Record, Vol. 37, p. 136, Jackson County Courthouse, Independence, Missouri; and *Westport Border Star*, June 23, 1860.

19. "Daniel's Planing Machine," *Scientific American*, Nov. 4, 1848; and *Westport Border Star*, June 23, 1860.

20. Carolyn C. Cooper, "A Patent Transformation: Woodworking Mechaniza-

tion in Philadelphia, 1830–1856," in Judith A. McGaw, ed., *Early American Technology: Making and Doing Things from the Colonial Era to 1850* (Chapel Hill: University of North Carolina Press, 1994), 296.

21. William L. Sims, *Two Hundred Years of History and Evolution of Woodworking Machinery* (Burton Lazaras, Leicestershire, England: Walders Press, 1985), 54.

22. J. Richards, *A Treatise on the Construction and Operation of Wood-Working Machines* (London: E. & F. N. Spon, 1872), 185–86. For an excellent illustration of a heavy swing saw from 1904, see Dana M. Batory, *Vintage Woodworking Machinery, An Illustrated Guide to Four Manufacturers* (Mendham, N.J.: Astragal Press, 1997), 73–74.

23. M. Powis Bale, *Woodworking Machinery: Its Rise, Progress, and Construction* (1880; repr. ed., Lakewood, Colo.: Glen Moor Press, 1992), 203.

24. *Westport Border Star*, June 23, 1860.

25. "Daniel's Planing Machine," *Scientific American*, Nov. 4, 1848.

26. Fitchburg Foundry and Machine Co. broadside, Henry Stevens Collection, Special Collections, University of Vermont Libraries, Burlington, Vermont; and C. L. Fleischmann, *Trade, Manufacture, and Commerce in the United States of America* (Stuttgart, Germany, 1852; English trans., Jerusalem: Israel Program for Scientific Translations, 1970), 124.

27. Richards, *A Treatise*, 53.

28. "Daniel's Planing Machine," *Scientific American*, Nov. 4, 1848.

29. Freedley, *Philadelphia and its Manufactures . . . in 1857*, 451; and *Eighty Years' Progress*, 1:367.

30. Freedley, *Philadelphia and its Manufactures . . . in 1857*, 448.

31. T. G. Turner, *Gazetteer of the St. Joseph Valley, Michigan and Indiana, with a View of its Hydraulic and Business Capacities* (Chicago: Hazlitt & Reed, 1867), 126.

32. Stephen Longstreet, *A Century on Wheels: The Story of Studebaker, A History, 1852–1952* (New York: Henry Holt and Company, 1952), 43.

33. *Rocky Mountain News*, Mar. 18, 1874. Two-thirds of the Studebaker factory burned in 1874, after which they immediately rebuilt on a larger scale. In 1895, Studebaker Brothers was "the largest wagon and carriage manufacturers in the world." Longstreet, *A Century on Wheels*, 43; and Chauncey Thomas, "American Carriage and Wagon Works," in Chauncey Depew, ed., *One Hundred Years of American Commerce*, 2 vols. (New York: D. O. Haynes & Co., 1895), 2:519.

34. Walker, *Ninth Census—Volume III*, 687.

35. *U.S. Census: Products of Industry*, 1870, Jackson County, Missouri, Kansas City First Ward, 1.

36. *U.S. Census: Products of Industry*, 1870, Jackson County, Missouri, City of Independence, 1. Robert Weston's partner was Bailey P. Strode, who had started working in Weston's shop at age fourteen. See Pearl Wilcox, *Jackson County Pioneers* (1975; repr. ed., Independence, Mo.: Jackson County Historical Society, 1990), 173.

37. Walker, *Ninth Census—Volume III*, 689.

38. *U.S. Census: Products of Industry*, 1870, St. Louis County, Missouri, Subdivision 9, p. 5; Subdivision 18, pp. 27, 49, and 64; and Subdivision 20, p. 3.

39. For example, Semple, Birge & Co. of St. Louis, agents for the Whitewater wagon manufactured in Whitewater, Wisconsin, advertised Whitewater farm, plantation, and freight wagons in the *Trinidad Enterprise* (Colorado) of July 25, 1873. For a description of Semple, Birge & Co., see J. A. Dacus and James W. Buel, *A Tour of St. Louis; or the Inside Life of a Great City* (St. Louis: Western Publishing Company, 1878), 250–53.

40. Francis A. Walker and Chas W. Seaton, comps., *Report on the Manufactures of the United States at the Tenth Census (June 1, 1880) . . .* (Washington, D.C.: Government Printing Office, 1883), 280 and 432–33.

41. Ibid., 231 and 432.

42. Ibid., 242; and W. S. Burke and J. L. Rock, *The History of Leavenworth, the Metropolis of Kansas, and the Chief Commercial Center West of the Missouri River* (Leavenworth: The Leavenworth Times Book and Job Printing Establishment, 1880), 35–36.

43. The contract entered into between the penitentiary and the officials of the Kansas Manufacturing Company is found in Frank M. Gable, "The Kansas Penitentiary," in William E. Connelley, ed., *Collections of the Kansas State Historical Society, 1915–1918*, vol. 14 (Topeka: Kansas State Printing Plant, 1918): 399–402. The average daily wage for Murphy's workers is in *U.S. Census: Products of Industry*, 1880, City of St. Louis, St. Louis County, Missouri.

44. Burke and Rock, *History of Leavenworth*, 35–36; and *The Leading Industries of Leavenworth, Kansas* (Leavenworth, Kans.: Commercial and Manufacturing Publishing Company, 1883), 9.

45. Quoted in Gable, "The Kansas Penitentiary," 407.

46. W. R. Holloway, *Indianapolis: A Historical and Statistical Sketch of the Railroad City* (Indianapolis: Indianapolis Journal Print, 1870), 364.

47. *Eighty Years' Progress*, 1:367.

48. *U.S. Census: Products of Industry*, 1870, St. Louis County, Missouri, City of St. Louis, subdivision 15, p. 6.

49. Richard Hegel, *Carriages from New Haven: New Haven's Nineteenth-Century Carriage Industry* (Hamden, Conn.: Archon Books, 1974), 49.

50. "The Wagon Hardware Trade," *Scientific American*, Dec. 6, 1879.

51. Burke and Rock, *The History of Leavenworth*, 35.

52. Don Peloubet, ed., *Wheelmaking: Wooden Wheel Design and Construction* (Mendham, N.J.: Astragal Press, 1996), 54.

53. See Charles Eckhart, "How Carriages Were Built in Early Days," in John Thompson, *The Wheelwright's Trade* (Fleet, Hampshire, U.K.: John Thompson, 1983), 19.

Chapter 6

1. This issue of the *Western Journal of Commerce* has not survived. However, the article was reprinted in the Prairie City, Kansas, *Freemen's Champion* of June 24, 1858. It is reproduced in its entirety in this volume's appendix A.

2. *Westport Border Star*, June 23, 1860.

3. In a letter dated Independence, June 6, 1859, Charles W. Fribley wrote of the "Santa Fe Wagon (as all the largest sized freight wagons are called in this country)." Charles W. Fribley, "Charles W. Fribley's Trail Diary and Letters, 1857–1859," ed. David L. Richards, pt. 2, *Wagon Tracks* (Quarterly of the Santa Fe Trail Association) 13 (November 1998): 24.

4. C. L. Fleischmann, *Trade, Manufacture, and Commerce in the United States of America* (Stuttgart, Germany, 1852; English trans., Jerusalem: Israel Program for Scientific Translations, 1970), 93–94.

5. J. Richards, *A Treatise on the Construction and Operation of Wood-Working Machines* (London: E. & F. N. Spon, 1872), 125. Mark Twain expressed similar thoughts. Writing in his notebook in 1883, Twain commented that an Englishman was a "person who does things because they have been done before," and an American was a "person who does things because they haven't been done before." Albert Bigelow Paine, ed., *Mark Twain's Notebook* (New York: Harper & Brothers, 1935), 169.

6. There exists another photograph of this particular warehouse, which was taken immediately before or after Fig. 6.3. It features a wider view of the warehouse and wagons at the loading dock. This photograph is in the collections of the Kansas State Historical Society, Topeka.

7. The Pioneer Village Museum of Salt Lake City was purchased several years ago by the Lagoon Corporation and moved to Farmington, Utah. According to the current curator, Mr. Howard Freed, some artifacts did not make the transfer, and the wagon in question appears to fall into that category. However, Mr. Freed states that there are three similar freight wagons in his collection, although they are in very poor condition. Telephone conversation with the author, Nov. 13 and 21, 1996.

8. A wonderful painting of a Santa Fe Trail freight train, circa 1872, is "Ships of the Plains" by Samuel Colman (1832–1920). A work of oil on canvas, 48 x 92 inches, it depicts several ox-drawn wagons and teamsters in action. The lead vehicle, a Santa Fe wagon, has the words "Kit Carson" painted on the front of the canvas cover. This may denote the town of Kit Carson, Colorado Territory, established as a railhead on the Kansas Pacific in 1870. Marked on one of the wooden crates in this wagon is the word *Trinidad*. Trinidad, Colorado Territory, was one of the stops on the route from Kit Carson to Santa Fe. Colman is known to have been in the West during this period. His "Ships of the Plains" is the property of the Union League Club of New York City, and although it has been reproduced several times in modern publications, it has never been correctly identified as a Santa Fe Trail caravan.

9. Homer W. Wheeler, *The Frontier Trail, or from Cowboy to Colonel* (Los Angeles: Times-Mirror Press, 1923), 52.

10. George Curry, *George Curry, 1861–1947: An Autobiography*, ed. H. B. Hening (Albuquerque: University of New Mexico Press, 1958), 8.

11. Sometimes several empty wagons were connected in order to reduce the number of teams and teamsters needed. In 1862, Robert M. Wright was "going east with one of Majors, Russell and Waddell's large ox trains. I think we had thirty or

forty wagons, with six yoke of oxen to the wagon. Our wagons were strung five or six together and one team of six yoke cattle attached to each string." Wright, "Personal Reminiscences of Frontier Life in Southwest Kansas," in George W. Martin, ed., *Transactions of the Kansas State Historical Society, 1901–1902*, vol. 7 (Topeka: W. Y. Morgan, 1902): 51.

12. See William E. Lass, *From the Missouri to the Great Salt Lake: An Account of Overland Freighting*, Nebraska State Historical Society Publications, vol. 26 (Lincoln: Nebraska State Historical Society, 1972), 14–16; and Michael H. Piatt, "Hauling Freight into the 20th Century by Jerk Line," *Journal of the West* 36 (January 1997): 87–88.

13. As quoted in Lloyd Espenschied, "Louis Espenschied and His Family," *Bulletin of the Missouri Historical Society* 18 (January 1962): 96.

14. *Factura* prepared by Glasgow & Brother, March 31, 1863, José Felipe Chaves Papers, University of New Mexico Library, Special Collections, Albuquerque. In 1858, Glasgow & Brother purchased twenty wagons (132 dollars each) of maker Jacob Kern for Felipe Chaves. See *Factura* in Glasgow & Brother statement of June 30, 1858.

15. *U.S. Census: Products of Industry*, 1880, City of St. Louis, St. Louis County, Missouri (microfilm), State Historical Society of Missouri, Columbia.

16. Espenschied, "Louis Espenschied and His Family," 101 and 103.

17. *U.S. Census: Products of Industry*, 1880, City of St. Louis, St. Louis County, Missouri.

18. James Cox, *Old and New St. Louis: A Concise History of the Metropolis of the West and Southwest, with a Review of its Present Greatness and Immediate Prospects* (St. Louis: Central Biographical Publishing Co., 1894), 491.

19. William F. Cody, *Buffalo Bill's Own Story of His Life and Deeds*, "Memorial Edition" (N.p.: John R. Stanton, 1917), 46.

20. Las Animas County Deed Record, vol. 2, p. 451, Las Animas County Courthouse, Trinidad, Colorado. An advertisement in the *Leavenworth Daily Times* of May 16, 1866, offered "Heavy Freight Wagons for sale, very low, designed to carry sixty hundred pounds."

21. Testimony of Dudley Crittenden, in Thomas J. Seehorn, Administrator of Hiram Young vs. U. S., Cong. Jurisdiction Case File no. 7320, Records of the United States Court of Claims (Record Group 123), National Archives.

22. See Charles Collins, *Collins' City Directory of Leavenworth* (Leavenworth, Kans.: Charles Collins, 1866), 225.

23. *U.S. Census: Products of Industry*, 1870, First Ward, City of Independence, Jackson County, Missouri, 1; Ninth U.S. Census, First Ward, City of Independence, Jackson County, Missouri, 267; and *U.S. Census: Products of Industry*, 1880, Independence, Jackson County, Missouri, Enumeration Dist. No. 26.

24. *Westport Border Star*, Dec. 31, 1858, and May 20, 1859.

25. *Westport Border Star*, May 20, 1859, and June 23, 1860.

26. Jackson County Deed Record, vol. 37, pp. 136–38, Jackson County Clerk's Office, Independence, Missouri.

27. Testimony of Henry Crump, in Thomas J. Seehorn, Administrator of Hiram Young vs. U. S., Cong. Jurisdiction Case File no. 7320, Records of the United States Court of Claims (Record Group 123), National Archives.

28. *U.S. Census: Products of Industry*, 1870, Third Ward Westport, Jackson County, Missouri, 1.

29. Ibid.

30. *The History of Jackson County, Missouri* (1881; repr. ed., Cape Girardeau, Mo.: Ramfre Press, 1966), 752.

31. Inventories, Sale & Appraise Bills, Book B, 165 and 168, Jackson County Probate Records, Independence, Missouri.

32. Inventories, Sale & Appraise Bills, Book B, 197–98, Jackson County Probate Records, Independence, Missouri; and *U.S. Census: Products of Industry*, Kansas City Division 35, Jackson County, Missouri, 1.

33. T. G. Turner, *Gazetteer of the St. Joseph Valley, Michigan and Indiana, with a View of its Hydraulic and Business Capacities* (Chicago: Hazlitt & Reed, 1867), vii.

34. Reprinted 1967 by Newburg-Historical Publishers, Cleveland, Ohio. It should be noted that this same engraving is also reproduced on another page of the price list and given the title of "The Nevada Iron Axle Wagons."

35. Eugene F. Ware, *The Indian War of 1864* (1911; repr. ed., New York: St. Martin's Press, 1960), 102.

36. Gerhard Stullken, *My Experience on the Plains* (Wichita, Kans.: The Grit Printery, 1913), 9.

37. *Out West* (Colorado Springs), July 18, 1872, quoted from the St. Louis *Missouri Republican*.

38. Howard Louis Conard, *"Uncle Dick" Wootton: The Pioneer Frontiersman of the Rocky Mountain Region* (Chicago: W. E. Dibble & Co., 1890), 327.

39. Turner, *Gazetteer of the St. Joseph Valley*, 55. As early as 1879, there was a Milburn Wagon Company manufacturing wagons in Toledo, Ohio. An 1899 promotional notepad from the company states that the firm "commenced building Farm Wagons in 1848." Did George Milburn & Co. relocate to Toledo, less than 150 miles from Mishawaka? Did the Indiana company sell its name to the Toledo firm? Or is it simply that the Toledo factory took its name from another Milburn, one with no relationship to George Milburn of Indiana?

40. Ken Wheeling, "Trans-Mississippi Transport: Part VII—The Schuttler Wagons: Triumph and Tragedy," *The Carriage Journal* 30 (Spring 1993): 154–55.

41. William B. Horner, *The Gold Regions of Kansas and Nebraska* (Chicago: Wm. H. Tobey & Co., 1859).

42. Smith & DuMoulin, *Illinois State Business Directory, 1860* (Chicago: J. C. W. Bailey & Co., 1860), 460.

43. *The Daily Chieftain* (Pueblo, Colo.), Apr. 28, 1872.

44. Wheeling, "Trans-Mississippi Transport: Part VII," 155.

45. John Warner Barber and Henry Howe, *Our Whole Country: or the Past and Present of the United States, Historical and Descriptive*, 2 vols. (Cincinnati: Henry Howe, 1861), 2:1289.

46. Austin, Tomlinson & Webster Mfg. Co., Jackson, Mich., 1883 Price List, author's collection; and Wheeling, "Trans-Mississippi Transport: Part VII," 156.

47. William Henry Jackson, *The Diaries of William Henry Jackson, Frontier Photographer*, ed. LeRoy R. Hafen and Ann W. Hafen, The Far West and the Rockies Historical Series, vol. 10 (Glendale, Calif.: 1959), 34.

48. *Gazetteer and Directory of the State of Kansas* (Lawrence, Kans.: Blackburn & Co., 1870), 197.

49. The University of Virginia library has in its collections an 1890 price list for Austin, Tomlinson & Webster.

50. U.S. Congress, Senate, *Letter From the Secretary of the Interior, Transmitting, in response to a resolution of the Senate relative to the rejection of certain bids for wagons for the Indian service, a report of the Commissioner of Indian Affairs and accompanying correspondence*, S. Ex. Doc. 210, 46th Cong., 2d sess., 1880 (Serial 1886), 18 and 23.

51. W. S. Burke and J. L. Rock, *The History of Leavenworth, the Metropolis of Kansas, and the Chief Commercial Center West of the Missouri River* (Leavenworth: The Leavenworth Times Book and Job Printing Establishment, 1880), 35.

52. Burke and Rock, *The History of Leavenworth*, 37; Seventh U.S. Census, Manchester Borough, Allegheny County, Pennsylvania, 331; and Tenth U.S. Census, Leavenworth County, Kansas, Enum. Dist. 161, 25.

53. U.S. Congress, Senate, *Letter from the Secretary of the Interior*, 25.

54. Ibid., 26.

55. Ibid., 27.

56. William Hyde and Howard L. Conard, *Encyclopedia of the History of St. Louis*, 4 vols. (St. Louis: Southern History Company, 1899), 2:802.

57. August Santleben, *A Texas Pioneer: Early Staging and Overland Freighting Days on the Frontiers of Texas and Mexico*, ed. I. D. Affleck (New York: The Neal Publishing Company, 1910), 109–11.

58. A William Henry Jackson photograph of Chihuahua City's Guadalupe Street, taken circa 1883, shows several carretas and, in the distance, some large freight wagons. See Museum of New Mexico (Palace of the Governors) photo negative number 54088.

59. As quoted in R. R. Olmsted, ed., *Scenes of Wonder & Curiosity from Hutchings' California Magazine, 1856–1861* (Berkeley, Calif.: Howell-North, 1962), 379.

60. The negative of this photograph, No. P-153, is on file in the National Museum of American History's Transportation Division. It is also in the collections of the Library of Congress (Neg. No. USZ62-13355). My thanks to Lonn Taylor, historian at the National Museum, for alerting me to this image.

61. Nick Eggenhofer, *Wagons, Mules and Men: How the Frontier Moved West* (New York: Hastings House, 1961), 83.

62. See Nick Eggenhofer, *Horses, Horses, Always Horses: The Life and Art of Nick Eggenhofer* (Cody, Wyo.: Sage Publishing Co., 1981), 148.

CHAPTER 7

1. Jackson W. Moore, *Bent's Old Fort: An Archeological Study* (Denver: State Historical Society of Colorado and Pruett Publishing Co., 1973), 36–37.

2. These artifacts are currently housed in a museum storage facility at Bent's Old Fort National Historic Site, near La Junta, Colorado.

3. I am speaking primarily of the pipe boxes found in level six of Room NW 1. See Moore, *Bent's Old Fort*, 18.

4. Object No. T-66, Missouri State Society Daughters of American Revolution, Old Tavern, Arrow Rock, Missouri, Museum Catalog Record, 410, now part of the collections of Arrow Rock State Historic Site.

5. Raymond W. Settle and Mary Lund Settle, *Empire on Wheels* (Stanford, Calif.: Stanford University Press, 1949), 4; and Alexander Majors, *Seventy Years on the Frontier*, ed. Prentiss Ingraham (Chicago: Rand, McNally & Co., 1893). 15.

6. I have also examined another large wagon running gear not far from Fort Garland, at the Fort Francisco Plaza Museum in La Veta, Colorado, but have not yet been able to take measurements.

7. Museum Catalog Sheet, Frontier Army Museum, Fort Leavenworth, Kansas.

8. Richard M. Davis, "Where have all the wagons gone? (Part II)," *Overland Journal* 16 (Summer 1998): 38–39.

9. Lloyd Espenschied, "Louis Espenschied and His Family," *Bulletin of the Missouri Historical Society* 18 (January 1962): 98. Henry Espenschied was a brother, and competitor, of Louis.

10. Marc Simmons, *Murder on the Santa Fe Trail: An International Incident, 1843* (El Paso: Texas Western Press, 1987), 74.

11. Richard F. Burton, *The City of the Saints and across the Rocky Mountains* (1862; repr. ed.; Niwot: University Press of Colorado, 1990), 22.

12. Inventories, Sale & Appraise Bills, Book B, 199, Jackson County Probate Records, Independence, Missouri.

13. D. M. Draper, "The Santa Fe Trail in '61: Personal reminiscences [*sic*] of a 'train' conductor before the railroads came," Denver Public Library, Western History Collection. The tools provided for Draper's train were "an old axe that was no longer of any use at the wood pile, a brace, some bits, an auger and a chisel."

CHAPTER 8

1. Meredith Miles Marmaduke, "Santa Fe Trail: M. M. Marmaduke Journal," ed. Francis A. Sampson, *Missouri Historical Review* 6 (October 1911): 3.

2. John Russell Bartlett, *Dictionary of Americanisms* (Boston: Little, Brown and Company, 1860), 117.

3. Don H. Berkebile, *Carriage Terminology: An Historical Dictionary* (Washington, D.C.: Smithsonian Institution Press, 1978), 121.

4. John A. Paxton, *The St. Louis Directory and Register* (St. Louis: John A. Paxton, 1821).

5. Berkebile, *Carriage Terminology*, 121.

6. John Glover, "Westward along the Boone's Lick Trail in 1826, The Diary of Colonel John Glover," ed. Marie George Windell, *Missouri Historical Review* 39 (January 1943): 193.

7. As quoted in Nicholas Perkins Hardeman, *Wilderness Calling: The Hardeman Family in the American Westward Movement* (Knoxville: University of Tennessee Press, 1977), 102.

8. John Russell Bartlett, *Dictionary of Americanisms* (1848; repr. ed., New York: Crescent Books, 1989), 65.

9. Mathew C. Field, *Matt Field on the Santa Fe Trail*, ed. John E. Sunder, collected by Clyde and Mae Reed Porter (Norman: University of Oklahoma Press, 1960), 74–75.

10. George W. Kendall, *Narrative of an Expedition across the Great South-Western Prairies, from Texas to Santa Fe*, 2 vols. (London: David Bogue, 1845), 1:72 and 85.

11. Louise Barry, *The Beginning of the West: Annals of the Kansas Gateway to the American West, 1540–1854* (Topeka: Kansas State Historical Society, 1972), 1099.

12. Frederick Adolphus Wislizenus, *Memoir of a Tour to Northern Mexico, Connected with Col. Doniphan's Expedition, in 1846 and 1847* (1848; repr. ed., Albuquerque: Calvin Horn, 1969), 5.

13. Mark L. Gardner, ed., *Brothers on the Santa Fe and Chihuahua Trails: Edward James Glasgow and William Henry Glasgow, 1846–1848* (Niwot: University Press of Colorado, 1993), 78. Another reference to a dug out can be found in a letter written by Joseph P. Hamelin from Chihuahua, Mexico, in 1847. See James Aull and Robert Aull, "Letters of James and Robert Aull," ed. Ralph P. Bieber, *Missouri Historical Society Collections* 5 (1928): 297.

14. Invoice Book (Owens & Aull), Feb. 14, 1846–1847, p. 36, in James Aull Business Records, 1825–1851, Coll. no. 3001 (microfilm), Western Historical Manuscript Collection, Columbia, Missouri.

15. St. Louis *Daily Reveille*, Sept. 8, 1846.

16. Bartlett, *Dictionary of Americanisms* (1848), 52. In the 1860 edition of this work, Bartlett changed his definition to read "one or two horses."

17. *Jefferson Inquirer* (Jefferson City, Mo.), June 24, 1846; and St. Louis *Daily Reveille*, July 3, 1846.

18. John Greiner, "Private Letters of a Government Official in the Southwest," ed. Tod B. Galloway, *Journal of American History* 3 (1909): 542.

19. Susan Shelby Magoffin, *Down the Santa Fe Trail and into Mexico: The Diary of Susan Shelby Magoffin, 1846–1847*, ed. Stella M. Drumm (New Haven: Yale University Press, 1926), 25 and 4. I am indebted to Marc Simmons for bringing this reference to my attention and to Doug Thamert for providing me with much useful material on Rockaways.

20. Berkebile, *Carriage Terminology*, 151. An 1865 advertisement for Clarke's Carriage Repository and Wagon Depot of Leavenworth, Kansas, lists both Rockaways and "Germantown Wagons." Braunhold & [?], *Leavenworth City Directory and Business Mirror for 1865–66* (Leavenworth, Kams.: Braunhold & [?]), 52.

21. Henry William Herbert, *Hints to Horse-Keepers, A Complete Manual for Horsemen* (New York: A. O. Moore & Company, 1859), 379–80.

22. These curtains and even the tops of the carriages were not all that helpful in truly severe weather. Thomas J. Farnham writes of his efforts to weatherproof a carryall upon the approach of a storm in 1839: "I drew the carryall . . . close to the Santa Fe wagons, secured the curtains as firmly as I was able to do, spread blankets over the top and around the sides, and lashed them firmly with ropes passing over, under, and around the carriage in every direction; but to little use. The penetrating powers of that storm were not resisted by such means." Farnham and his companion were "thoroughly drenched." Thomas J. Farnham, *Travels in the Great Western Prairies, the Anahuac and Rocky Mountains, and in the Oregon Territory* (New York: Greeley & McElrath, 1843), 18.

23. For a discussion of the history of the Rockaway, see Ezra M. Stratton, *The World on Wheels; or Carriages, with their Historical Associations from the Earliest to the Present Time* (1878; repr. ed., New York: Benjamin Blom, 1972), 444–46.

24. Kendall, *Narrative of an Expedition,* 1:351.

25. George A. F. Ruxton, *Adventures in Mexico and the Rocky Mountains* (London: John Murray, 1847), 110.

26. See Anna Belle Cartwright, ed., "William James Hinchey: An Irish Artist on the Santa Fe Trail," *Wagon Tracks* (Quarterly of the Santa Fe Trail Association) 10 (May 1996): 11–23; (August 1996): 12–22; and 11 (November 1996): 10–18.

27. "Carriage Building in America," *Carriage Journal* 2 (Summer 1964): 31.

28. Edward K. Eckert and Nicholas J. Amato, eds., *Ten Years in the Saddle: The Memoir of William Woods Averell, 1851–1862* (San Rafael, Calif.: Presidio Press, 1978), 89.

29. See Berkebile, *Carriage Terminology,* 18.

30. Julius Froebel, *Seven Years' Travel in Central America, Northern Mexico, and the Far West of the United States* (London: Richard Bentley, 1859), 239.

31. Mamie Bernard Aguirre, "Spanish Trader's Bride," *The Westport Historical Quarterly* 4 (December 1969): 10.

32. Howard Louis Conard, *"Uncle Dick" Wootton: The Pioneer Frontiersman of the Rocky Mountain Region* (Chicago: W. E. Dibble & Co., 1890), 325.

33. *Kansas City Directory, and Business Mirror, for 1860–61* (Indianapolis, Ind.: James Sutherland, 1860), 68. According to the 1860 industrial census, Wiley's "New Carriage Factory" was a rather small operation. He employed two men and produced eight carriages worth sixteen hundred dollars. If Wiley's "factory" was indeed new in 1860, however, that might explain these low figures. *U.S. Census: Products of Industry,* 1860, Jackson County, Missouri, Kansas City Division 35, 1 (microfilm), State Historical Society of Missouri, Columbia.

34. *U.S. Census: Products of Industry,* 1850, Fourth Ward, City of St. Louis, St. Louis County, Missouri, 271.

35. Barton H. Barbour, ed., *Reluctant Frontiersman: James Ross Larkin on the Santa Fe Trail, 1856–57* (Albuquerque: University of New Mexico Press, 1990), 4, 124, and 137 n.2.

36. *Kansas City Enterprise*, Mar.1, 1856; and *U.S. Census: Products of Industry*, 1860, Sixth Ward, City of St. Louis, 14.

37. *Edwards' Annual Directory to the . . .City of St. Louis, for 1866* (St. Louis: Edwards' Directory Office, 1866), 331; and *U.S. Census: Products of Industry*, 1870, Subdivision no. 15, City of St. Louis, 18. Robert Dougherty is not found in the industrial census for 1880. However, James Dougherty, Robert's brother, is listed as a manufacturer of carriages.

38. Berkebile, *Carriage Terminology*, 132 and 134.

39. This sketch is reproduced in Cartwright, "William James Hinchey," 15.

40. Randy Steffen, *The Horse Soldier, 1776–1943* (Norman: University of Oklahoma Press, 1978), 2:202 and 204; and *Manual for the Quartermaster Corps, United States Army, 1916, Appendix* (Washington, D.C.: Government Printing Office, 1917), 299.

41. Day Book, 1847–1853, 525, Joseph Murphy Collection (microfilm), Missouri Historical Society, St. Louis.

42. Barry, *The Beginning of the West*, 642.

43. Magoffin, *Down the Santa Fe Trail*, 25.

44. *The Kansas Press* (Council Grove), Mar. 19, 1860. Parker's train also had fourteen passengers, "six of whom were ladies."

45. *Missouri Intelligencer*, June 19, 1825.

CHAPTER 9

1. See Walter Blair, *Tall Tale America: A Legendary History of Our Humorous Heroes* (New York: Coward, McCann & Geoghegan, 1944); Wilbur Schramm, *Windwagon Smith and Other Yarns* (New York: Harcourt, Brace and Co., 1947); Vera J. Prout, *Prairie Windwagon* (New York: Dodd, Mead & Company, 1958); Mary Calhoun, *High Wind for Kansas* (New York: William Morrow & Co., 1965); Ennis Rees, *Windwagon Smith* (Englewood Cliffs, N.J.: Prentice Hall, 1966); and Ramona Maher, *When Windwagon Smith Came to Westport* (New York: Coward, McCann & Geoghegan, 1977). The Disney cartoon is *The Saga of Windwagon Smith*, released in 1961 with a running time of thirteen minutes. See Dave Smith, *Disney A to Z: The Official Encyclopedia* (New York: Hyperion, 1996), 428.

2. See "Westport's Dry-Land Navy," *Kansas City Star*, Aug. 6, 1905.

3. Patent File no. 23277 for William Thomas, Records of the Patent Office (Record Group 241) (hereafter cited as Thomas patent file).

4. Jackson County Deed Record, Vol. 5, p. 600, Jackson County Courthouse, Independence, Missouri (I am grateful to the late Pauline Fowler for a copy of this deed record); and "A Wind-Wagon," *Missouri Historical Review* 31 (October 1936): 85. Allen T. Ward had been experimenting with a windmill design as early as 1850. He wrote his sister on September 1 of that year that his "last model was very sattisfactory [*sic*] & proved that it is the proper power for this country . . . it is on the self adjusting principle, it turns itself to face the wind, & the sails are so arranged with springs that they yield to the force of the wind when it blows hard, so that it will not run much faster in a hurricane than in a light breeze, if I was going to build

a mill for grinding grain or sawing lumber, I would use wind power." Ward moved to Paola, Kansas, in 1855. Allen T. Ward, "Letters of Allen T. Ward, 1842–1851, From the Shawnee and Kaw (Methodist) Missions," ed. Lela Barnes, *Kansas Historical Quarterly* 33 (Autumn 1967): 371 and 322.

5. St. Louis *Missouri Republican*, Apr. 20, 1859, as quoted in LeRoy R. Hafen, ed., *Colorado Gold Rush: Contemporary Letters and Reports, 1858–1859* (Glendale, Calif.: Arthur H. Clark Co., 1941), 297.

6. Eighth U.S. Census, Division 35, Jackson County, Missouri, 166; and Hattie E. Poppino, ed., *Census of 1860, Population Schedules for Jackson County, Missouri* (Kansas City, Mo.: Mrs. Hattie E. Poppino, 1964), 242–43.

7. Ibid.

8. Rocky M. Thomas is also listed in the 1870 census, living in the household of his brother, Benton Thomas. Ninth U.S. Census, Westport Township, Jackson County, Missouri, 47.

9. Ninth U.S. Census, Westport Township, Jackson County Missouri, 53.

10. LeRoy R. Hafen, ed., *Overland Routes to the Gold Fields, 1859, from Contemporary Diaries* (Glendale, Calif.: Arthur H. Clark Co., 1942), 29.

11. *Westport Border Star*, Apr. 22, 1859.

12. Louise Barry, *The Beginning of the West: Annals of the Kansas Gateway to the American West, 1540–1854* (Topeka: Kansas State Historical Society, 1972), 650–51.

13. St. Louis *Weekly Reveille*, May 10, 1847.

14. The *Tri-Weekly Post* of Springfield, Mass., picked up the *Republican*'s article and ran it in its issue of Dec. 19, 1846. I am grateful to Marc Simmons for alerting me to this article.

15. St. Louis *Weekly Reveille*, Nov. 30, 1846.

16. Ward, "Letters of Allen T. Ward," 347.

17. St. Louis *Daily Union*, Apr. 12, 1847. Like previous reports, the *Daily Union* copied its information from the Independence *Western Expositor*.

18. *Jefferson Inquirer* (Jefferson City, Mo.), July 17, 1847.

19. St. Louis *Daily Reveille*, July 30, 1847.

20. As quoted in William A. Goff, *Old Westport* (N.p., 1977), 17.

21. *Westport Border Star*, Apr. 22, 1859.

22. Ibid.

23. Sager is listed in the 1850 census as a miller. He is best known, however, as a Westport cabinet maker and furniture dealer. Interestingly, his first wife, Mary Matney, was born in Benton County, Arkansas, in 1823. Seventh U.S. Census, Kaw Township, Jackson County, Missouri, 239; Eighth U.S. Census, Westport Div. 35, Jackson County, Missouri, 120; and Ancestral File, Church of Jesus Christ of Latter-day Saints database, 1996.

24. "Westport's Dry-Land Navy," *Kansas City Star*, Aug. 6, 1905.

25. John S. Hough, "Old Westport," typescript in Adrienne Tinker Christopher Papers, Western Historical Manuscript Collection, Columbia, Missouri. Hough resided in Westport from 1855 to 1865. See Mark L. Gardner, "John Simpson

Hough: Merchant on the Trail," *Wagon Tracks* (Quarterly of the Santa Fe Trail Association) 2 (February 1988): 10.

26. *Jefferson Examiner* (Jefferson City, Mo.), Apr. 30, 1859. *Westport Border Star* editor H. M. McCarty may also have been an investor in the windwagon. See the Kansas City *Daily Journal of Commerce*, Aug. 30, 1859.

27. W. L. Webb, *The Centennial History of Independence, Mo.* (Independence: Lambert-Moon Printing Co., 1927), 235–36.

28. St. Louis *Missouri Republican*, Apr. 20, 1859, as quoted in Hafen, *Colorado Gold Rush*, 297.

29. *Jefferson Examiner*, Apr. 30, 1859.

30. Hafen, *Overland Routes to the Gold Fields*, 29.

31. George A. Storz, "My First Trip to the Rocky Mountains at Age 18," in *Las Animas County, Interviews Collected during 1933–34 for the State Historical Society of Colorado*, vol. 2 (DeBusk Memorial), Colorado Historical Society, Denver, Colorado.

32. Don H. Berkebile, *Carriage Terminology: An Historical Dictionary* (Washington, D.C.: Smithsonian Institution Press, 1978), 205.

33. Ibid., 205–7.

34. *Westport Border Star*, Apr. 22, 1859.

35. Thomas patent file.

36. "Windwagon Was Too Speedy for These Pioneers of Old Westport," *Kansas City Journal-Post*, Jan. 4, 1931.

37. Thomas patent file.

38. Ibid.

39. St. Louis *Missouri Republican*, Nov. 30, 1846.

40. Thomas patent file.

41. Ibid.; and Brooke Hindle and Steven Lubar, *Engines of Change: The American Industrial Revolution, 1790–1860* (Washington, D.C.: Smithsonian Institution Press, 1986), 79. As part of the patent application process, not only were a written description and drawings required, but also a model. William Thomas's application shows that a model of his windwagon was indeed submitted. After 1880, however, when the Patent Office dropped the model requirement, all the patent models were disposed of in various ways. The Smithsonian Institution has many patent models in its collections but not, unfortunately, the model for the windwagon. Its current location is unknown. See Barbara Suit Janssen, ed., *Icons of Invention: American Patent Models* (Washington, D.C.: Smithsonian Institution, 1990).

42. *Westport Border Star*, Apr. 22, 1859.

43. Kansas City *Daily Journal of Commerce*, Apr. 21, 1859.

44. *Westport Border Star*, Apr. 22, 1859.

45. Hafen, *Overland Routes to the Gold Fields*, 29.

46. Kansas City *Daily Journal of Commerce*, Aug. 30, 1859.

47. *The Weekly Western Argus* (Wyandotte City, Kans.), June 4, 1859.

48. Kansas City *Daily Journal of Commerce*, Aug. 30, 1859.

49. "Westport's Dry-Land Navy," *Kansas City Star*, Aug. 6, 1905.

50. "Windwagon Was Too Speedy for These Pioneers of Old Westport," *Kansas City Journal-Post*, Jan. 4, 1931.

51. Hough, "Old Westport."

52. Storz, "My First Trip to the Rocky Mountains at Age 18."

53. *Lawrence Republican* (Lawrence, Kans.), Aug. 16, 1860.

54. Richard and Mary Ann Gehling, "Windwagons West," *Overland Journal* 11 (Winter 1993): 4–9. See also David Dary, *True Tales of the Old-Time Plains* (New York: Crown Publishers, 1979), 33–41.

55. Frank A. Root and William E. Connelley, *The Overland Stage to California* (Topeka, Kans.: Crane & Co., 1901), 430–31.

Bibliography

ARCHIVAL MATERIALS

Arrow Rock State Historic Site, Arrow Rock, Missouri.

Museum Catalog Records.

Baker Library, Harvard University
Graduate School of Business Administration.

R. G. Dun & Co. Collection.

Bent's Old Fort National Historic Site, La Junta, Colorado.

Museum Catalog Records.
Photograph Collections.

Colorado Historical Society, Denver.

Las Animas County, Interviews Collected during 1933–34 for the State Historical Society of Colorado, vol. 2 (DeBusk Memorial).

Denver Public Library, Western History Collection.

D. M. Draper, "The Santa Fe Trail in '61: Personal reminisences [*sic*] of a 'train' conductor before the railroads came."

Huntington Library, San Marino, California.

William Fairholme Journal (HM 40696).
Edward Kern Diary, 1851 (HM 4276).

Jackson County Courthouse, Independence, Missouri.

Jackson County Deed Records.
Jackson County Probate Records.

Las Animas County Courthouse, Trinidad, Colorado.

Las Animas County Deed Records.

Missouri Historical Society, St. Louis.

Joseph Murphy Collection (microfilm): Account Books, 1825–1836, 1836–1840;
    Day Book, 1847–1853; Inventories, 1881–1892.

State Historical Society of Missouri, Columbia, Missouri.

U.S. Census: Products of Industry, Missouri, 1850, 1860, 1870 and 1880 (microfilm).
Photograph Collections.

National Archives, Washington, D.C.

Thomas J. Seehorn, Administrator of Hiram Young vs. U.S., Cong. Jurisdiction
    Case File no. 7320, Records of the United States Court of Claims (Record
    Group 123).
Patent File no. 23277 for William Thomas, Records of the Patent Office
    (Record Group 241).
U.S. Census: Population Schedules, Seventh, Eighth, Ninth, and Tenth (microfilm).

New Mexico State Records Center and Archives, Santa Fe.

District Court Records, Santa Fe County.

Platte County Courthouse, Platte City, Missouri.

Platte County Circuit Court Records.

University of New Mexico Library, Special Collections, Albuquerque.

José Felipe Chaves Papers.

University of Vermont Libraries, Special Collections, Burlington.

Henry Stevens Collection.

Western Historical Manuscript Collection, Columbia, Missouri.

James Aull Business Records, 1825–1851, Coll. no. 3001 (microfilm).
Adrienne Tinker Christopher Papers.
Lucy Wortham James Collection.
Lead Mining Companies, Washington County, Missouri, Records, 1809-1954,
    Coll. no. 3893 (microfilm).

Recorded Materials

Taped comments of Doug Thamert, April 10, 1996, and January 17, 1998.
    Author's collection.

Wagon and Carriage Catalogs

Austin, Tomlinson & Webster Mfg. Co., Jackson, Mich., 1883 Price List.
Birdsell Manufacturing Co., South Bend, Ind., c. 1885.
John Burg & Sons, Burlington (?), Iowa, c. 1880.
J. M. Childs & Co., Utica, N.Y., 1886.
G. & D. Cook & Co.'s llustrated Catalogue of Carriages and Special Business
    Advertiser, New Haven, Conn., 1860.
Luedinghaus-Espenschied Wagon Co., St. Louis, Mo., c. 1902.
Mitchell, Lewis & Co., Racine, Wisc., 1884 Annual.
Peter Schuttler Company, Chicago, Ill., 1920.
Sligo Iron Store Company, St. Louis, Mo., c. 1890.
Star Wagon Company, Cedar Rapids, Iowa, c. 1880.
Studebaker Bro's Manufacturing Company, South Bend, Ind., 1876 Price List.
Weber & Damme Wagon Company, St. Louis, Mo., 1908.
Winchester & Partridge Manufacturing Co., Whitewater Wisc., 1874.

Wagon Plans

"Specifications for Six-Mule United States Army Wagon," 1878. On file at Fort
    Union National Monument, Watrous, New Mexico.
Thompson, John. "Conestoga Waggon in the Collection of the American Mu-
    seum in Britain" (3 sheets), 1977.

Newspapers and Periodicals

Chronicle-News (Trinidad, Colo.)
Council Grove Press (Council Grove, Kans.)
Daily Chieftain (Pueblo, Colo.)
Daily Journal of Commerce (Kansas City, Mo.)
Daily Tribune (Denver)

Daily Reveille (St. Louis)
Freemen's Champion (Prairie City, Kans.)
Globe-Democrat (St. Louis)
Jefferson Examiner (Jefferson City, Mo.)
Jefferson Inquirer (Jefferson City, Mo.)
Kansas City Enterprise
Kansas City Journal-Post
Kansas City Star
Kansas Press (Council Grove)
Lawrence Republican (Lawrence, Kans.)
Le Tour Du Monde (Paris, France)
Leavenworth Daily Times (Leavenworth, Kans.)
Merchants' Magazine and Commercial Review
The Missouri Magazine
Missouri Intelligencer (Franklin, Fayette, and Columbia)
Missouri Republican (St. Louis)
Niles' National Register
Out West (Colorado Springs)
Pittsburgh Morning Chronicle
Rocky Mountain News (Denver)
Sacramento Daily Union
San Antonio Express (Texas)
Scientific American
Trinidad Enterprise (Colorado)
Wagon Tracks (Quarterly of the Santa Fe Trail Association)
Weekly Mercury and Manufacturer (Pittsburgh, Pa.)
Weekly Reveille (St. Louis)
The Weekly Western Argus (Wyandotte City, Kans.)
The Western Expositor (Independence, Mo.)
Western Journal of Commerce (Kansas City, Mo.)
Westport Border Star (Westport, Mo.)

CITY AND STATE DIRECTORIES

Braunhold & [?]. *Leavenworth City Directory and Business Mirror for 1865–66.*
    Leavenworth, Kans.: Braunhold & ?, 1865.
Collins, Charles. *Collins' City Directory of Leavenworth.* Leavenworth, Kans.:
    Charles Collins, 1866.
———. *Collins' Business and Resident Directory of Leavenworth.* Leavenworth,
    Kans.: Charles Collins, 1868.
Corbett, Hoye & Co.'s Leavenworth City Directory for 1873. Leavenworth, Kans.:
    Corbett, Hoye & Co., 1873.
Edwards' Annual Directory to the . . .City of St. Louis, for 1866. St. Louis: Edwards'
    Directory Office, 1866.

Fahnestock, Samuel. *Fahnestock's Pittsburgh Directory for 1850.* Pittsburgh: Geo. Parkin & Co. Book and Job Printers, 1850.

Foley, M. S., & Co. *Leavenworth City Directory, for 1868–9.* Leavenworth, Kans.: M. S. Foley & Co., 1868.

Gazetteer and Directory of the State of Kansas. Lawrence, Kans.: Blackburn & Co., 1870.

Green, James. *The Saint Louis Business Directory for the Year of Our Lord 1850.* St. Louis: M'Kee Printer, 1850.

Harris, Isaac. *Harris' General Business Directory, of the Cities of Pittsburgh and Allegheny.* Pittsburgh: A. A. Anderson, 1841.

———.*Harris' Business Directory of the Cities of Pittsburgh and Allegheny.* Pittsburgh: A. A. Anderson, 1844.

———. *Harris's General Business Directory of the Cities of Pittsburgh and Allegheny.* Pittsburgh: A. A. Anderson, 1847.

———. *Harris' Pittsburgh & Allegheny Directory.* Pittsburgh: A. A. Anderson, 1839.

———. *Harris' Pittsburgh Business Directory, for the Year 1837.* Pittsburgh: Isaac Harris, 1837.

Jones, S. *Pittsburgh in the Year Eighteen Hundred and Twenty-Six.* Pittsburgh: Johnston & Stockton, 1826.

Kansas City Directory, and Business Mirror, for 1860–61. Indianapolis, Ind.: James Sutherland, 1860.

Leavenworth City Directory, and Business Mirror, for 1863–64. Leavenworth, Kans.: Hume & Prescott, 1863.

Lyford, William G. *The Western Address Directory: Containing the Cards of Merchants, Manufacturers, and Other Business Men, in Pittsburgh, (Pa); Wheeling, (Va.); Zanesville, (O.); Portsmouth, (O.); Dayton, (O.); Cincinnati (O.); Madison, (Ind.); Louisville, (K.); St. Louis, (Mo.) . . .* Baltimore: Jos. Robinson, 1837.

Merwin's Leavenworth City Directory for 1870–71. Leavenworth, Kans.: Heman Merwin, 1870).

O'Brien, John G. *O'Brien's Philadelphia Wholesale Business Directory . . . for the Year 1844.* Philadelphia: King & Baird, Printers, 1844.

———. *O'Brien's Philadelphia Wholesale Business Merchants and Manufacturer's Directory . . . for the Year 1853.* Philadelphia: John G. O'Brien, 1853.

———. *O'Brien's United States Advertising Circular, and City and Country Merchants' Directory, to the . . . City of Philadelphia, for the Year 1843.* Philadelphia: King & Baird, Printers, 1843.

Paxton, John A. *The St. Louis Directory and Register.* St. Louis: John A. Paxton, 1821.

Pittsburgh Business Directory and Merchants and Travelers' Guide. Pittsburgh: Jones & Co., 1854.

Smith & DuMoulin. *Illinois State Business Directory, 1860.* Chicago: J. C. W. Bailey & Co., 1860.

Sutherland & McEvoy. *The Missouri State Gazetteer and Business Directory.* St. Louis: Sutherland & McEvoy, 1860.

Turner, T. G. *Gazetteer of the St. Joseph Valley, Michigan and Indiana, with a View of its Hydraulic and Business Capacities.* Chicago: Hazlitt & Reed, 1867.

GOVERNMENT DOCUMENTS
AND PUBLICATIONS

Boyle, Susan Calafate. *Commerciantes, Arrieros, y Peones: The Hispanos and the Santa Fe Trade.* Southwest Cultural Resources Center Professional Papers No. 54. Santa Fe, N.M.: National Park Service, 1994.

Comer, Douglas C. *1976 Archeological Investigations; Trash Dump Excavations, Area Surveys, and Monitoring of Fort Construction and Landscaping; Bent's Old Fort National Historic Site, Colorado.* Washington, D.C.: U.S. Department of the Interior/National Park Service, 1985.

Gardner, Mark L. *Wagons on the Santa Fe Trail, 1822–1880.* Santa Fe, N.M.: National Park Service, 1998.

Manual for the Quartermaster Corps, United States Army, 1916, Appendix. Washington, D.C.: Government Printing Office, 1917.

Report of the Commissioner of Patents, volumes for 1846 through 1870.

Risch, Erna. *Quartermaster Support of the Army: A History of the Corps, 1775– 1939.* Washington, D.C.: Center of Military History, U.S. Army, 1989.

Thomas, Tom. *Special History Study: The Evolution of Transportation in Western Pennsylvania.* Denver, Colo.: Denver Service Center, National Park Service, 1994.

U.S. Congress, House. *Findings in Case of Thomas J. Seehorn, Administrator of Hiram Young.*H.R. Doc. 409, 60th Cong., 1st sess., 1907 (Serial 5376).

———. Report of the Quartermaster General. In H.R. Ex. Doc. 2, 32dCong., 1st sess., 1851 (Serial 634).

———. *Thomas S. J. Johnson. Mr. Ready, from the Committee of Claims, made the following Report.* H.R. Rep. 85, 33d Cong., 1st sess., 1854 (Serial 742).

U.S. Congress, Senate. *Answers of Augustus Storrs, of Missouri, to Certain Queries upon the Origin, Present State, and Future Prospect, of Trade and Intercourse between Missouri and the Internal Provinces of Mexico, Propounded by the Hon. Mr. Benton.* S. Doc. 7, 18th Cong., 2d sess., 1825 (Serial 108).

———. *Letter From the Secretary of the Interior, Transmitting, in response to a resolution of the Senate relative to the rejection of certain bids for wagons for the Indian service, a report of the Commissioner of Indian Affairs and accompanying correspondence.* S. Ex. Doc. 210, 46th Cong., 2d sess., 1880 (Serial 1886).

Walker, Francis A., comp. *Ninth Census—Volume III: The Statistics of the Wealth and Industry of the United States . . . from the Original Returns of the Ninth Census . . .* Washington, D.C.: Government Printing Office, 1872.

Walker, Francis A., and Chas. W. Seaton, comps. *Report on the Manufactures of the United States at the Tenth Census (June 1, 1880) . . .* Washington, D.C.: Government Printing Office, 1883.

BOOKS AND ARTICLES

Abert, Lieut. James W. *Abert's New Mexico Report, 1846–'47.* Albuquerque: Horn & Wallace, 1962.

———. *Through the Country of the Comanche Indians in the Fall of the Year 1845.* Edited by John Galvin. San Francisco: John Howell, 1970.

Aguirre, Mamie Bernard. "Spanish Trader's Bride." *The Westport Historical Quarterly* 4 (December 1969): 5–23.

Antisell, Thomas. *Hand-book of the Useful Arts.* New York: George P. Putnam, 1852.

Asher & Adams' Pictorial Album of American Industry, 1876. 1876. Reprint, New York: Rutledge Books, 1976.

Atherton, Lewis E. "Business Techniques in the Santa Fe Trade." *Missouri Historical Review* 34 (April 1940): 335–41.

———. *The Frontier Merchant in Mid-America.* Columbia: University of Missouri Press, 1971.

Aull, James, and Robert Aull. "Letters of James and Robert Aull." Edited by Ralph P. Bieber. *Missouri Historical Society Collections* 5 (1928): 267–310.

Bale, M. Powis. *Woodworking Machinery: Its Rise, Progress, and Construction.* 1880. Reprint, Lakewood, Colo.: Glen Moor Press, 1992.

Barber, John Warner, and Henry Howe. *Our Whole Country: or the Past and Present of the United States, Historical and Descriptive.* 2 vols. Cincinnati: Henry Howe, 1861.

Barbour, Barton H., ed. *Reluctant Frontiersman: James Ross Larkin on the Santa Fe Trail, 1856–57.* Albuquerque: University of New Mexico Press, 1990.

Barry, Louise. *The Beginning of the West: Annals of the Kansas Gateway to the American West, 1540–1854.* Topeka: Kansas State Historical Society, 1972.

Bartlett, John Russell. *Dictionary of Americanisms.* 1848. Reprint, New York: Crescent Books, 1989.

———. *Dictionary of Americanisms.* Boston: Little, Brown and Company, 1860.

———. *Personal Narrative of Explorations and Incidents in Texas, New Mexico, California, Sonora, and Chihuahua . . .* 2 vols. 1854. Reprint, Chicago: The Rio Grande Press, 1965.

Batory, Dana M. *Vintage Woodworking Machinery, An Illustrated Guide to Four Manufacturers.* Mendham, N.J.: Astragal Press, 1997.

Beachum, Larry M. *William Becknell: Father of the Santa Fe Trade.* Southwestern Studies Monograph No. 68. El Paso: Texas Western Press, 1982.

Berkebile, Don H. *Carriage Terminology: An Historical Dictionary.* Washington, D.C.: Smithsonian Institution Press, 1978.

———. "Conestoga Wagons in Braddock's Campaign, 1755." In *Contributions from the Museum of History and Technology,* 142–153. United States National Museum Bulletin 218. (Washington D.C.: Smithsonian Institution, 1959).

———. *Horse-Drawn Commercial Vehicles.* Mineola, N.Y.: Dover Publications, 1977.

Berkebile, Don H., ed. *American Carriages, Sleighs, Sulkies, and Carts.* Mineola, N.Y.: Dover Publications, 1977.

Bishop, J. Leander. *A History of American Manufactures from 1608 to 1860*. 2 vols. Philadelphia: Edward Young & Co., 1864.

The Book of English Trades, and Library of the Useful Arts. London, Sir Richard Phillips and Co., c. 1830.

Bott, Emily Ann O'Neil. "Joseph Murphy's Contribution to the Development of the West." *Missouri Historical Review* 47 (October 1952): 18–28.

Boucher, John Newton, ed. *A Century and a Half of Pittsburgh and Her People*. 4 vols. New York: The Lewis Publishing Company, 1908.

Bourne, Russell. *Americans on the Move: A History of Waterways, Railways, and Highways*. Golden, Colo.: Fulcrum Publishing, 1995.

Boutros, David. "The West Illustrated: Meyer's Views of Missouri River Towns." *Missouri Historical Review* 80 (April 1986): 304–20.

Boyle, Susan Calafate. *Los Capitalistas: Hispano Merchants and the Santa Fe Trade*. Albuquerque: University of New Mexico Press, 1997.

Breckenridge, William Clark. "Freighters' Wagons Commonly Called Conestoga Wagons." In James Malcolm Breckenridge, *William Clark Breckenridge: Historical Research Writer and Bibliographer of Missouriana; His Life, Lineage and Writings*, 233-234. St. Louis: J. M. Breckenridge, 1932.

Burke, W. S., and J. L. Rock. *The History of Leavenworth, the Metropolis of Kansas, and the Chief Commercial Center West of the Missouri River*. Leavenworth: The Leavenworth Times Book and Job Printing Establishment, 1880.

Burnes, Brian. "The Journey of Hiram Young—Ox Yokes lift Slavery's Chains." *Kansas City Star* (undated newspaper clipping).

Burton, Richard F. *The City of the Saints and Across the Rocky Mountains to California*. 1862. Reprint,Niwot: University Press of Colorado, 1990.

Capps, Michael A. "Wheels in the West: The Overland Wagon." *Overland Journal* 8, no. 4 (1990): 2–11.

"Carriage Building in America." (1860) *The Carriage Journal* 2 (Summer 1964): 30–33.

Carroll, H. Bailey, and J. Villasana Haggard, eds. and trans. *Three New Mexico Chronicles*. 1942. Reprint, New York: Arno Press, 1967.

Cartwright, Anna Belle, ed. "William James Hinchey: An Irish Artist on the Santa Fe Trail." *Wagon Tracks* (Quarterly of the Santa Fe Trail Association) 10 (May 1996): 11–23; (August 1996): 12–22; and 11 (November 1996): 10–18.

Chandler, Alfred D., Jr. *The Visible Hand: The Managerial Revolution in American Business*. Cambridge, Mass.: Belknap Press of Harvard University Press, 1977.

Cody, William F. *Buffalo Bill's Own Story of His Life and Deeds.*, "Memorial Edition." N.p.: John R. Stanton, 1917.

Condron, H. David. "The Knapheide Wagon Company, 1848–1943." *The Journal of Economic History* 3 (May 1943): 32–41.

Cook, John R. *The Border and the Buffalo: An Untold Story of the Plains*. Edited by Milo Milton Quaife. Chicago: The Lakeside Press, 1938.

"The Cover." *Bulletin of the Missouri Historical Society* 8 (April 1952): 225.

Cox, James. *Old and New St. Louis: A Concise History of the Metropolis of the West and Southwest, with a Review of its Present Greatness and Immediate Prospects.* St. Louis: Central Biographical Publishing Co., 1894.

Cranmer, Tom C. *Rules and Regulations, By which to Conduct Wagon Trains.* Kansas City: Commercial Advertiser Job Rooms, 1866.

Curry, George. *George Curry, 1861–1947: An Autobiography.* Edited by H. B. Hening. Albuquerque: University of New Mexico Press, 1958.

Dacus, J. A., and James W. Buel. *A Tour of St. Louis; or the Inside Life of a Great City.* St. Louis: Western Publishing Company, 1878.

Dana, Charles A., ed. *The United States Illustrated.* 2 vols. New York: Herrmann J. Meyer, 1853.

Dary, David. *True Tales of the Old-Time Plains.* New York: Crown Publishers, 1979.

Davis, Richard M. "Where have all the wagons gone? Gone, gone long ago, or very nearly so (Part I)." *Overland Journal* 15 (Autumn 1997): 16–39.

———. "Where have all the wagons gone? (Part II)." *Overland Journal* 16 (Summer 1998): 24–42.

Davis, William Watts Hart. *El Gringo; or, New Mexico and Her People.* 1857. Reprint, Lincoln: University of Nebraska Press, 1982.

Day, Sherman. *Historical Collections of the State of Pennsylvania.* Philadelphia: George W. Gorton, 1843.

Dewitt, Melvin L. *Wheels, Wheels, Wagons & More.* Moscow, Idaho: Melvin Dewitt, 1984.

Dines, Glen. *Bull Wagon: Strong Wheels for Rugged Men—The Frontier Freighters.* New York: The Macmillan Company, 1963.

Downing, Paul H. "A History of Carriages." *The Carriage Journal* 6 (Autumn 1968): 78–82.

———. "A History of the Rockaway." *The Carriage Journal* 4 (Winter 1967): 99–110.

Duggan, Edward P. "Machines, Markets, and Labor: The Carriage and Wagon Industry in Late-Nineteenth-Century Cincinnati." *Business History Review* 51 (Autumn 1977): 308–25.

Dunbar, Seymour. *A History of Travel in America.* New York: Tudor Publishing Company, 1937.

Eckert, Edward K., and Nicholas J. Amato, eds. *Ten Years in the Saddle: The Memoir of William Woods Averell, 1851–1862.* San Rafael, Calif.: Presidio Press, 1978.

Edwards, Richard, and M. Hopewell. *Edwards's Great West and Her Commercial Metropolis, Embracing a View of the West, and a Complete History of St. Louis . . .* St. Louis: Edwards's Monthly, 1860.

Eggenhofer, Nick. *Horses, Horses, Always Horses: The Life and Art of Nick Eggenhofer.* Cody, Wyo.: Sage Publishing Co., 1981.

———. *Wagons, Mules and Men: How the Frontier Moved West.* New York: Hastings House, 1961.

Eighty Years' Progress of the United States: A Family Record of American Industry,
    Energy and Enterprise. 2 vols. Hartford, Conn.: L. Stebbins, 1867.

Elder, Jane Lenz and David J. Weber, eds. *Trading in Santa Fe: John M. Kings-*
    bury's Correspondence with James Josiah Webb, 1853–1861. Dallas: Southern
    Methodist University Press, 1996.

Espenschied, Lloyd. "Louis Espenschied and His Family." *Bulletin of the Missouri*
    Historical Society 18 (January 1962): 87–103.

Fairholme, William. *Journal of an Expedition to the Grand Prairies of the Missouri,*
    1840. Edited by Jack B. Tykal. Spokane, Wash.: The Arthur H. Clark
    Co., 1996.

Farnham, Thomas J. *Travels in the Great Western Prairies, the Anahuac and Rocky*
    Mountains, and in the Oregon Territory. New York: Greeley & McElrath, 1843.

Field, Mathew C. *Matt Field on the Santa Fe Trail.* Edited by John E. Sunder,
    collected by Clyde and Mae Reed Porter. Norman: University of Okla-
    homa Press, 1960.

Fleischmann, C. L. *Trade, Manufacture, and Commerce in the United States of*
    America. Stuttgart, Germany, 1852. English translation, Jerusalem: Israel
    Program for Scientific Translations, 1970.

Foggett, John S. "The Manufacture of Carriage Wheels." *The Carriage Journal*
    15 (Summer 1977): 236–42.

Forest, E. S., and L. H. Houck. "Last Wagons to Santa Fe." *The Westport His-*
    torical Quarterly 3 (November 1967): 3–13.

Frederick, J. V. *Ben Holladay, The Stagecoach King: A Chapter in the Development*
    of Transcontinental Transportation. Glendale, Calif.: The Arthur H. Clark
    Co., 1940.

Freedley, Edwin T. *A Treatise on the Principal Trades and Manufactures of the*
    United States. 1856. Reprint, New York: Garland Publishing,1974.

———. *Philadelphia and its Manufactures: A Hand-Book Exhibiting the Develop-*
    ment, Variety, and Statistics of the Manufacturing Industry of Philadelphia in
    1857. Philadelphia: Edward Young, 1858.

———. *Philadelphia and its Manufactures: A Hand-Book of the Great Manufactories*
    and Representative Mercantile Houses of Philadelphia in 1867. Philadelphia:
    Edward Young & Co., 1867.

Fribley, Charles W. "Charles W. Fribley's Trail Diary and Letters, 1857–1859."
    Edited by David L. Richards. *Wagon Tracks* (Quarterly of the Santa Fe Trail
    Association) 12 (August 1998): 14–23; and 13 (November 1998): 18–25.

Froebel, Julius. *Seven Years' Travel in Central America, Northern Mexico, and the*
    Far West of the United States. London: Richard Bentley, 1859.

Gabbert, L. C. "Conestoga Wagons." *Bulletin of the Missouri Historical Society* 8
    (July 1952): 371–73.

Gable, Frank M. "The Kansas Penitentiary." In William E. Connelley, ed.,
    Collections of the Kansas State Historical Society, 1915–1918, vol. 14, 379–
    437. Topeka: Kansas State Printing Plant, 1918.

Gardner, Mark L. "Conestogas on the Santa Fe Trail." In Gardner, ed., *The Mexican Road: Trade, Travel, and Confrontation on the Santa Fe Trail*, 88–97. Manhattan, Kans.: Sunflower University Press, 1989.

———. "Discovered: Rare Independence-made Ox Yoke." *Wagon Tracks* (Quarterly of the Santa Fe Trail Association) 6 (May 1992): 16–17.

Gardner, Mark L., ed. *Brothers on the Santa Fe and Chihuahua Trails: Edward James Glasgow and William Henry Glasgow, 1846–1848*. Niwot: University Press of Colorado, 1993.

Garrard, Lewis. *Wah-to-Yah and the Taos Trail*. 1850. Reprint, Norman: University of Oklahoma Press, 1955.

Gehling, Richard, and Mary Ann Gehling. "Windwagons West," *Overland Journal* 11 (Winter 1993): 2–11.

Giulvezan, Isabel Stebbins, ed. *A Collection of Letters Written by the Scholl Family and Their Kin, 1836–1897*. St. Louis, 1959.

Glover, John. "Westward along the Boone's Lick Trail in 1826, The Diary of Colonel John Glover." Edited by Marie George Windell. *Missouri Historical Review* 39 (January 1943): 184–99.

Goff, William A. *Old Westport*. N.p., 1977.

Gordon, Robert B., and Patrick M. Malone. *The Texture of Industry: An Archaeological View of the Industrialization of North America*. New York: Oxford University Press, 1994.

Greeley, Horace, et al. *The Great Industries of the United States*. Hartford, Conn.: J. B. Burr & Hyde, 1872.

Greene, J. Everts. *The Santa Fe Trade: Its Route and Character*. Worcester, Mass.: Press of Charles Hamilton, 1893.

Gregg, Josiah. *Commerce of the Prairies*. Edited by Max L. Moorhead. Norman: University of Oklahoma Press, 1954.

Gregg, Kate L., ed. *The Road to Santa Fe: The Journal and Diaries of George Champlin Sibley*. Albuquerque: University of New Mexico Press, 1952.

Greiner, John. "Private Letters of a Government Official in the Southwest." Edited by Tod B. Galloway. *Journal of American History* 3 (1909): 541–54.

Hafen, LeRoy, ed. *Colorado Gold Rush: Contemporary Letters and Reports, 1858–1859*. Glendale, Calif.: Arthur H. Clark Co., 1941.

———. *Overland Routes to the Gold Fields, 1859, From Contemporary Diaries*. Glendale, Calif.: Arthur H. Clark Co., 1942.

Hall, James. *Letters from the West; Containing Sketches of Scenery, Manners, and Customs; and Anecdotes Connected with the First Settlements of the Western Sections of the United States*. 1828. Reprint, Gainesville, Fla.: Scholars' Facsimiles & Reprints, 1967.

[Hallock, Charles]. "The Seige of Fort Atkinson." *Harper's New Monthly Magazine* 15 (October 1857): 638–48.

Hardeman, Nicholas Perkins. *Wilderness Calling: The Hardeman Family in the American Westward Movement, 1750–1900*. Knoxville: University of Tennessee Press, 1977.

Hardingham, Martin. *The Fabric Catalog.* New York: Pocket Books, 1978.

Hawke, David Freeman. *Nuts and Bolts of the Past: A History of American Technology, 1776–1860.* New York: Harper & Row, 1988.

Hawkins, Bruce R., and David B. Madsen. *Excavation of the Donner-Reed Wagons: Historic Archaeology along the Hastings Cutoff.* Salt Lake City: University of Utah Press, 1990.

Hazen, Edward. *Popular Technology; or, Professions and Trades.* 2 vols. New York: Harper and Brothers, 1846.

Hegel, Richard. *Carriages from New Haven: New Haven's Nineteenth-Century Carriage Industry.* Hamden, Conn.: Archon Books, 1974.

Herbert, Henry William. *Hints to Horse-Keepers, A Complete Manual for Horsemen.* New York: A. O. Moore & Company, 1859.

Hindle, Brooke. *Technology in Early America: Needs and Opportunities for Study.* Chapel Hill: University of North Carolina Press, 1966.

Hindle, Brooke, ed. *America's Wooden Age: Aspects of its Early Technology.* Tarrytown, N.Y.: Sleepy Hollow Restorations, 1975.

Hindle, Brooke, and Steven Lubar. *Engines of Change: The American Industrial Revolution, 1790–1860.* Washington, D.C.: Smithsonian Institution Press, 1986.

History of the Arkansas Valley, Colorado. Chicago: O. L. Baskin & Co., 1881.

The History of Jackson County, Missouri. 1881. Reprint, Cape Girardeau, Mo.: Ramfre Press, 1966.

Holling, Holling Clancy. *Tree in the Trail.* Boston: Houghton Mifflin Company, 1942.

Holloway, W. R. *Indianapolis: A Historical and Statistical Sketch of the Railroad City.* Indianapolis: Indianapolis Journal Print, 1870.

Honig, Louis O. *Westport: Gateway to the Early West.* Kansas City, Mo.: Industrial Press, 1950.

Hounshell, David A. *From the American System to Mass Production, 1800–1932: The Development of Manufacturing Technology in the United States.* Baltimore: John Hopkins University Press, 1984.

Howard, Robert West. *The Wagonmen.* New York: G. P. Putnam's Sons, 1964.

Hyde, William, and Howard L. Conard. *Encyclopedia of the History of St. Louis.* 4 vols. St. Louis: Southern History Company, 1899.

Jackson, William Henry. *The Diaries of William Henry Jackson, Frontier Photographer.* Edited by LeRoy R. Hafen and Ann W. Hafen. The Far West and the Rockies Historical Series, vol. 10. Glendale, Calif.: The Arthur H. Clark Co., 1959.

Janssen, Barbara Suit, ed. *Icons of Invention: American Patent Models.* Washington, D.C.: Smithsonian Institution, 1990.

Jenkins, J. Geraint. *The English Farm Wagon, Origins and Structure.* Newton Abbot, England: David & Charles, 1981.

Kendall, George W. *Narrative of an Expedition across the Great South-Western Prairies, from Texas to Santa Fe.* 2 vols. London: David Bogue, 1845.

————. *Narrative of the Texan Santa Fe Expedition.* 2 vols. New York: Harper and Brothers, 1847.

Kerr, K. Austin, Amos J. Loveday, and Mansel G. Blackford. *Local Businesses: Exploring Their History.* The Nearby History Series, vol. 5. Nashville: Tenn.: American Association for State and Local History, 1990.

Klinkenborg, Verlyn. "If It Weren't For the Ox, We Wouldn't be Where We Are," *Smithsonian* (September 1993): 83–93.

Kroupa, B. *An Artist's Tour: Gleanings and Impressions of Travels in North and Central America.* London: Ward and Downey, 1890.

Kuykendall, Judge W. L. *Frontier Days: A True Narrative of Striking Events on the Western Frontier.* N.p. [probably Denver]: J. M. and H. L. Kuykendall, 1917.

Lane, Lydia Spencer. *I Married a Soldier, or Old Days in the Old Army.* 1893. Reprint, Albuquerque: Horn & Wallace, 1964.

Lass, William E. *From the Missouri to the Great Salt Lake: An Account of Overland Freighting.* Nebraska State Historical Society Publications, vol. 26. Lincoln: Nebraska State Historical Society, 1972.

The Leading Industries of Leavenworth, Kansas. Leavenworth, Kans.: Commercial and Manufacturing Publishing Company, 1883.

Little, James A. *What I Saw on the Old Santa Fe Trail.* Plainfield, Ind.: The Friends Press, 1904.

Longstreet, Stephen. *A Century on Wheels: The Story of Studebaker, A History, 1852–1952.* New York: Henry Holt and Company, 1952.

Lowe, Percival G. *Five Years a Dragoon ('49 to '54) and Other Adventures on the Great Plains.* 1906. Reprint, Norman: University of Oklahoma Press, 1965.

Lucia, Ellis. *The Saga of Ben Holladay: Giant of the Old West.* New York: Hastings House, 1959.

McGaw, Judith A., ed. *Early American Technology: Making and Doing Things from the Colonial Era to 1850.* Chapel Hill: University of North Carolina Press, 1994.

MacGill, Caroline E., et al. *History of Transportation in the United States before 1860.* Edited by Balthasar Henry Meyer. Washington, D.C.: Carnegie Institution of Washington, 1917.

Magoffin, Susan Shelby. *Down the Santa Fe Trail and into Mexico: The Diary of Susan Shelby Magoffin.* Edited by Stella M. Drumm. New Haven: Yale University Press, 1926.

Majors, Alexander. *Seventy Years on the Frontier.* Edited by Prentiss Ingraham. Chicago: Rand, McNally & Co., 1893.

Marcy, Randolph B. *The Prairie Traveler, A Hand-Book for Overland Expeditions.* New York: Harper & Brothers, 1859.

Marmaduke, Meredith Miles. "Santa Fe Trail: M. M. Marmaduke Journal." Edited by Francis A. Sampson. *Missouri Historical Review* 6 (October 1911): 1–10.

Mayr, Otto, and Robert C. Post, eds. *Yankee Enterprise: The Rise of the American System of Manufactures.* Washington, D.C.: Smithsonian Institution Press, 1981.

Meline, James F. *Two Thousand Miles on Horseback.* 1868. Reprint, Albuquerque: Horn & Wallace, 1966.

Moorhead, Max L. *New Mexico's Royal Road: Trade and Travel on the Chihuahua Trail.* Norman: University of Oklahoma Press, 1958.

———. "Spanish Transportation in the Southwest, 1540–1846." *New Mexico Historical Review* 32 (April 1957): 107–22.

Morgan, Dale, ed. *Overland in 1846: Diaries and Letters of the California-Oregon Trail.* 2 vols. 1963. Reprint, Lincoln: University of Nebraska Press, 1993.

Napton, W. B. *The Santa Fe Trail, 1857.* 1905. Reprint, Arrow Rock, Mo.: The Friends of Arrow Rock, 1991.

O'Brien, William Patrick "Hiram Young: Black Entrepreneur on the Santa Fe Trail." *Wagon Tracks* (Quarterly of the Santa Fe Trail Association) 4 (November 1989): 6–7.

———. "Hiram Young: Pioneering Black Wagon Maker for the Santa Fe Trade." *Gateway Heritage* 14 (Summer 1993): 56–67.

Oliva, Leo E. *Soldiers on the Santa Fe Trail.* Norman: University of Oklahoma Press, 1967.

Olmsted, R. R., ed. *Scenes of Wonder & Curiosity from Hutchings' California Magazine, 1856–1861.* Berkeley, Calif.: Howell-North, 1962.

Omwake, John. *The Conestoga Six-Horse Bell Teams of Eastern Pennsylvania* (Cincinnati: The Ebbert & Richardson Co., 1930).

Parkman, Francis. *The Oregon Trail.* Edited by E. N. Feltskog. Madison: University of Wisconsin Press, 1969.

Peloubet, Don, ed. *Wheelmaking: Wooden Wheel Design and Construction.* Mendham, N.J.: Astragal Press, 1996.

Peterson, John M. "The Lawrence Windmill." *Kansas History* 3 (Autumn 1980): 147–64.

Piatt, Michael H. "Hauling Freight into the 20th Century by Jerk Line." *Journal of the West* 36 (January 1997): 82–91.

"Pittsburgh: Her Manufactures, Commerce, and Railroad Position." *Merchants' Magazine and Commercial Review* 30 (June 1854): 683–702.

Poppino, Hattie E., ed. *Census of 1850, Jackson County, Missouri.* Kansas City, Mo.: Mrs. Hattie E. Poppino, 1959.

———. *Census of 1860, Population Schedules for Jackson County, Missouri.* Kansas City, Mo.: Mrs. Hattie E. Poppino, 1964.

Powell, Richard E., Jr. "The Early Carryall." *The Carriage Journal* 27 (Spring 1990): 192–94.

Purcell, Carroll W., Jr. *Early Stationary Steam Engines in America: A Study in the Migration of a Technology.* Washington, D.C.: Smithsonian Institution Press, 1969.

Reiser, Catherine Elizabeth. *Pittsburgh's Commercial Development, 1800–1850.* Harrisburg: Pennsylvania Historical and Museum Commission, 1951.

Reist, Arthur L. *Conestoga Wagon: Masterpiece of the Blacksmith.* Lancaster, Pa.: Forry and Hacker, 1975.

Richards, J. *A Treatise on the Construction and Operation of Wood-Working Machines*. London: E. & F. N. Spon, 1872.

Richardson, M. T. *Practical Carriage Building*. 1892. Reprint, Mendham, N.J.: The Astragal Press, 1994.

Richardson, William H. *Journal of William H. Richardson, a Private Soldier in Col. Doniphan's Command*. Baltimore, J. W. Woods, printer, 1848.

Rittenhouse, Jack D. *American Horse-Drawn Vehicles*. Los Angeles: Floyd Clymer, 1951.

———. *The Santa Fe Trail: A Historical Bibliography*. Albuquerque: University of New Mexico Press, 1971.

Rondé, M. "Voyage Dans L'Etat de Chihuahua, (Mexique)." *Le Tour Du Monde* 4 (1861): 129–60.

Root, Frank A., and William E. Connelley. *The Overland Stage to California*. Topeka, Kansas: Crane & Co., 1901.

Rosenberg, Nathan, ed. *The American System of Manufactures: The Report of the Committee on the Machinery of the United States, 1855, and the Special Reports of George Wallis and Joseph Whitworth, 1854*. Edinburgh: Edinburgh University Press, 1969.

Ruxton, George A. F. *Adventures in Mexico and the Rocky Mountains*. London: John Murray, 1847.

Sage, Rufus. *Scenes in the Rocky Mountains*. Edited by LeRoy R. Hafen and Ann W. Hafen. The Far West and the Rockies Historical Series, vols. 4 & 5. Glendale, Calif.: Arthur H. Clark Co., 1956.

Santleben, August. *A Texas Pioneer: Early Staging and Overland Freighting Days on the Frontiers of Texas and Mexico*. Edited by I. D. Affleck. New York: The Neal Publishing Company, 1910.

Scenes of American Wealth and Industry in Produce, Manufactures, Trade, The Fisheries, &c. &c. for the Instruction and Amusement of Children. Boston: Allen and Ticknor, 1833.

Searight, Thomas B. *The Old Pike: A History of the National Road*. Uniontown, Pa.: T. B. Searight, 1894.

Settle, Raymond W. and Mary Lund Settle. *Empire on Wheels*. Stanford, Calif.: Stanford University Press, 1949.

Shumway, George, and Howard C. Frey. *Conestoga Wagon, 1750–1850: Freight Carrier for 100 Years of America's Westward Expansion*. York, Pa.: George Shumway, 1968.

Simmons, Marc. "Carros y Carretas: Vehicular Traffic on the Camino Real." In Marta Weigle, ed., *Hispanic Arts and Ethnohistory in the Southwest, 325–34*. Santa Fe: Ancient City Press, 1983.

Simmons, Marc, and Frank Turley. *Southwestern Colonial Ironwork: The Spanish Blacksmithing Tradition from Texas to California*. Santa Fe: Museum of New Mexico Press, 1980.

Sims, William L. *Two Hundred Years of History and Evolution of Woodworking Machinery*. Burton Lazaras, Leicestershire, England: Walders Press, 1985.

Steffen, Randy. *The Horse Soldier, 1776–1943.* Vol. 2. Norman: University of Oklahoma Press, 1978.

Stepp, Steven Lee. *"The Old Reliable": The History of the Springfield Wagon Company, 1872–1952.* N. p., 1972).

Storrs, Augustus, and Alphonso Wetmore. *Santa Fe Trail First Reports: 1825.* Houston, Tex.: Stagecoach Press, 1960.

Stratton, Ezra M. *The World on Wheels; or Carriages, with their Historical Associations from the Earliest to the Present Time.* 1878. Reprint, New York: Benjamin Blom, 1972.

Stullken, Gerhard. *My Experiences on the Plains.* Wichita, Kans.: The Grit Printery, 1913.

Swift, Roy L., and Leavitt Corning, Jr. *Three Roads to Chihuahua: The Great Wagon Roads that Opened the Southwest, 1823–1883.* Austin, Tex.: Eakin Press, 1988.

Taylor, Benjamin Franklin, ed. *Short Ravelings from a Long Yarn, or Camp March Sketches of the Santa Fe Trail; from the Notes of Richard L. Wilson.* Chicago: Geer & Wilson, Daily Journal Office, 1847.

Taylor, George Rogers. *The Transportation Revolution, 1815–1860.* New York: Harper & Row, 1968.

Taylor & Crooks. *Sketch Book of Saint Louis.* St. Louis, Mo.: George Knapp & Co., 1858.

Thomas, Chauncey. "American Carriage and Wagon Works." In Chauncey Depew, ed., *One Hundred Years of American Commerce,* 2 vols., 2:516–20. New York: D. O. Haynes & Co., 1895.

Thomas, James. *From Tennessee Slave to St. Louis Entrepreneur: The Autobiography of James Thomas.* Edited by Loren Schweninger. Columbia: University of Missouri Press, 1984.

Thompson, John. *The Wheelwright's Trade.* Fleet, Hampshire, U.K.: John Thompson, 1983.

"The Trade and Commerce of St. Louis in 1850." *Merchants' Magazine and Commercial Review* 24 (March 1851): 298–316.

Turners' Guide from the Lakes to the Rocky Mountains . . . South Bend, Ind.: T. G. & C. E. Turner, 1868.

Vineyard, Ron. *Virginia Freight Waggons, 1750–1850.* Colonial Williamsburg Foundation Library Research Report Series no. 345. Williamsburg, Va.: Colonial Williamsburg Foundation Library, 1994.

Walden, Arthur Treadwell. *Harness and Pack.* New York: American Book Company, 1935.

Walker, Henry Pickering. *The Wagonmasters: High Plains Freighting from the Earliest Days of the Santa Fe Trail to 1880.* Norman: University of Oklahoma Press, 1966.

Ward, Allen T. "Letters of Allen T. Ward, 1842–1851, From the Shawnee and Kaw (Methodist) Missions." Edited by Lela Barnes. *Kansas Historical Quarterly* 33 (Autumn 1967): 321–76.

Ware, Eugene F. *The Indian War of 1864.* 1911. Reprint, New York: St. Martin's Press, 1960.

Webb, James Josiah. *Adventures in the Santa Fe Trade, 1844–1847.* Edited by Ralph P. Bieber. Southwest Historical Series, vol. 1. Glendale, Calif.: Arthur H. Clark Co., 1931.

Webb, W. L. *The Centennial History of Independence, Mo.* Independence: Lambert-Moon Printing Co., 1927.

Wells, Eugene T. "The Growth of Independence, Missouri, 1827–1850." *Bulletin of the Missouri Historical Society* 16 (October 1959): 33–46.

Wheeler, A. C. *The Iron Trail.* New York: F. B. Patterson, 1876.

Wheeler, Homer W. *The Frontier Trail, or from Cowboy to Colonel.* Los Angeles: Times-Mirror Press, 1923.

Wheeling, Ken. "Trans-Mississippi Transport: Part IV—Wheeled Transport: The Wagons that Went West." *The Carriage Journal* 30 (Summer 1992): 29–32.

———. "Trans-Mississippi Transport: Part V—Louis Espenschied and his Freight Wagons." *The Carriage Journal* 30 (Fall 1992): 66–69.

———. "Trans-Mississippi Transport: Part VI—Joseph Murphy and the 'Murphy Wagons.'" *The Carriage Journal* 30 (Winter 1992): 115–19.

———. "Trans-Mississippi Transport: Part VII—The Schuttler Wagons: Triumph and Tragedy." *The Carriage Journal* 30 (Spring 1993): 154–59.

Wilcox, Pearl. *Jackson County Pioneers.* 1975. Reprint, Independence, Mo.: Jackson County Historical Society, 1990.

Wilson, Edward James. *The Artist's and Mechanic's Encyclopedia, or, A Complete Exposition of the Arts and Sciences, As Applicable to Practical Purposes . . .* Newcastle upon Tyne: Mackenzie and Dent, c. 1830.

Winther, Oscar O. *The Transportation Frontier, Trans-Mississippi West, 1865–1890.* New York: Holt, Rinehart & Winston, 1964.

Wippold, Barney. "St. Louisan's Wagons Carried Settlers Westward." St. Louis *Globe-Democrat,* Nov. 2, 1978.

Wistar, Isaac Jones. *Autobiography of Isaac Jones Wistar, 1827–1905.* Philadelphia: The Wistar Institute of Anatomy and Biology, 1937.

Wood, Dean Earl. *The Old Santa Fe Trail from the Missouri River: Documentary Proof of the History and Route of the Old Santa Fe Trail.* Panoramic Edition. Kansas City, Mo.: E. L. Mendenhall, 1955.

Wood, Frances, and Dorothy Wood. *I Hauled These Mountains in Here.* Caldwell, Idaho: The Caxton Printers, 1977.

Woodward, Arthur. *Ox Carts and Covered Wagons.* Los Angeles County Museum, 1951.

Wright, Robert M. "Personal Reminiscences of Frontier Life in Southwest Kansas." In George W. Martin, ed., *Transactions of the Kansas State Historical Society, 1901–1902,* vol. 7, 47–83. Topeka: W. Y. Morgan, 1902.

Wyman, Walker D. "Bullwhacking: A Prosaic Profession Peculiar to the Great Plains." *New Mexico Historical Review* 7 (October 1932): 297–310.

————. "Freighting: A Big Business on the Santa Fe Trail." *The Kansas Historical Quarterly* 1 (November 1931): 17–27.

Youatt's History, Treatment, and Diseases of the Horse . . . with a Treatise on Draught. Philadelphia: J. B. Lippincott & Co., 1874.

UNPUBLISHED STUDIES

Givens, W. Earl. "An Introduction to Joseph Murphy and his Wagons." Author's collection.

McLaughlin, Marilyn Ruth Crosswhite. "Independence, Jackson County, Missouri, c. 1827–1844: With Emphasis on Independence as Staging Area for Westward Commercial Movements." Master's thesis, University of Washington, 1971.

Newton, Dwight Bennett. "Techniques of Overland Freighting in the Trans-Missouri West." Master's thesis, University of Kansas City, 1942.

O'Brien, William Patrick. "Independence, Missouri's Trade with Mexico, 1827–1860: A Study in International Consensus and Cooperation." Ph.D. diss., University of Colorado, 1994.

Wyman, Walker D. "Freighting on the Santa Fe Trail, 1843–1866." Master's thesis, State University of Iowa, 1931.

Index